Metaracial

Metaracial

HEGEL, ANTIBLACKNESS, AND POLITICAL IDENTITY

Rei Terada

The University of Chicago Press   Chicago and London

The University of Chicago Press, Chicago 60637
The University of Chicago Press, Ltd., London
© 2023 by The University of Chicago
Published 2023
Printed in the United States of America

32 31 30 29 28 27 26 25 24 23   1 2 3 4 5

ISBN-13: 978-0-226-82369-0 (cloth)
ISBN-13: 978-0-226-82371-3 (paper)
ISBN-13: 978-0-226-82370-6 (e-book)
DOI: https://doi.org/10.7208/chicago
/9780226823706.001.0001

Library of Congress Cataloging-in-Publication Data
Names: Terada, Rei, 1962– author.
Title: Metaracial : Hegel, antiblackness, and political identity /
Rei Terada.
Other titles: Hegel, antiblackness, and political identity
Description: Chicago ; London : The University of Chicago
Press, 2023. |
Includes bibliographical references and index.
Identifiers: LCCN 2022036025 | ISBN 9780226823690 (cloth) |
ISBN 9780226823713 (paperback) | ISBN 9780226823706 (e-book)
Subjects: LCSH: Hegel, Georg Wilhelm Friedrich, 1770–
1831. | Anti-racism. | Racism against Black people. | Slavery. |
Enlightenment. | BISAC: SOCIAL SCIENCE / Ethnic Studies /
American / African American & Black Studies | PHILOSOPHY /
Movements / Phenomenology
Classification: LCC B2948.T44 2023 | DDC 193—dc23/
eng/20220906
LC record available at https://lccn.loc.gov/2022036025

♾ This paper meets the requirements of ANSI/NISO Z39.48-1992
(Permanence of Paper).

CONTENTS

TRANSLATIONS AND
ABBREVIATIONS

References to Hegel in German are from G. W. F. Hegel, *Werke in zwanzig Bänden*, edited by Eva Moldenhauer and Karl Markus Michel, Frankfurt: Suhrkamp, 1970.

It has been necessary to use three translations, which are different assemblages of the text, of Hegel's *Lectures on World History*:

Brown and Hodgson   *Lectures on the Philosophy of World History.* Vol. 1. Edited and translated by Robert F. Brown and Peter C. Hodgson. Oxford: Oxford University Press, 2011.

Nisbet   *Lectures on the Philosophy of World History. Introduction: Reason in History.* Translated by H. B. Nisbet. Cambridge, UK: Cambridge University Press, 1975.

Sibree   *Philosophy of History.* Translated by J. Sibree [1857]. Kitchener, Ontario: Batoche Books, 2001.

Other works by Hegel are abbreviated as follows:

EPR   *Elements of the Philosophy of Right.* Translated by H. B. Nisbet, edited by Allen Wood. Cambridge, UK: Cambridge University Press, 1991.

LPS   *Lectures on the Philosophy of Spirit 1827–28.* Edited and translated by Robert R. Williams. Oxford: Oxford University Press, 2007.

LPR   *Lectures on the Philosophy of Religion.* Vol. 2, *Determinate Religion.* Edited by Peter C. Hodgson, translated by R. F. Brown, P. C. Hodgson, and J. M. Stewart. Berkeley: University of California Press, 1987.

Letters   *The Letters*. Translated by Clark Butler and Christiane
           Seiler. Bloomington: Indiana University Press, 1984.

PS   *The Phenomenology of Spirit*. Translated by A. V. Miller. Ox-
           ford: Oxford University Press, 1977.

   Works by others are abbreviated as follows:

CPR   Kant, Immanuel. *Critique of Pure Reason*. Translated by
           Norman Kemp Smith. New York: St. Martin's Press, 1965.

CHPR   Marx, Karl. *Critique of Hegel's Philosophy of Right. In Writ-
           ings of the Young Marx on Philosophy and Society*, edited and
           translated by Lloyd D. Easton and Kurt H. Guddat, 151–202.
           New York: Anchor/Doubleday, 1967.

OJQ   "On the Jewish Question." In *Collected Works*, vol. 3, by Karl
           Marx and Friedrich Engels, translated by Clemens Dutt,
           146–174. London: Lawrence Wishart, 1974.

Introduction

The citizen is thus the synthesis of the master and the slave.

FRANÇOIS REGNAULT, "Hegel's Master and
Slave Dialectic in the Work of Lacan"

What were we doing in the night that just ended? Well, we were
dreaming in German fashion, that is, we were philosophizing.

HEINRICH HEINE, "From the Introduction to
'Kahldorf on the Nobility in Letters to Count M. von Moltke'"

Sylvia Wynter tells the story of how a racial hierarchy of peoples remained in place after "1492" (more than an event) across epistemological epochs, shifting "genre[s] of the human" all the while.[1] She assigns
the European enlightenment to a genre she calls Man$_2$ or "homo politicus, or the political subject of the state." Supplanting Man$_1$, the theo-
cratic human, by shedding the medieval idea of heterogeneous kinds of
matter, Man$_2$ claimed unlimited global relation (Wynter, "Unsettling,"
272, 281). Rather than heterogeneous beings, Man$_2$ now perceived beings who fulfilled a single model of humanity either more or less. Man$_2$
therefore legitimated conquest by asserting an organizational mission
and an increasingly systematic racial science. Wynter sees the "political"
functioning here as a quasi-transcendental limit for the enlightenment.
It becomes a frame with which to make dynamic sense out of the very
existence of positions that, torn from theological explanations, were
only now experienced as an alarming disorder.

Wynter's argument exposes the enlightenment's fear of parataxis—
positions of indeterminate conjunction—its defensive use of philosophical systematization, and its treatment of political relation as a

---

1. Sylvia Wynter, "Unsettling the Coloniality of Being/Power/Truth/ Freedom: Towards the Human, After Man, Its Overrepresentation—An Argument," *CR: The New
Centennial Review* 3 (2003): 269.

greater logic exceeding dilemmas of government. Wynter calls attention to the racial effects of humanity's new political orientation: while
the rise of political organization as a justifying logic would seem to be
a productive way to think about social beings, Wynter depicts the expansion of political logic as a defense, a conservation of racial hierarchy
on new grounds. In her analysis, the French Revolution helps to create
Man$_2$—it is part of the opening of the colonial world. No threat to projects of racial order, the Rights of Man open "an even more far-reaching
paradox": Napoleon's troops empowered by the Rights of Man land in
Haiti "to reinslave the former slaves freed now by their own efforts."[2]

I consider the problem that Wynter frames, the problem of racism
for radicals, in texts of the radical enlightenment, all by inspirers and
supporters of the French Revolution—Hegel most of all, as well as
Rousseau, Kant, Mary Shelley, and Marx. What it means to be "radical" in the eighteenth and nineteenth centuries is vexed and changes
with its present signification. Currently, the qualities of the radical Hegel are highly valued, and as an index of lasting radical principle I will
focus on how Hegel stabilizes an epistemology that supports radical
subjects' political orientation by limiting their nascent conceptions of
racial slavery. Crucially, racial slavery appears in the texts I study not as
a historical event, nor a given set of conditions, but as the problem of
slavery's indefinite origin and causally ambiguous relationship to blackness, as a great deal of Black Studies scholarship has explored.[3]

In part 1, I study the limits of Hegelian antiracism by examining
Hegel's relational reality, his emphasis on negativity, and his figure of

2. Sylvia Wynter, "'A Different Kind of Creature': Caribbean Literature, the Cyclops
Factor, and the Second Poetics of the Propter Nos," *Annals of Scholarship* 12 (2002): 154.

3. "Black" in upper case may express parity with other categories and/or symbolic
determination. I write Black in upper case and blackness (less determined) in lower
case.

Questions about racial slavery's origin run through writing from the eighteenth century, if not before. Threads in contemporary criticism that I've found to be especially
helpful on this score include Nahum Chandler's call for the patient "desedimentation"
of the philosophical record on blackness ("The Economy of Desedimentation: W. E. B.
Du Bois and the Discourses of the Negro," *Callaloo* 19 [1996]: 78–93); Lindon W. Barrett's attention to circularity of blackness and value (*Blackness and Value: Seeing Double*
[Cambridge, UK: Cambridge University Press, 1999]); and David S. Marriott's and Jared
Sexton's psychoanalytic complications of the ontological stakes of Black Studies since
Marriott's *Haunted Life: Visual Culture and Black Modernity*, especially the signal essay
"That Within" (New Brunswick, NJ: Rutgers University Press, 2007, 33–68); and Sex-
ton's *Amalgamation Schemes: Antiblackness and the Critique of Multiracialism* (Minneap-
olis: University of Minnesota Press, 2008).

the slave. Then in part 2, I consider anxieties about slavery and global relation that haunt European political hope in romantic thought. These are the anxieties that Hegel's philosophy acknowledges and processes in negativity—the disquiets he manages by successfully transforming terms. In part 3, I return to Hegel's work to review his own apprehensions of European unfreedom, looking at how Hegel's epistemology emerges both from and for his domestic political desires from a different angle. The last section of part 3 considers early Marx and his "On the Jewish Question" (1843), which pauses symptomatically on some costs of Hegel's political reality. In the afterword, I repeat the method I've presented by returning to Hegel after Wynter, briefly suggesting a series of problems illuminated by recent Black thought in order to assess radical enlightenment legacies. The structure of the book's three parts is almost circular: part 3 on nonpolitical foils to Hegel's political identity can be seen as part of the matrix for part 1; part 2 can be seen as the less systematic matrix for parts 1 and 3; and part 1 presents the movement from which the book as a whole takes its name. The prologue to each part discusses the part's content and interrelation; in this introduction, I focus on conclusions that are most forcefully expressed in part 1.

Hegel's philosophy accomplishes a "metamorphosis of the static, metaphysical concept of totality"[4] into a contingent, speculative, and open-ended historical reality, antiracist in its anti-essentiality and relationality. Wynter suggests, though, that like Christian structures that continue in and through secularization, racial structures inhabit enlightenment radicals' theories of reality. Those theories constitute reality as relational and take that to mean that reality is nonracial. Within a relational and contingent reality, racism cannot appear as an operative and integral feature of the *exemplary* radical subject.[5] This repudiation is aspirational but also defensive. To the radical political identity, racism now appears outside the self, in people of insufficient understanding and worse politics. Further, because reality is now conceived as non-

---

4. John Grumley, *History and Totality: Radical Historicism from Hegel to Foucault* (London and New York: Routledge, 2016), 7.

I accept the account of Hegel presented in such works as Gillian Rose, *Hegel Contra Sociology* [1981] (New York: Verso Books, 2009); Nick Nesbitt, *Universal Emancipation: The Haitian Revolution and the Radical Enlightenment* (Charlottesville: University of Virginia Press, 2008); and Todd McGowan, *Emancipation after Hegel: Achieving a Contradictory Revolution* (New York: Columbia University Press, 2019).

5. I will consider nationalism in time.

racial to the core, in the radical enlightenment racialized people begin to appear not as raced but as "racialist"[6]—that is, *immaturely political*, damaged or held back by their political failures and incapacities.

In the hundred or so years of philosophy and literature that I discuss (1755–1843, dates that take a sample rather than indicate a particular necessity), opposition to Atlantic slavery and unease about its origins and implications, the classical opposition between slaves and citizens, and the necessity to overturn natural law strictures on political rights for Europeans all made it urgent to manage the destabilizing effects of racial slavery so as to secure the terms of society.[7]

How might terms of analysis have to shift, however, to register the difference of the radical enlightenment? In part following in Wynter's steps, Denise Ferreira da Silva's *Toward a Global Idea of Race* (2007) also narrates the persistence of "analytics of raciality" in Continental philosophy.[8] Ferreira da Silva characterizes Hegel as the major architect of "engulfment," a strategy of historical ontology that "explain[s] other human conditions as variations of those found in post-Enlightenment Europe" (xvii) in a "movement toward transparency" (238). Ferreira da Silva locates Hegel in the midst of a series of philosophical works that reproduce racial fantasies in postracial modes. Implicitly, in her argument, these works' features—their overinvestment, repetition, and condensation of figures—have the qualities of an enchanted reality. Under the weight of their own seemingly interminable unfreedom, European philosophy labors as though under a "spell," to borrow Adorno's

6. "Racialism," like "postracial," is a term of art I am interested in as an object of study, not a term I recommend. Meaning any positive use of race—for example, to mobilize a politics—it isolates a group's purported *beliefs and practices* from social, political, and legal *imposition*. While it is not overtly pejorative like "racist," that distinction is difficult to maintain. The initial distinction (soon to break down) between racialism and raciality functions in many writers to mark their entry into a metalevel of discourse—a discourse about someone else's discourse—where "racialist" holds the place formerly held by the attribution of a racial trait, and I am interested in these instances. Imperfectly, I've tried to preserve these various aspects by writing "rac(ial)ism," "racial(ist)," and so on where the move can be seen being made yet breaking down. For discussions of "racialism," see Ben Yagoda, "Racists and Racialists—What's the Difference?" *Chronicle of Higher Education* (June 9, 2016), and Robert Johnson, "Was the British Empire Racist or Racialist?" in *British Imperialism* (Houndmills, UK: Palgrave Macmillan, 2003), 107–121.

7. Scholarship on the concept of the human shows similar dynamics in various eras, as in Aimé Césaire, *Discourse on Colonialism* [1955] (New York: New York University Press, 2001).

8. Denise Ferreira da Silva, *Toward a Global Idea of Race* (Minneapolis: University of Minnesota Press, 2007), 262.

metaphor, to "act in line with the inevitable,"[9] that is, to repeat patterns
of violence. I proceed more interpretively and less schematically than
Wynter and Ferreira da Silva have, hoping to complement their conclusions by drawing out the play of unconsciousness implied in their
work. For Ferreira da Silva, perhaps my closest interlocutor on similar
terrain, interiority often appears as the cognitive realm posited by idealism—a fictive safe space in which which the idealist imagines power
to reside. While the schematism of interiority and exteriority and the
metaphor of inner life are violent technologies of colonial objectifica-
tion, in Kant and Hegel interiority is not only an architecture of ra-
tionalist idealism. It's also the mythic site of extreme self-difference,
of turbulence, and a whole suite of nonrational resources for violence.
These aspects cannot be discarded along with the metaphor of inner
location or even of subjectivity because they are operational to saturation in contemporary society. The radical enlightenment already requires for itself the nonhumanist insights that can be read inside eigh-
teenth- and nineteenth-century philosophy. Thought of the period was
not only invested in reason and coherence; its ideas of constitutive crisis, negativity, nonteleological history, and social construction also imply new and problematic forms of materialism, antiracism, and antihu-
manism. These forms work differently from humanist ones *and* work in
the same matrix—the questions for unfreedom raised by slavery—to
similar ends. In doing so, they generate an epistemology that is, however paradoxically, orienting for a political identity, this time a radical
one closer to a subjectivity of the present-day left.

In the context of hopes for radical transformation, anxieties raised
by slavery questioned the nature of the reality on which such hopes de-
pended. This situation made the Atlantic slave a figure that needed to
be incorporatable into a political imaginary for the benefit of the exemplary radical subject. A radical subjectivity in search of reorienta-
tion is the "political identity" of this book's subtitle. In political theory "political identity" usually designates a group seeking rights and
advancement. I do not mean that. By political identity I mean a model
of subjectivity like Wynter's *homo politicus* with which certain individuals interact, with which they negotiate as individualities within a collective when, after Hegel, they describe themselves as "shapes" being
formed and broken down by historicity.[10] I call this character an "iden-

9. T. W. Adorno, *Negative Dialectics* [1966], trans. E. B. Ashton (London and New
York: Routledge & Kegan Paul, 1973), 344.

10. Hegel treats kinds of knowledge in *The Phenomenology of Spirit* as "shapes" of consciousness. Each appears as a personification struggling to realize itself and coming up to

tity" ironically, since nonidentity is one of its slogans. But the irony is fair because political identity embodies itself precisely and only on the far side of whatever is, to it, identity politics—to which it cleaves, in the second or third person, attributing identity politics to someone else who believes in it. To adopt a political identity is to inhabit a reality organized by a political frontier, and to *assume* one's nonidentical shape. Robert Meister thoughtfully unfolds Marx's acknowledgment that "politics is not merely a set of transcendent ideas or goals ... one's politics is a matter of identity that is not wholly given, and not wholly chosen"[11] that "*underlies* Marx's discussion of class" (2). When "the process of forming a self-conscious identity is the inner dimension of the way in which society individuates us" (28), as Meister observes it is in Marx, political identity can be a guide to the same extent that its emergence is an "epistemological process" of reality construction (27). Now, to assume a side is also to assume a common, if negative, ground.

Chantal Mouffe's "Citizenship and Political Identity" is a fair example of such a reference to political identity. She notes that "the 'we' of the radical democratic forces is created by the delimitation of a frontier, the designation of a 'them'" worth fighting;[12] the "we" will be constellated by an only conjunctural reality, and to the extent that it may speak of itself, it now underlines the benefits of this "only." With a stronger effect of amalgamation, Jodi Dean's "comrade" is "a generic figure, a figure of sameness, the symbolic identity that attends to those belonging on the same side."[13] Each political identity creates another figure, one who is not excluded from the group but rather seems to disavow or be unaware of the force that constructs the "frontier" or the "side." When applied to those who are overly concerned with racial antagonism as it cuts across any side, the creation of such a prop or foil becomes the radical's way of reinforcing former hierarchies. Perhaps beginning with Hegel's negative turn, political identity projects "racialist" identity somewhere else. After Hegel, political identity is a matter of desire and/or capacity to avow a historical reality—the reality that is, in the radical enlightenment, no more or less than the play of contingent forces in total relation, whose best awarenesss lies open, by the contingent and unpredictable nature of *reality itself*, to strategic connection and severance.

a moment of truth. On "shapes," see Allen W. Wood, "Hegel on Education," in *Philosophers on Education*, ed. Amélie Rorty (London: Routledge, 2005), 312–329.

11. Robert Meister, *Political Identity: Thinking Through Marx* (Cambridge, MA: Blackwell, 1990), 24.

12. Chantal Mouffe, "Citizenship and Political Identity," *October* 61 (1992): 32.

13. Jodi Dean, *Comrade: An Essay on Political Belonging* (New York: Verso Books, 2019), 71.

This concatenation of assumptions ends by re-racializing the same previously racialized people on a metalevel in antiracist language.

Critical archaeology can find such a dynamic in Hegel's various fig-
urations of the slave. For Hegel learned from the ancient Romans that
he needed to account for slaves. "In Roman law, for example," he opines
in *Elements of the Philosophy of Right,* "no definition of a human being
would be possible, because the slave could not be subsumed under it;
indeed, the status [*Stall*] of the slave does violence to that concept."[14]
Hegel is objecting to slavery, yet he is highlighting the effect of Roman
slavery *on Roman jurisprudence*; the violence is to the concept. Voicing
Wynter's script for the enlightenment human, Hegel absorbs the missed
advantage *for the Roman state* of an open approach to the human. The
stakes are especially high because the "state" for Hegel is not only a particular historical form but a harbinger of any collective to come. Thus
he goes beyond political form to criticize the bases of Roman law's mistake. Definitions of man cannot just be about man: they must express a
relational, historical reality in which they participate and by which they
stand or fall, the chance of a polity to come swinging in the balance. As
in Rome, in these new terms the chance does not exist if it does not exist for the slave. This must be a true conclusion. But is racial slavery exhausted by it? And what is the relation to the polity of any remainder?
What if this is also emblematic: whatever conservatives may continue
to believe, the *Hegelian radical* desperately desires the participation in
principle of a certain slave and therefore desires the answer to be that
the bracketed remainder of racial slavery, its uncertain borders and origins, is not relevant to the chance of collective freedom, for either better or worse. *Whether it is possible* for this wish to be true; whether the
racial slave exists to Hegel as more than a figure, and whether the separation of person and figure is a possible question where racial slavery is
concerned; and whether or not it is possible for an enslaved person to
complete Hegel's vision of political training, the *way* the left political
subject *desires* it to be true already predicts the antiblack legacy of the
scenario. What if the slave in the lead of the master-slave dialectic is an
enlightenment version of a problem greater than Hegel's—an enduring dispositive with the desire to manage the racial slave built into it?
What if it's still not possible to see around this desire, so that its presence is a cost that my study also pays—the reason that a lot of us are
here? What if it's still not possible for the left Hegelian to do otherwise
than Hegel does?

14. *Elements of the Philosophy of Right,* trans. H. B. Nisbet, ed. Allen Wood (Cambridge, UK: Cambridge University Press, 1991), 27; henceforward EPR.

Writing about the metaphorization of waged labor as slavery, Sara-Maria Sorentino points out that the metaphor generates "good slaves and bad slaves": those who "demonstrat[e] their anthropological political potential" and those who don't.[15] Similarly, it will turn out that the desire to establish a radical epistemology while dealing with the figure of the slave splits the slave into two versions again and again. One is a much-desired political identity in waiting, indeed the exemplar of political identity in formation that is the best, not yet materialized chance of dialectic. Overinvested desire generates an equally fantasmatic object—in the case of figures of slavery, "constitutes a mere prop," to borrow from Calvin Warren's discussion of the Black fetish object[16]—who absorbs the anxiety that racial slavery's origin raises for political relation as a logic of reality. The difference the radical epistemology of relation makes is that the foil and prop are no longer depicted in racial terms: they are racia*list*, and either insufficiently political or subpolitical altogether. The "bad" slave of Sorentino's analysis is one artifact of the radical enlightenment—a recurring impediment who does not yet sufficiently grasp contingent reality. While slavery is not the only entry into radical anxiety about unfreedom, tendentious figures of the sub-Saharan African, the Atlantic slave, and the dangerous "free Black" mediate the political and the nonpolitical even within Europe, at a distance from the colonies, as we will see. The strictly psychoanalytic splitting[17] of the figure of the slave manages what would otherwise appear as an unbound ambiguity of racial slavery's springs. At the same time, it turns attention from slavery and toward political unfreedom.

So while there has been a great deal of scholarship on liberal[18] and

15. Sara-Maria Sorentino, "The Idea of Slavery: Abstraction, Analogy, and Anti-Blackness" (PhD diss., University of California, Irvine, 2018), 177. See also Sorentino, "The Abstract Slave: Anti-Blackness and Marx's Method," *International Labor and Working-Class History* 96 (2019): 17–37.

16. Calvin Warren, "Barred Objects (o): Police Brutality, Black Fetishes, and Perverse Demonstrations," *Comparatist* 45 (2021): 29–40, 31. I will distinguish between instrumental props and social foils.

17. See Melanie Klein, *Envy and Gratitude and Other Works, 1946–1963* (New York: Free Press, 1975); *Love, Guilt, and Reparation and Other Works, 1921–1945* (New York: Free Press, 1975); and D. W. Winnicott, *Playing and Reality* [1971] (New York: Routledge, 1991). The great object relations essay on this topic, awaiting analysis, is W. D. Fairbairn's "The Repression and the Return of Bad Objects (with Special Reference to the 'War Neuroses')," in *Psychoanalytic Studies of the Personality* (London: Routledge, 1994), 59–81. Thanks to Arlene Keizer for alerting me to it years ago.

18. Domenico Losurdo finally construes the issue as one of self-preservation. Pinned between theological naturalism that included divine rights to sovereignty and property and their fear of slave rebellion, writers like Jefferson endorsed armed revolution in

humanist contributions to slavery and the crisis that slavery presented for those philosophical systems, we cannot leave it there without noticing that radicalism follows suit. The writers I study treat figures of the slave largely in parallel to their liberal counterparts: as important *for radical political subjects* and our hopes for collectivity. Slaves are presumed to be included, yet the relationship between slavery and political freedom remains unresolved. This can be difficult to notice because, as thinkers with relational theories of reality altogether, radical writers do not treat racial slavery as natural law racists do, nor as Victorian scientific racists do. Let's underline Hegel's achievement again: a disjunctive historical ontology, empty so as to be open, negative so as to be real. Because reality just is a relational ontology, the slave must be a participant in the relational totality, not in the sense that enslaved people are already political subjects but in the sense that racial slavery cannot be seen to raise a problem for reality as relational ontology: the theory of such a reality cannot be seen as an effect of slavery, for example. Slaves must be able to be found on the path for the sake of the path, and the result is that slavery comes to be seen as "the threshold of the political world," as Jared Sexton observes.[19] My claim is not that radical writers' imaginative engagements with slavery are or are not successful. Complementarily, I am not claiming that I can turn the picture around and find a key to construing reality differently for the very reason that racial slavery is not reconciled into arguments: it may be. Rather, the desire of radical Hegelian political identity to reconcile a figure of the slave *is readable* and is *a problem in itself.*

This desire to enable a figure of the slave on one's political side, and so to be confirmed in one's political reality, takes the place of analysis of the new terms of racism within political identity itself, for those who hold to neither the essentialism of conservatives nor the humanism of liberals. It is true that these new terms do not fit within the former racism, and even that they are antiracist. But this truth promptly rediscovers the necessity of the term "antiblack." If racism conflates slavery with blackness, for the antiracist the slave is contingently a slave and not identical with blackness, as politically exemplary slaves seem

France at any cost—even if it "would have seen half the earth desolated"—while invoking the moral panic of race war to support repression of slave uprisings (*A Brief History of Liberalism* [2006], trans. Gregory Elliott [New York: Verso Books, 2011], 177). For consonant work, see Susan Buck-Morss, *Hegel, Haiti, and Universal History* (Pittsburgh, PA: University of Pittsburgh Press, 2009), and Tyler Stovall, *White Freedom: The Racial History of an Idea* (Princeton, NJ: Princeton University Press, 2021).

19. Jared Sexton, "The *Vel* of Slavery: Tracking the Figure of the Unsovereign," *Critical Sociology* 42 (2014): 583–597, 11.

to confirm. Under these conditions, however, another slave is likely to appear, an inconvenient slave on the margin of the master-slave dialectic who is not maturely political. Enlightenment antiracism is now liable to conflate blackness, not with slavery itself—which is treated as a possible incubator of political identity—but with the racial*ism* of insufficiently politico-historical people who, for whatever reasons, adhere to an incorrect understanding of reality. To develop Wynter's parallel between the secularization of Christianity and the continuation of racial order, racial order is now transposed to a metalevel: to the perception of a stance taken to express, be the result of, or be in a feedback loop with, someone's inadequately historico-political grasp. This elevation to a metalevel can be called *metaracial*: one no longer attributes a racial trait, but attributes "racialism" in place of a racial trait.

Hegel's master-slave dialectic illustrates preparation for liberation through a metaracial splitting of the Black Atlantic slave. Moreover, this figure emerges from and supports the systematized entirety of Hegel's philosophy. Hegel is therefore the key thinker in this book; however, it isn't completely obvious who "Hegel" is. He is ubiquitous, as readers will know, and as shadowy figures populate his writings, he is one in mine—a "shape" of repudiation and identification too. The question of how far "Hegel" extends needs to be left open, but not infinitized. I can say that my arguments remain Hegelian, but I cannot say that anyone or no one can be Hegel, nor prescribe anyone to be or not be in a celebratory fashion. This stopping place registers Hegel's radical mode as a problem, a problem in the way that it has been a solution. Hegel ascribes political identity by conceiving it as a recognition of relationality that no real understanding being can fail to avow. That is a problem because it transposes what was, one level down, a racial hierarchy of sensibility.

This isn't exactly a Hegelian book, in the sense that I don't sift Hegel's works, interrelating their vast internal subtleties—although I think that could be done with my questions in mind and it would produce something interesting. Rather, I dwell on basic Hegelian notions of negativity, self-negation, realization, and sublation, pointed by Hegelians toward a politics cleansed of "identity politics," to illuminate what are in Hegelian texts political, subpolitical, and nonpolitical spaces organized by "good" and "bad" slaves. Around Hegel, in his antecendents and in Marx as his respondent, I consider the dilemmas set for radical aspirations by slavery and how these writers address them with a variety of maneuvers. All manage disquiet about what kind of reality could support the missing origins and causes of racial slavery. The problem of how to place the slave emerges as one that Hegel "solves" by passing from racism to antiblackness.

The naturalization of political reality, the antiracist legacy of Hegelianism, debilitates critical purchase on slavery by making negativity and disjunctive self-realization features shared by political identity and Hegelianism itself. I descriptively agree that these features *are* quasi-transcendental at this time, but that is a situation to analyze, rather than assume, celebrate, or recommend. In dialogue with the recent emphasis of Black thought on antiblackness' processes of abstraction, I will argue that the assuming, celebrating, recommending modes of Hegelianism continue to gloss over dilemmas shown by Atlantic slavery in a kind of stretch for the figure of the slave. If social transformation depends on working forward from the forms modernity has managed to manifest, what does slavery's prominence and recalcitrance among those forms imply? What is lost when radical longing leaves aside the disappearing origins of a "racination" whose roots are "never touching the soil"?[20] I am clearly writing because I care about radical political community and its antiracist capacities; my own stance does not externalize anything beyond political identity and political attachment. What I can offer is the deformalization of a naturalized phenomenon, a formation of antiracism around antiblackness, that can't be discussed if it is defined out of existence.

20. Jacques Derrida, *Of Grammatology* [1967], trans. Gayatri Chakravorty Spivak (Baltimore, MD: Johns Hopkins University Press, 1976), 101.

PART 1

Metaracial Logic

The misery of this contradiction is the *Discipline of the World*. "Zucht" (discipline) is derived from "Ziehen" (to draw) ... the subject of it is being trained, in order that the standard of attainment may be reached. A renunciation, a disaccustoming, is the means of leading to an absolute basis of existence. That contradiction which afflicts the Roman World is the very state of things which constitutes such a discipline—the discipline of that culture which compels personality to display its nothingness. But it is reserved for us of a later period to regard this as a training.

HEGEL, *Lectures on the Philosophy of World History*

In *The Rooster's Egg* (1995), Patricia J. Williams identifies a certain mechanism of postracial fantasy. She remarks that a "dilemma many people of color face" is that they attract the charge of racism: in their case "talking about" race gets to be "considered an act of war."[1] Casting redistribution as "reverse discrimination" is part of the phenomenon, she remarks (14). The practice she points out does not necessarily express universalist ideology, nor only disregard of racist violence. Rather, for her postracialist interlocutors, Williams's concern with race merges into racism, or at least unfortunate "racialism"—and already functions as a racial trait.

This practice adopts a secondary position. It claims only to cite someone else's misbegotten racialism. But it is also secondary in another, logical sense: the perspective it promotes must take charge of what race is and assume the responsibility for deciding what counts as it to characterize a reference to it. This implies a previous account of race itself. As Barnor Hesse remarks, many theses of social construction "rel[y] for coherence on the rhetorical force of refuting the meanings given to race by biological associations and at the same time . . . silently reinscribe those same biological associations as [their] only account of race."[2] Such discourse acts as though racist associations always belong to others—as though, in J. L. Austin's vocabulary, it only cites

---

1. Patricia J. Williams, *The Rooster's Egg: The Persistence of Prejudice* (Cambridge, MA: Harvard University Press, 1995), 40.

2. Barnor Hesse, "Preface: Counter-Racial Formation Theory," in *Conceptual Aphasia in Black: Displacing Racial Formation*, ed. P. Khalil Saucier and Tryon P. Woods (Lanham, MD: Lexington Books, 2016), vii. See also, although her conclusions diverge, Michelle Wright, *Physics of Blackness: Beyond the Middle Passage Epistemology* (Minneapolis: University of Minnesota Press, 2015).

or "mentions" inherited assumptions instead of "using" them.[3] But the certainty that racism comes from outside is part of the problem.

When the normative discourse is not postracialist, but antiracist, these patterns persist in the absence of even tacit biologism, with another twist. Antiracism points out that postracial discourse is *actually too racial(ist)*. In naive postracial discourse, race supposedly is mentioned only when someone else has brought it up. Now, racism is someone else's problem again: the problem is the still-racial practice that has been uncovered in the naive liberal postracialist and needs to be radically transformed politically. In this now metaracial logic, divorced from any biologism, the properly political antiracist is likely to attack both the liberal postracialist who is cryptically invested in whiteness and the radical rival who appears, from this perspective, overinterested in antiblackness. We must now use a vocabulary of antiblackness rather than racism, since antiblackness here continues through antiracism, projecting blackness as an excess of political identity. As the critic's emphasis shifts to "regressive implications for politics and policy," as Sexton (*Amalgamation*, 87) points out, "in this schema, it is black people in particular who prove guilty."[4] Annie Olaloku-Teriba (2018) characteristically makes antiracism the field of a battle between political and racialist antiracism in which concern with antiblackness is a symptom: "the exceptionalism with which 'anti-black' racism is treated, along with the territoriality over what are deemed particularly Black registers of resistance ... stands in stark contrast to the most prevalent traditions of Black anti-imperialist organizing of the 1960s and 1970s."[5] What there's too much of now is not reference to racism, which antiracists analyze as capitalist and nationalist technology, but *to antiblackness*.[6] Blackness is split into a world of politics and an unnamed space, neither political

3. J. L. Austin's "use" and "mention" distinguish one's own content from what appears in quotation marks, so to speak (*How to Do Things with Words*, 2nd ed., ed. J. O. Urmson and Marina Sbisà [Cambridge, MA: Harvard University Press, 1975]). Saidiya Hartman's work is a demolition of use and mention, as mention not only represents but re-enacts use (*Scenes of Subjection: Terror, Slavery, and Self-Making in Nineteenth-Century America* [Oxford: Oxford University Press, 1997]).

4. In Hegelian terms, what is institution and "policy" but a mode of historical "self-awareness"?

5. Annie Olaloku-Teriba, "Afro-Pessimism and the (Un)logic of Anti-Blackness," *Historical Materialism* 26 (2018): 96–122. The "stark" splitting of a "good," especially political Black actor from another echoes Hegel.

6. Thus Adolph Reed Jr. opines that "antiracists ... reproduce a key premise of racialist thinking" when they supposedly make racism "a transhistorical force." For Reed "an ideological program is the sole condition of existence for race" ("The Post-1965 Trajectory of Race, Class, and Urban Politics in the United States Reconsidered," *Labor Stud-*

nor nonpolitical in the given terms, that appears regressive in the radical imaginary. Reference to antiblackness becomes a quantity of which
there can be too much as a second-order reflection of slavery's location
at Sexton's "threshold of the political world" (Sexton, "The *Vel* of Slavery," 11).

Similarly, the history of "political blackness" in the United Kingdom
suggests that the benefits of political blackness are difficult to articulate without evoking another blackness that is not beneficial. As Claire
Alexander comments, the concept of political blackness, an "inclusive
'black' category" for South Asian and Black citizens of the Windrush
generation in Britain, was never regarded as unified, even in its heyday.
Nonetheless Alexander's sketch of its distinction from a later construction of "British 'black'" continues to draw its merit from proximity to a
properly sophisticated politics: "the first [construction] should be understood as a political stance, and represents a coalition of groups and
concerns, the second privileges identity."[7] Again, a thematic turn substitutes politico-philosophical *"stance[s]" for identities*, while preserving
the long-standing assumption that blackness needs to be wedded to the
political to attain legitimacy (Sexton, *Amalgamation*, 66).

While Sexton doesn't address "political blackness" per se, *Amalgamation Schemes* addresses the pressures that form it and diagnoses
an antiblack defensive function of political identity. Writing of multiracialism, Sexton notes its desire "to condemn identification with racial
blackness as the source of social crisis." Extending the fantasy of misce-
genation, Sexton argues, blackness appears as needing to be "purified"
by coalition, even "in the name of preeminent black political formation"
(Sexton, *Amalgamation*, 65–66). Recently, for Asad Haider, for example, a presumed racialism divides "expressions of racial ideology" from
revolutionary Black radicalism. Haider's exemplary radicals are Black
and his exemplary racialists are people who say *"anti-blackness* in the
place of *racism."*[8] But gathering Black revolutionary models makes a
difference only if antiblackness is demographically reduced in the first
place. In this splitting of good from bad Black actors, the same logic
persists: the former are properly radical to the extent that they aren't
mainly concerned with blackness.

---

ies Journal 41 [2016]: 260–291), while the relations of production undergirding class
politics are real.

7. Claire Alexander, "Breaking Black: The Death of Ethnic and Racial Studies in Britain," *Ethnic and Racial Studies* 41 (2018): 1034–1054, 1038.

8. Asad Haider, *Mistaken Identity: Race and Class in the Age of Trump* (New York:
Verso Books, 2018), 36.

In these scenes what might, in another language, have been the phenomenalization of a primitive figure consigned to identity and isolation
gets expressed instead as the perception of a regressive position of "racial ideology,"[9] the rac(ial)ism of an interlocutor who may or may not
be Black, but in any case serves as the conduit for an antiblackness for
which Black people will pay.[10] The turn to stance here is a metaracial
one. But, as metalevels of consciousnesses may be necessary for first-
order experience, second-order logics aren't necessarily second in time
or lower powered causally. The turn to stance, with its political twist—
how deep does it go, how wide is its circle, and how far back?

Metaracial logic—the substitution of stance for identity and its transposition of racial hierarchy—is not a technique of the post–civil rights
era but a complement to scientific racism that rises alongside it as a hab-
itable form for antiblackness on the left to take. I shall offer that Hegel's
philosophical project is not the sole origin, but is the consolidation of
metaracial logic, accomplishing its successful elaboration, psychologi-
zation, and institutionalization. Of course, Hegel should not be read as
an engineer of teleology but rather as an acerbic analyst of restlessness
and self-conflict. Not in spite but because of these qualities, the name
of "Hegel" signs a metaracial retrojection of "racialism." Both first- and
second-order figures of blackness and racialism assuage anxieties about
the bases of collectivity and the limitations of history.

9. On the twentieth-century history of Black radicals accused of racialism, see Michael Dawson, *Blacks in and out of the Left* (Cambridge, MA: Harvard University Press,
2013), 47–48. See also Dawson's criticism of the argument that antiracist efforts divided
a previously unified workers' left (171–174).

10. Fred Moten points out the "racialized responsibility for de-racialization" imposed
as a veritable "critique of blackness" ("Notes on Passage [The New International of Sovereign Feelings]," *Palimpsest: Journal on Women, Gender, and the Black International* 3
[2014]: 51–74, 53).

§ 1

The Metaracial

The West came to conveive of peoples whose self-realization could only exist as a function of securing its own (i.e., the West's) and ... its own people's self-realization ... it had also done so only by re-projecting its own agency and authorship onto entities that, while no longer supernatural, were no less extra-human.

SYLVIA WYNTER, "On How We Mistook the Map for the Territory, and Re-Imprisoned Ourselves in Our Unbearable Wrongness of Being, of *Désêtre*: Black Studies Toward the Human Project"

The philosopher ... sets himself up as the measuring rod of the alienated world.

MARX, *Economic and Philosophic Manuscripts of 1844*

Contemporary societies are not the first to confuse their desires not to be racist with their desires to minimize the scope of race. In 2014 the University of California Humanities Research Institute workshop, "Archives of the Non-Racial," noted:

> By the 19th century, the "non-racial" emerged as an intellectual, political, and ethical category, assuming a variety of interpretations. Indexed to different intellectual, social, and political contexts, at times the non-racial has stood for the idea of "a shared human nature." At others, it has gestured toward the idea of "abolition." Sometimes it has meant the erasure of "difference" and its substitution by "sameness" alongside the commitment to a set of universal moral principles.[1]

1. UC Humanities Research Institute, "Session 2014: Archives of the Non-Racial: A Mobile Workshop in South Africa." UCHRI Seminar in Experimental Critical Theory IX / Johannesburg Workshop in Theory and Criticism, http://sect.uchri.org/apply.

This institutional description presents the "non-racial" as divided into good, bad, and neutral-sounding forms. At best, the "non-racial" belongs to a vision of abolition; at worst, it is postracial in the cynical sense, a vision of sameness that disavows difference and, with it, racism.

Whatever is thought of as racial(ist), by contrast, is not ordinarily accorded a similar ambiguity and scope. Being unwelcome, it is presumed to belong to others, who are tasked with moving on from it. For the exemplary political identity, it is an object only of second-order complaint. This presumption is held in common by the radical vision of heterogeneous social relations and the liberal vision of placid human sameness. This notion that from within a desirable political project racialism must not belong to the political at its most exemplary is characteristic of both liberalism and radicalism and is a principle embedded in the philosophical sources of current constructions of collectivity. In a certain radical philosophy, the radical philosopher's foils and props are portrayed as unwilling to let go of a racial attachment. The radical philosopher's own role in the perceived situation is subtracted. The exchange does not appear as a dynamic but as the fault of other people who have the wrong commitments. The "tribal" attachment of the philosopher's foil or prop operates contrary to collective need: this need may be "the goal of authentic democracy"[2] or of communism. The pattern is a general one that constricts the spirit of radical movement as such. I'll explore this pattern within Hegel and will argue that the left interpretation of Hegel, following in his tracks, exposes the overlap between antiracism and antiblackness in and through its preparation for collectivity.

Negativity and Racialism

In Kant's and Hegel's constructions of actuality, reality becomes aligned with the nonracial. In Hegel, relation as a "discipline of the world" entails affirmation of a self created by and participating in a historically contingent process of negativity. On the whole, Hegel places what he imagines to be racially organized societies at history's margins— marginal in the sense that they have poor access to connections. As we'll see, Hegel attributes racialism primarily to non-Europeans: he is preoccupied by the "tribal" nadir of sub-Saharan Africa.[3] As I'll explore

2. Paul Gilroy, *Against Race: Imagining Political Culture Beyond the Color Line* (Cambridge, MA: Harvard University Press, 2002), 12.

3. Eric Williams is thus concerned to turn around Hegel's implications about the causes of slavery: slavery is an explanation of economic results (*Capitalism and Slavery* [1944] [Chapel Hill: University of North Carolina Press, 2021], 26). On slavery as a

in § 6, Hegel *aims* these remarks at German-speaking nations, whose disunity is "reflected to a significant degree" in the "career of the concept of spirit," as Stuart Hall points out.[4] Hegel insinuates that they shouldn't become like Africans—a version of the familiar trope that compares European workers to slaves in order to move them toward action. Hegel's stereotypical depictions of Africans, however, and even the global hierarchizations in his *World History*, are not the significant locations of his antiblackness. It is rather his second-order logic that pits open relation against an anxiety that he deflects with images of Black subpolitical existence. Yet this line of thought is characterized by Hegelians *as his antiracist potential*.

These implications bear on the radical, negative, nonteleological, "left" Hegel specifically. The problem with the consensus that Hegel's dialectical subtlety triggers "right" and "left" interpretations is that left Hegelians often assume that anti-Hegelians are objecting to the rightist Hegel and that their own task is therefore to explain the resources that Hegel nonetheless offers to the left. This gesture leaves no room for left criticism of left Hegelianism. Instead, it locates left racism only in other leftists making mistakes of exclusion. My goal here isn't to rehearse right/left arguments, and so I start with the following understandings:

1. Hegel is radically historical rather than dogmatic. He is opposed to nature and essence, even as he preserves the extent to which communities may require some notions of nature and essence. Further, his vision of history is neither progressive nor simply teleological, because
2. Hegelian subjectivity and historicity center self-division, aporia, disarticulation, and negativity, and are radically nonidentitarian;
3. Hegel promotes radical openness to historical ontology as structurally necessary positive and negative relation; relation and speculation should be understood as the media of openness and are themselves incomplete and open;
4. the speculative proposition is the container of relation in flux, and the template for all Hegelian propositions; and

---

problem that historical causality cannot solve "because it conditions the very tools [that historians] have at their disposal to think slavery at all," see Parisa Vaziri, "No One's Memory: Blackness at the Limits of Comparative Slavery," *Racial Formations in Africa and the Middle East: A Transregional Approach* 44 (2021): 14–19. See also Vaziri, "Arba'in and Bakhshū's Lament: African Slavery in the Persian Gulf and the Violence of Cultural Form," *Antropologia* 7 (2020): 191–214, and "On 'Saidiya': Indian Ocean World Slavery and Blackness beyond Horizon," *Qui Parle* 28, no. 2 (2019): 241–280.

4. Stuart Hall, *Essential Essays, vol. 1: Foundations of Cultural Studies* (Durham, NC: Duke University Press, 2018), 116.

5. relation in Hegel is grounded in nonrelation, the Absolute of the system, and this Absolute is absolutely the opposite of the "given."

It is *in these philosophical choices* that Hegel's antiblackness emerges *together with* his antiracism. They matter particularly much because they continue to characterize left preferences. Despite their inadequacies, I cannot help preserving the ambiguity of the terms *progressive*, *left*, and *radical* for the time being, not only because it's as difficult to say whether Hegel was radical or liberal as it is to say whether he was right or left but also because the logic consolidated in his philosophy affects the range of so-called progressive views from liberal to radical. I'm concerned to make the point that radicals cannot distinguish themselves from liberals in this regard—even as I am invested in what happens on the radical side. My argument pertains, then, to the post-Hegelian left especially. Its antiblackness acts *in and through* the values above, which can be shared across demographics. While philosophical parameters chosen by Hegel, Kant, and others make it difficult to perceive the antiblack inheritances of the post-Hegelian left, radical philosophy integrally cultivates these difficulties. When "racialism" is discovered in order to cast someone as *less political*, metaracial logic solidifies the former racial categories in the guise of stances. At issue are not Black people, now, but people who talk about blackness too much—and, therefore, Black people again at no more than one degree of separation. It follows that antiracist activity finds an enemy on one side and a prop or foil on the other: racists who are still practicing "racialism" and its errors, and those who take antiblackness as the main issue. Distinguishing antiblackness from racism helps to break this circle.

Hegel's Colonial Opening

The frantic negrophobia of Hegel's depiction of sub-Saharan Africa in *Lectures on the Philosophy of World History* is well known. Building on that familiarity, I'd like to explore Hegel's curious use of ideals of relation there and in the less discussed *Philosophy of Religion*. If Africa is "savage," it's because "Africa proper" is "self-enclosed" (Brown and Hodgson, 196).[5] According to Hegel, North Africa, being coastal and

---

5. G. W. F. Hegel, *Lectures on the Philosophy of World History*, vol. 1, ed. and trans. Robert F. Brown and Peter C. Hodgson (Oxford: Oxford University Press, 2011), 196. The question of which translation to use of Hegel's *Lectures on the Philosophy of World History*, assembled from sets of student notes, is not really solvable. Brown and Hodgson is the most recent translation. J. Sibree's 1858 translation of the introduction and lectures

oriented toward Europe, "is not independent on its own account…
Spain is said to belong to Africa. But it is just as correct to say that this
part of Africa belongs to Europe" (Brown and Hodgson, 197). Egypt,
meanwhile, is riparian and associates with the Mediterranean (Brown
and Hodgson, 197). Coastal rims, blue states of openness, "benefit from
the connecting aspect of the sea" (204); indeed, water "makes communication possible" (194). In the *Philosophy of Right* the sea "enlivens"
"relations to the external world … and for the ties of the soil and the
limited circles of civil life with its pleasures and desires, it substitutes
the element of fluidity, danger, and destruction" (EPR, § 247). Quite
explicitly, Hegel's sea embodies global relation as "medium": "Through
this supreme medium of communication, it also creates trading links
between distant countries, a legal [*rechtlichen*] relationship which gives
rise to contracts; and at the same time, such trade [*Verkehr*] is the greatest educational asset [*Bildungsmittel*], and the source from which commerce derives its world-historical significance" (EPR, § 247). Offering
states access to one another, ocean channels accelerate the projects of
"all great and enterprising nations" (EPR, § 247) and so, we can add in
this mercantile context,[6] ocean channels enhance relation and access

---

together is still the only place to find English versions of certain material (*Philosophy of
History*, trans. J. Sibree [Kitchener, Ontario: Batoche Books, 2001]). I use Brown and
Hodgson where possible and fall back on Sibree as necessary. Further, H. B. Nisbet's less
apologetic edition is sometimes indispensable (*Lectures on the Philosophy of World History. Introduction: Reason in History*, trans. H. B. Nisbet [Cambridge, UK: Cambridge
University Press, 1975]). These three translations of *World History* are henceforward referred to by the names of the translators.

As Nicholas Walker concludes, Brown and Hodgson's claims to have modernized
the translation are problematic and "in the last analysis most of the old and many of the
new problems associated with this controversial work remain largely impervious to such
textual and editorial changes and revisions" ("Review of Brown and Hodgson's Translation of Hegel, *Lectures on World History*," *Notre Dame Philosophical Reviews* [Decem-
ber 14, 2011]: unpaginated, https://ndpr.nd.edu/news/lectures-on-the-philosophy-of
-world-history-vol-i-manuscripts-of-the-introduction-and-the-lectures-of-1822–3/).
I find Brown and Hodgson's translation bland but use it as a control.

6. One entry point into the emphasis on open relation in German enlightenment
thought is the fact that German connections to the Atlantic slave trade and its economic
benefit are mercantile. Heike Raphael-Hernandez and Pia Wiegmink observe that although "for the longest time, Germany has entertained the notion that the transatlantic
slave trade and New World slavery involved only *other* European players," "turn[ing]
from a micro- to macro-economic level" finds German traders and shareholders sup-
porting the plantation economy and encouraging imperialism later in the century—
that is, a situation in which mercantile movement leads imperialism ("German Entanglements in Transatlantic Slavery: An Introduction," *Atlantic Studies* 14 [2017]:
419–495. On Hegel's notion of movement as an ambivalent response to global capital's

themselves as valued properties of anything. Thus, although North Africa remains African because it does not yet "stand on its own two feet" (Brown and Hodgson, 197), Hegel opines that it has access to influences that are likely to allow it to do so (Nisbet, 174), as previous civilizations also did before they became historical. Sub-Saharan Africa, in contrast, has no such access to relation, not even to other parts of Africa, such that the continent as a whole suffers from poor interrelation between its geographical regions (Brown and Hodgson, 196; Nisbet, 173).[7] African sparsity of relation is explicitly the obverse of Europe's frustrated access to Africa: "the Europeans ... have not yet penetrated into the highland, where riches are to be found in the most inaccessible conditions" (Brown and Hodgson, 196–197). Such is Africa's geographical destiny as a "highland" region.[8]

If Hegel's geographical materialism predicts cultural backwardness for Africa, his theory of historical realization, and particularly its emphasis on openness and negativity, registers his geographical materialism. For Hegel's account of Africa to be what it is, it must be able to indict African societies for being racial(ist). That is, "racial" practices are already a hallmark of the inadequately political. The key element of African societies' inferiority is their self-enclosure and "government ... patriarchal in character" (Nisbet, 185), by which Hegel means their

---

movement, see M. A. R. Habib, *Hegel and Empire: From Postcolonialism to Globalism* (New York: Palgrave McMillan, 2017), e.g., 59, 78.

7. Marx's *Grundrisse* explains how in early capitalist societies density of connection becomes aesthetically prized and metaphysically invested, and how indexes of relational density come to hierarchize forms of life: "it is always a certain social body, a social subject, which is active in a *greater or sparser* totality of branches" (*Grundrisse: Introduction to the Critique of Political Economy*, trans. Martin Nicolaus [New York: Vintage Books, 1973], 86).

8. Hegel subtextually implicates Prussia's discontinuous territory, its landlocked regions such as Bavaria and Austria. Felix Brahm and Eve Rosenhaft call German-speaking Europe a "hinterland" of slavery: a largely "inland area that is economically or politically related to a port city or a coastal area and connected via different transport routes" (*Slavery Hinterland: Transatlantic Slavery and Continental Europe, 1680–1850* [Woodbridge, UK: Boydell and Brewer, 2016], 4). Such regions of Europe worried about how to maximize their benefit from global trade (4n4). Brahm and Rosenhaft call these regions hinterlands in riposte to the common use of the term: "during the course of the 'Scramble for Africa' ... the Germans even introduced the term into colonial diplomacy to encompass and to claim a reputedly 'natural' sphere of interest behind the coastal area, one oriented towards both physical and human geographical criteria" (4). The "hinterlands" of Europe were not disconnected from the slave trade: they were insecure about *whether they were connected enough.* They may have felt an intensified desire for the profits of relation—and a particular urgency to be unlike sub-Saharan Africa.

reliance on kinship structures, or what he assumes are kinship structures.[9] Self-enclosure and kinship centeredness collapse into one: Hegel's causal reasoning here is that African societies, having no access to the foreign influences that would expand their scope, fall back into themselves and reproduce the prehistoric family unit.[10] Insofar as kinship structures are blood ties (Hegel does not explore the possibility of a difference between the two), Hegel's African societies are cast as racial in the way that later political science would criticize them for being "tribal."[11] The series abstract-nonracial-open and familial-racial-closed renews the racial hierarchy mythologized in travel literature.

Hegel's open reality, *and use of it to reproduce antiblack images of Africans*, is writ large in his philosophy altogether. It is metaracial: it targets "racialism" in general to embody it in racialized peoples specifically, with blackness mediating its organization. This point is lost if Hegel's internal conflicts and domestic interests are seen as contradictory with his antiblackness, or if he is seen as disingenuous. What if, instead, the antiblackness of Hegel's imagination and enclosure of sub-Saharan Africa *requires his antiracism*? Hegel mentions, for example, that "the original organization that created social distinctions" in India "immediately became set in stone as natural determinations (the castes)" (Brown and Hodgson, 116). In Hegel's account of India, "distinctions imposed by nature" capture the imagination of social relations at the first available moment (Brown and Hodgson, 116). Such periods of entrapment, he explains, may occur whenever "peoples may have had a long life without a state before they finally reach their destination" (Brown and Hodgson, 114).

In Hegel's Africa, by contrast, no impulse ever arises to make what is happening into a conscious social system, so that "even the family ethos

9. Hegel perceives what would count as kinship structures if they occurred in the German-speaking nations.

10. At this moment Hegel fails to extend to sub-Saharan Africans the dynamism he attributes to "natural organisms" whose "existence is not simply an immediate one which can be altered only by external influences" (Brown and Hodgson, 108).

11. Talal Asad argues that scholarship defaults to "kinship" as though it were the only way to describe "a category of societies variously labeled in classical anthropological literature as 'primitive,' 'acephalous,' 'tribal,' 'kin-based,' et cetera" ("Are There Histories of Peoples Without Europe? A Review Article," *Comparative Studies in Society and History* 29 [1987]: 504–607, 600.) Sifting the distinctions among groups classified in this way, Asad "suggest[s] a more radical conclusion: that *nothing* can be deduced about the structure and development of local economies from the fact that they employ kinship as the general principle for claims to social labor" (602; my italics). See also Asad, *Genealogies of Religion: Discipline and Reasons of Power in Christianity and Islam* (Baltimore, MD: Johns Hopkins University Press, 1993).

is lacking in strength" (Nisbet, 184–185). What Hegel imagines to precede social organization is a reproductive primal horde that, if it *were*
to be systematized, would generate a merely natural order, as in the example of Hegel's imagination of caste. Hegel's sub-Saharan Africa does
not even get that far. These imaginations function as justifications for
colonization, explicitly—and this justification serves as a warning to
the provincial German-speaking states. Hegel's Africans are collateral in
the antiracist cause of moving Germans toward abstraction. Yet, Hegel's
disapproval of "natural" orders is taken to be something he gets right
and as evidence for the extent to which he is antiracist. As Joseph Mc-
Carney writes, defending Hegel from Bernasconi's explanations of his
racism, "history is precisely, in one aspect at least, the escape of spirit
from nature, its overcoming of all natural determinants such as common descent or blood relationship."[12]

What is usually discussed as Hegel's development of abstract polity
out of negativity calls for the development of systems of access to colonies, first in the name of their stimulation and ultimately in the name
of a global society. *Relation after Hegel is not just interaction but interaction valued in this educative way.*[13] At the same time, it is also an unchosen totality for all, secured by the Absolute of nonrelation and productive of negativity. Affirming the relation/nonrelation axis in this way
bridges humanism and posthumanism and their two lines of left politics. In both, "disaccustoming" (Sibree, 339) prescribes customarily racial locations as surely as myths of modernity prescribe locations of
the primitive.

Nonrelation and Coerced Relation

In the informal pedagogy of the *Lectures on the Philosophy of World History*, which, readers are constantly reminded as an apology for them, are

12. Joseph McCarney, "Hegel's Racism? A Response to Bernasconi," *Radical Philosophy* 119 (2003): 32–37, 33.

13. Opacity in Edouard Glissant's *Poetics of Relation* is porous and never challenges
the Relation that "the world makes and expresses *of itself*" (my italics) through the "absolute" self-realization of movement (*Poetics of Relation*, trans. Betsy Wing [Ann Arbor:
University of Michigan Press, 1997], 160, 171). But Wynter offers a Fanonian reading of
Glissant in "Beyond the Word of Man: Glissant and the New Discourse of the Antilles,"
World Literature Today 63 (1989): 637–648, while Winfried Siemerling suggests that Glissant's opacity is a transformation of Du Bois's "veil" ("Du Bois, Hegel, and the Staging
of Alterity," *Callaloo* 24 [2001]: 325–333, 330). Both complicate what *Poetics of Relation*
overtly presents.

university lectures that were never published,[14] prescribed relationality can take on the trivial appeal of college breadth requirements. Relation in nonrelation must be affirmed to cultivate human potential. But although the register and sophistication of arguments changes from text to lecture (e.g., from *Logic* to *World History*), Hegel's posthumanist and humanist notions of nonrelation and relation alike are shaped by his "extraordinary stress on 'negativity,' becoming other to self, doubling or division."[15]

At its most uncontroversial, Hegelian subjectivity depends on the self's ability to be at odds with itself and the world, to feel the friction of situation, difference, and aggressivity ("abstract" or "simple" negation) and then, on reflection ("absolute" or double negation), to find actuality in complicity: "Living substance ... is in truth actual only as the movement of self-positing, or is the mediation of its becoming other than itself with itself. As subject, it is pure, simple negativity, and thereby the division of the simple, or a doubling which opposes, which is again the negation of this indifferent differentiation and its opposition."[16] Negativity generates an educated and invigorated subject of historical actuality, fit for action to the same extent that it is no longer preoccupied with "indifferent differentiation." Negativity is especially able to legitimate a radical stance because the political subject is shattered in it, displaying the complex objectivity of historical process.[17] Marx's early complaint that Hegel's philosophy sounded to him like "a grotesque melody of the rocks [Felsenmelodie]" contains this meaning: the world calls to the subject with a siren's song of necessary breakage emphasized with a strange pleasure.[18] Acting collectively depends fundamentally on the capacity to be educated toward the Absolute. But the capacity to learn from wreck, it turns out, can't be taken for granted. Rather, a new dilemma emerges.

---

14. For apologetics on this point, see Timothy Brennan, *Borrowed Light: Hegel, Vico, and the Colonies* (Stanford, CA: Stanford University Press, 2014), 98, 103.

15. Robert Pippin, *Idealism as Modernism: Hegelian Variations* (Cambridge, UK: Cambridge University Press, 1997), 389.

16. G. W. F. Hegel, *The Phenomenology of Spirit*, trans. A. V. Miller (Oxford: Oxford University Press, 1977), 10; henceforward PS.

17. "But what enables us to differentiate ourselves from the objects that we thus invent? Hegel's surprising answer is that we must find some other purposive intelligence, outside of ourselves, capable of viewing us instrumentally—in other words, capable of objectifying us" (Guyora Binder, "Mastery, Slavery, and Emancipation," *Cardozo Law Review* 10 [1989], 1435–1480, 1437).

18. *First Writings of Karl Marx*, edited by Paul M. Schafer (Brooklyn: Ig Publishing, 2006).

From this perspective, strata of Hegel's dialectic appear as follows. As *Lectures on the Philosophy of Religion* points out, relation is both built on top of "natural or necessary connection" and qualitatively distinct from it.[19] Even "natural organisms" split internally before they "engage with other things and thereby undergo a process of change" (LPR, 109). So, as I mentioned above, for Hegel, Indian society recognizes natural connection primarily. Relations can occur and be helpful for development, but remain narrow without wider contacts to develop them: "the precocious development of language and the progress and diffusion of nations [may] have acquired their significance and interest for concrete reasons, *partly in so far as the nations in question have had contact with other states*, and partly as they have begun to form constitutions of their own" (Nisbet 138; see also Brown and Hodgson 117; my italics).

But no amount of linguistic and mercantile finesse will make these peoples historical if they fail to be disturbed by friction. As Werner Hamacher writes, *something* "must be perceived as a non-given, something that holds itself back, something 'foreign' to which spirit entertains no 'positive' relation, and that means an absence of any determinate relation of positing: no positing relation at all. The relation to the 'natural' is thus at first the aporetic relation to the relationless."[20] Action begins with the "non-given": spirit depends on it. The radical Hegelian's journey in negativity discovers a disarticulation that is not confined to the inner nor to the outer. Without the "discipline of the world," there are realities, but no realization: "What has been reflection on our part must arise in the mind of the subject of this discipline [of the world] in the form of a consciousness that in himself he is miserable and null" (Sibree, 339).

Nonrelation connects the Hegel of organic growth to the radically anti-identitarian Hegel, the *Lectures* to the *Logic*. The disturbance of nonrelation provides the live element of historicity. Exposure to nonrelation, an "education" or "discipline" in the real, is uniquely catalytic, as its exposition in the vocabulary of the Absolute indicates. Historicity can exist only through contact with the "'foreign' to which spirit entertains no 'positive' relation" (Hamacher, *Premises*, 6).[21] Nonrelation occurs at any moment whatever. Yet, it's clear enough from Hegel's *World*

19. G. W. F. Hegel, *Lectures on the Philosophy of Religion*, vol. 2, *Determinate Religion*, ed. Peter C. Hodgson, trans. R. F. Brown, P. C. Hodgson, and J. M. Stewart (Berkeley: University of California Press, 1987), 364; henceforward LPR.

20. Werner Hamacher, *Premises: Essays on Philosophy and Literature from Kant to Celan*, trans. Peter Fenves (Cambridge, MA: Harvard University Press, 1999), 6–7.

21. Daniel Barber explains how *world* and *relation* are privileged terms of containment and binding. Through these superterms, "the *co*-existence, the *ensemble*, the *simul*-

History that not just anyone can realize its truth. Not scarce as opportunity, still "feel[ing oneself] as the negation of [one]self" (Sibree, 339) is precious and not to be assumed as a capacity.

Within this perspective, the sub-Saharan African is imagined not to understand negativity's rewards. In this way, "foreign" contact is both not actualized by everybody and required for all. The requirement makes access to others ethically possible to demand: the subject pays for it with the genuine abrasion of its own exposure to egoic destruction. Immediately, negativity is difficult to separate from the acquired taste for negativity, like a craving for the unfamiliarity of travel. Hegel's radically anti-identitarian movement of subjective undoing walks in the tracks laid by subject building, "rewriting the other as therapeutic environment."[22] Subject building and shattering are two kinds of "training" (Sibree, 116), humanist and posthumanist, with the same entrance requirements and effects.

This is something to remember, as contemporary criticism understandably flees the identitarian moment. Of course, it's fatal that Hegel substitutes pulp fiction images of Africa for something that he states he can't comprehend "because it is so totally different from our own culture, and so remote and alien in relation to our own mode of consciousness" (Nisbet, 176). It can seem clearly better for Hegel to focus on nonrelation, where the Absolute has no repeating properties and no prerequisites. In his best-known formulations Hegel calls precisely for staying with the negative, which renews itself at every moment. Yet, as soon as Hegel does this he makes "openness" into the measure of authentic development *and uses it to generate antiblack images of Africans who "lack" it.*

Do we want to say here that Hegel is insincere, that he doesn't "really" open up to relation and nonrelation, at least as soon as sub-Saharan Africa enters the picture? Or that there is a moment in this argument that does not yet affiliate the open with the global, so that it might be stopped at the right place? Or should we say, more inconveniently, that

---

taneous presence" of antagonistic terms is made to last ("World-Making and Grammatical Impasse," *Qui Parle* 25 [2016], 179–206, 187).

22. Erin Trapp shows how psychoanalytic projection "falls short" in describing this phenomenon ("Human Rights Poetry: Ferida Durakovic's *Heart of Darkness,*" *Journal of Narrative Theory* 44 [2014]: 367–394, 371). To go further, she mobilizes Denise Ferreira da Silva and Paula Chakravartty, "Accumulation, Dispossession, and Debt: The Racial Logic of Global Capitalism—an Introduction," *American Quarterly* 64 (2012): 361–385. See also Trapp, "Human Rights Poetry and the Poetics of Nonhuman Being: Dunya Mikhail's Writing of Disaster," *Social Text* 36.4 (2018): 81–110. These are essays with methodological significance beyond their contexts.

there's a problem in Hegelian negativity and actuality altogether which is exposed when Hegel makes disturbance criterial to actuality as such, however complexly understood?[23] Can a measure of someone's contact with reality not be a weapon? For Hegel's conclusion is literally that, because within their own societies Africans supposedly do not experience the dismemberment of negativity, and rather encounter negativity everywhere but without being disturbed by it, they remain at an irrational stage of "racialism."

This reasoning is metaracial in that it imputes racialism to Africans to demand access to Africa. Access claims to be nonracial because it desires opening. Here metaracial logic creates "racialist" elsewheres through complaints about overvaluation of kinship, attachment, and so forth on the part of the others of Europe: their lack of openness, their lack of access to or disinterest in relation and organization, and their failure to be properly troubled by nonrelation and enriched by negativity. As part of the same train of thought, Hegel complains that Africans "see nothing unbecoming" in being connected to Europeans only through their own slave trade (Sibree, 116). Quite literally, their racialism is why Africans must remain enslaved for a while longer.

In these texts, Black figures are not quite deployed to stand for nonrelation itself (as in Wilderson's hypothesis that blackness inhabits the nonrelational place of the Real[24]—although a similar logic is working at one remove). They are lined up before the Real along with others, but singularly fail to notice it, and so are distant from negativity by their own error. This imputed imperviousness to disarticulation implies that, as Donna Jones explores, "black people are not thought to die," dying being an achievement of individuality.[25] Without the productive dimensions of negativity, life in sub-Saharan Africa "consists of a series of contingent happenings and surprises" (Nisbet, 176)—

23. Pippin clarifies that "the point of Hegel's denying to finite, empirical reality the gold standard badge of true actuality is not to say that it 'possesses' a lesser degree of reality." Rather, "finite objects *viewed in their finitude* ... can never reveal the possibility of their own intelligibility." This clarification means, for him, that Hegel is not afflicted with "'degrees of reality' Platonism" (*Hegel's Realm of Shadows: Logic as Metaphysics in the* Science of Logic [Chicago: University of Chicago Press, 2019], 97, 96). My point is exactly that Hegel transfers the low "degree of reality" previously projected onto finite objects *into* the metalevel of proper *stances toward them*, where he reconstitutes the hierarchy.

24. Frank B. Wilderson III, *Red, White, & Black: Cinema and the Structure of U.S. Antagonisms* (Durham, NC: Duke University Press, 2010), 75.

25. Donna Jones, "Inheritance and Finitude: Toward a Literary Phenomenology of Time," *ELH* 85 (2018): 289–303, 300.

by which fact itself, however, Africans cannot, according to Hegel, be surprised.

Hegel's deployment of nonrelation and relation to verify the real historicity of the globalizing world adds a progressive twist to the common idea, descending from the open admissions policy of Pauline Christianity, that relation, the medium of intelligible existence, must be affirmed or the failure to affirm it be classified as lesser. From a Pauline perspective "the Jewish religion" lacks the "latitudinarian tolerance" (Sibree, 215) of international modernity (LPR, 372–274).[26] Discourses of globalization and open markets draw on the Christian ethics of the open;[27] similarly, Christianity moralizes and promulgates a struggle with Judaic "racialism" in offering itself as freedom from it. Hegel insists that he judges Judaism only by its weak commitment to open access: "it is only a limitation in this respect and not a limitation of the religion [as such]" (LPR, 374)—necessarily, or it would otherwise be Christianity! In this way Judaic "particularity" and "egoism,"[28] Muslim "excarnation"[29] and the provinciality of certain forms of Christianity are born together with the violence of their vaunted open alternative.[30] The Christian structure of Hegel's anti-identitarianism is as well known as his hostility to certain existing forms of Christianity *for still not being open enough.*

26. According to Hegel the nationalization of God is not exclusive to Judaism but integral to it. When Christians act this way, they are acting atypically and unnecessarily restricting Christianity (LPR, 372).

27. As the historian of time Vanessa Ogle shows, nineteenth-century coordinators of time schemes, building global capital, quickly came to perceive "peoples who do not partake" in the global effort as "guilty of the crime of opposing it" (*The Global Transformation of Time, 1870–1950* [Cambridge, MA: Harvard University Press, 2015], 24).

28. Literary and philosophical revolutionists of the period 1815–1848 commonly attacked "destructive self-love." But images of Jewishness were "reinterpreted as the personification of . . . egoism." In this secularization of a previous antisemitic script, rather than failing to love Christ, Jews were accused of "reject[ing] love itself" (Paul Lawrence Rose, *German Question/Jewish Question: Revolutionary Antisemitism in Germany from Kant to Wagner* [Princeton, NJ: Princeton University Press, 1990], 27–28).

29. Kathleen Biddick, *Make and Let Die: Untimely Sovereignties* (New York: Punctum Books, 2016), 81–106.

30. Paul Lawrence Rose's study bursts with examples of self-satisfied openness in the discourse of the German left, such as the exclamation of the philosopher Friedrich Wilhem Carové: "Is it not the most beautiful part of German national character to honor the rights also of *foreigners?*" (Rose, *German Question/Jewish Question,* 114). Carové, like Hegel, Bauer, Marx, and many others in this discourse, supported Jewish emancipation; but antisemitism is a lot more than a political position against Jewish emancipation. Derrida's analysis of Hegel's writings on Jewishness and Judaism is relentless and devastating on this point (*Glas* [1974], trans. John P. Leavey [Lincoln: University of Nebraska Press, 1986], esp. 40–85).

Radical philosophy can now reread Hegel's history of religion and the nineteenth century secularization movements of which it is part for their contribution to a global order, organizing state reforms but also informing revolutionary movement beyond issues of governmental form, with both domestic European and transnational implications. On the domestic front, the "latitudinarian tolerance" of religion at its best sharpens into "*political* union" (Sibree, 216), passage from nation to people. From here on, *political* joins the growing list of normative terms that mark the presence of modernity, as Robinson argues in *Terms of Order*.[31] From here on, there are political (modern, contingently historical) societies and nonpolitical or insufficiently political (primitive or "tribal," at most provincially national) societies. Hegel aligns them with the nonracial and the racialist: "nonracial" values take over and project a former hierarchy of beings. His exemplary political identity may now discover more and less mature fractions of populations against the background of groups that are not properly political, like so-called kinship societies. Of course, radicals in Hegel's society, as after, were working against reaction, including biological racism in many cases. My point is that they do that by reproaching racialized people with racialism. Unlike postracialists with crypto-biological theories, they are antiracists with antiblack political theories.

As practiced, Hegel's union of political citizens resembles "common participation" (Sibree, 349) in a church regulated by spirit's "authority for the truth and for the relation of each individual to the truth" (Sibree, 350). In a secular vocabulary, social reality is now regulated through each member's avowal of relations—regional, colonial, and international—in all the fullness possible. This collective web maintains individuals, as individuals are fulfilled only in relations. "Independent subjectivity," Hegel specifies, is "the soil on which grows the True" (Sibree, 352); but separated, the individual person or society falls into barbarism.

At the height of Hegel's secularization of Christianity, "the attributes of God are God's relation to the world" (LPR, 326). With great consistency, in secular terms the attributes of human beings are *only* their relations in the world: "The way in which one human being is related to another—that is just what is human, that is human nature itself. When we are cognizant of how an object is related [to everything else], then we are cognizant of its very nature. To distinguish between the two [i.e., relation and nature] is to make misguided distinctions that col-

31. Cedric Robinson, *Terms of Order: Political Science and the Myth of Leadership* [1980] (Chapel Hill: University of North Carolina Press, 2016).

lapse straightaway because they are productions of an understanding that does not know what it is doing" (LPR, 160). In a memorable footnote, Hegel compares the entity in relation to an element in chemical reaction: "the acid is nothing else than the specific mode of its relation to the base—that is the nature of the acid itself" (LPR, 162).

The metaphor of acid is a fine articulation of how positions in social relation are not congealed in objects, a view that wholly avoids both reification and idealization. A lot of radical philosophy is linked to this sentence; everyone will like it—I like it. And indeed, maintaining a relational view of the world is already for Hegel what it is for contemporary theory, a safeguard against reduction to identity. In the name of this safeguard, the relation must be utter, "nothing else than" relation relating to nonrelation in continual breakdown and transformation. "Nothing else" lays all attachments down at the door at considerable expense, so no complaint of easiness-on-the-self can be made. Inside the door, then, is the exemplary radical Hegelian and its future, and this threshold will have been hard-earned. But at such moments, Hegel tends to emphasize a failure to affirm difficult transformation, either by others or by an other within. That other can be part of oneself, and Hegel furnishes a range of foils and props who fulfill the function in ways that have consequences for each of them. All are primitivist figures in that their one-sidedness is what the primitive looks like within a philosophy that believes it has no stock in primitive substrates. Within Europe, Hegel's foil appears not in the form of an innocent given but of someone who must *want* to "go back" to one, or at least not be present. It is not a constitutively inferior being incapable of perceiving more than one side of reality, but a primiti*vist* subject disavowing the truth of complicity: "the evil consciousness in its one-sided insistence on itself" (PS, § 662).

In contrast to the domestic foils that I'll discuss in part 3—personae of perversity and apostasy—it's revealing that Hegel doesn't interpret sub-Saharan non-Christianity as either a refusal or a disavowal. It is as though, in Robinson's intriguing phrase, there were "political societies ... and those societies in which the question did not come up" (Robinson, *Terms*, 3). At the same time, there must be a possibility for political society that hasn't *yet* come up or hasn't been taken up. This horizon of possibility appears clearly in the *Phenomenology* as a dynamic between slavery, coloniality, and international relations. It just might be that bondage will produce the opportunity for freedom, as the master-slave dialectic intimates. By placing sub-Saharan Africans at the limit of history and showing the slave turning toward the political in the master-slave dialectic, Hegel materializes racial*ism* as a racial trait of the sub-Saharan manifested in their insufficient politicality: a racial trait left behind by fully political Black people.

Blank Reflections

Obviously, Hegel's view of African societies isn't based on familiarity. He assumes that their practices are what his travel reading sounds like to him. Unlike Rousseau, he never wonders how his ideas would be evaluated outside the West. The situation would not necessarily be improved if he did, and notably, neither does epistemic critique improve it, even as, at the same time, I have not reached the end of it. The end of it is the fact that Hegel's pejorative descriptions sketch alternative societies that Hegel imagines in order to reject them. By gathering ideas that recur across his descriptions of various regions (reflecting the fact that the descriptions never describe regions responsibly), it is possible to piece together, as fantastic literature, what the imaginary societies of *World History* and *Philosophy of Religion* would look like if they were not being classified as insensible and perverse, respectively. The blank pages of history aren't completely blank. A certain alternative vision inhabits Hegel's lectures ephemerally, an apparition reflected in his choices, and so it is also something to ponder.

Again and again, Hegel imagines a landscape populated by many and various groups, "specialised in idiosyncrasies" (Sibree, 338). The groups are polytheistic as an aggregate and internally, which makes for a proliferation of powers and imaginations (LPR, 366). These polytheisms do not strive beyond the situations in which they find themselves but seem to orient themselves to a local environment or community (Sibree, 216), reflecting places and groups and, sometimes, particular persons. In general people inhabit societies of "prosaic things" and "understanding beings" (Sibree, 364). Hegel supposes that no further ordering of practices takes place; "hap and genius" account for what there is (Sibree, 352). These societies may have no arts or may have merely "beautiful" ones that stress sensory pleasures. They support themselves in subsistence economies, often nomadic ones (Sibree, 216); they live day to day without interpreting difficulty and precarity as discipline and disarticulation. Hegel imagines these polities to be based on kinship structures. In these societies' notion of origin, springs of motion lie in objects. Hegel interprets that in India the creation of the world involves "going forth," meaning that creativity lies in beings that go forth on their own rather than in an originary force that expresses them (LPR, 360).

The gods go forth of their own accord, which implies that they are finite and that the origin is just any place at all.

This situation inhibits the development of value. Everything is "special," so nothing is.[32] Instead, there is texture and variety to the point of saturation. Meaningfulness, you might say, proliferates instead of value. The sun and the mountains possess mentality and volition (Sibree, 215), and it becomes easy for people to "relate themselves to the divine" (LPR, 364). Of this *accessibility* to the divine, which Hegel could be expected to admire if it were facilitated by a constructed relation, he remarks that it is "an identity cheaply obtained. In fact it is everywhere" (LPR, 364). Crucially, and consistently with all the above, people in such societies "let themselves be determined from without" (LPR, 356)—even from without the human. Their authorities are themselves aleatory. Hegel is particularly fascinated by the "oracles" that, he reads, were used in both Indian and Greek societies to "allow the decision to be given from without": "Here no articulated answer was given. Their [oracles'] manifestation is some sort of external transformation, metallic forms, the rustling of trees, the blowing of the wind, visions, examinations of sacrificial animals, and contingencies of that sort. People needed such things in order to reach decisions" (LPR, 356). The societies he imagines in his peripheral vision are both long lasting and ephemeral, slow to change and fragile. They may not leave much trace, nor care to.

The story is problematic, even as fiction. It is the unencountered, never negated other of Hegel's philosophy of history, which is to say that it is primitivist—not a lifestyle to save from historicity's destructiveness but the inside-out of the one Hegel organizes. Hegel's peripheral images of racial(ist) societies can do no more than raise the question of what he stands against. Whether such societies ever existed is not the question to ask, but why, regardless of whether they exist or not, Hegel is so avid to overcome these features of *possible* societies. Moreover, what does it mean that the principles of radical history that he develops espouse their subordination as desirable, and their elimination as possible, practices? It's not only that the worth placed on the familiar oppositions of development and "tradition," consciousness and "immediacy," and so on down the line could be different but also that their production constitutes the process of *realization altogether*. That's

32. Peter Park notes that Hegel feels obliged to distinguish his own totalization from pantheism (*Africa, Asia, and the History of Philosophy: Racism in the Formation of the Philosophical Canon, 1780–1830* [Albany, NY: SUNY Press, 2013], 146). As we'll see, Marx also accuses Hegel of secularized pantheism.

why translation into any terminology other than Hegel's own—*prosaic activity* instead of *immediacy*, for example—at least illuminates its costs even though there is no nonracist language to use instead. The momentary shift of language is enough to underline, with the disappearance of the nonracial, that it is not hunter-gatherer societies that need to be restored to Hegel's analysis but the specialness of relation within it that needs to be understood as rendering *any* other principle and practice impossible, including future ones.

In global complicity the landscape (this too will have been an invention) in which everything matters is replaced with a thrilling sense that indeed—as exchange value allows—none of it needs to mean anything. Then there come the terminal moves of which capitalism is so fond, in which the fact that, indeed, none of it *needs* to mean anything means that none of it does mean anything. "Nowhere are to be found such revolutionary utterances as in the Gospels; for everything that had been respected, is treated as a matter of indifference—as worthy of no regard" (Sibree, 345).

Hegel breathlessly fetishizes the radicality of this gesture in and of itself, focused on its power rather than its effects. The same ecstasis greets Hegel's torn and disarticulated exemplary subject; its dismemberment is told and retold as a graphic dazzle. The "severe" edge of the lines that caricature it mimics the "discipline of the world."[33] No one is a stranger to the elation of the gesture, and it can be a fine thing—for instance, to put it to work toward the destruction of all, under the name of civilization, that made it possible to eliminate life that seemed "nonhistorical." But the gesture, and more than gesture, the strategies that align with it, create praiseworthy complicity by transposing trait into stance. In series, those stances have included the "tribalism" of "primitive" societies, the stances of the slave as an exemplary political actor or its excess, the racialism of the nonpolitical and subpolitical identity, the stance of someone too concerned with antiblackness.

Hegel's philosophy of history is alluring because it makes negativity and complicity into badges of honor, but it may look different once one grasps that, in doing so, he makes them powerfully normative of reality for all. Dismemberment's power to legitimate a new subject is visible in the frequency with which contemporary Hegelians point to it, as though to say that no one would invent a subjectivity based on dismemberment. These negative forms of historical legitimation, too, become criteria for a hierarchy of stances molded to a previous racial

33. On "severity," see Rose, *Hegel Contra Sociology*, 55–62, 160–165.

hierarchy. Because anyone can affirm historical dislocation, everyone who is anyone must.

In·this way, contemporary historical subjectivity selects a political society with a nonracial (metaracial; conventionally racialized) horizon, whether or not that horizon is thought of as attainable. The complex that Hegel refines is not the only way to conserve racial hierarchy in the early nineteenth century or now. It is a way of organizing it consonant with an epistemology that allows for radical change, and a key to the limits of antiracism thereafter, for radical political identities must transmute any racial content into metaracial stances.

§ 2

Metaracial Logic and Nationalism

There is no bridge by which one can pass from the universal idea of the organism to the particular idea of the organism of the state ... nor will there ever be.

—MARX, *Critique of Hegel's Philosophy of Right*

Hegel's relation/nonrelation axis supports the discipline of international relations. Tracing its emergence in Hegel means understanding his deployment of Africa with a domestic end in mind, as I'll discuss more in § 8. For now, it may be helpful to ask what Hegel's construction of reality for radicals must add to thought about nation-states in the nineteenth century. Is there such a thing as a metaracial logic of nationalism and internationalism, given the former's claim to move from identity to stance, from ontology to policy?

Theories of state both assume that nationality must be transcended in the abstraction of the state and use the openness of Hegelian relation to legitimate international and domestic colonialism. The interest of the state here is that the state—again, in Hegel an abstract harbinger of future polities—stands to inadequately political society as ontology does to the ontic. It claims to overcome a racialism that it projects onto its predecessor. As Marx comments in his *Critique of Hegel's Philosophy of Right*, "Hegel is right, therefore, when he says: the political state is the constitution, that is, the material state is not political."[1] The sequence material state—political state uses the sequences abstract—real, ontic—ontological. Reflecting on various forms of state (feudal, classical), Marx insists that the "political state" presumes and relies on

1. Karl Marx, *Critique of Hegel's Philosophy of Right* [1843], in *Writings of the Young Marx on Philosophy and Society*, trans. and ed. Lloyd D. Easton and Kurt H. Guddat (New York: Anchor/Doubleday, 1967), 151–202, 175; henceforward CHPR.

"private" spheres that come into being only beside its own rise: it relies on them for its *perceptibility* and *intelligibility*. The implication is that as the ontological continues to project the ontic, the political state cannot do without its nonpolitical and subpolitical excesses (I will come back to this in § 9).

In movement from "content" to constitution in *The Philosophy of Right,* a nation's [eines Völkes] unity is realized in its relations as a state with other states. Hegel supports the "self-awareness which an autonomous nation possesses" while asserting that its individuality can only be expressed globally, "in relation to the others" (EPR, § 322). Crucially, this self-awareness *can't preserve itself merely in thought*, as it does in Kant. National self-awareness must be *invested in global actions to realize itself.* "The ethical health of nations" resides in their risking themselves in war (EPR, § 324). And national health only stays healthy when it's dynamic over time. The nation's desire to become itself demands that it desire, in and through its self-awareness, the material self-transformation of international exploits. Nor is "the violence in question ... merely equivalent to, or circumscribed by the national formation."[2]

Hegel explains that nations that are not transformational will *become racial.* Notoriously, Kant's teleology installs race as a suite of evolved characteristics. A race lives in a certain landscape with its set of capacities, and if by misfortune a population should be displaced, its people will eventually perish of their indelible limitations in unsympathetic geography.[3] Hegel replies: a nation that declines transformation will become a racial society, *through its failure to realize its abstraction.* This

2. Lindon Barrett, *Racial Blackness and the Discontinuity of Western Modernity,* ed. Justin A. Joyce, Dwight A. McBride, and John Carlos Rowe (Urbana: University of Illinois Press, 2014). 28.

3. Immanuel Kant, "On the Use of Teleological Principles in Philosophy" [1788], trans. G. Zoller, in *Anthropology, History, and Education,* ed. and trans. R. B. Louden and G. Zoller (Cambridge, UK: Cambridge University Press, 2007), 195–218. This essay and associated writings have been the focus of analyses of Kant's negrophobia. Mikkelsen summarizes scholarship in philosophy up to 2013 in his introduction to his translation of Kant's other essays on race (*Kant and the Concept of Race: Late Eighteenth-Century Writings* [Albany, NY: SUNY Press, 2013], 1–18). R. A. Judy, "Kant and the Negro," *Surfaces* 1, no. 8 (1991): 4–70, and "Kant and Knowledge of Disappearing Expression," in *A Companion to African-American Philosophy,* ed. Tommy L. Lott and John P. Pittman (Oxford: Blackwell, 2003), 110–224, are definitive.

The scholar I most associate with Kant's "On the Use of Teleological Principles," though, is Nahum Chandler; see Chandler, *X—The Problem of the Negro as a Problem for Thought* (Bronx, NY: Fordham University Press, 2013), 191, and "Paraontology: Or, Notes on the Practical Theoretical Politics of Thought," Cornell University, October 15, 2018. Chandler underscores the violence of closing down the possibility of others'

could occur through stupid recalcitrance, as in the case of German nations, or through lack of opportunity and its resulting insensibility, as
in the case of sub-Saharan Africa. It is possible for a population never
to have wanted transformation. A people's lack of national desire will
have shown in their weak domestic energy, their "failure to organize
the power of the state from within" (EPR, § 324). From the vantage of
The Philosophy of Right, they betray an absence of *"disposition to act in
close association" "toward a common end"*[4] (EPR, § 327; my italics). If nations that have no wars or colonies stagnate, these are the same nations
"which are reluctant or afraid to accept internal sovereignty."[5] With no
experience of sovereignty, they "may be subjugated by others." ("Unable to represent themselves, they must be represented," Marx writes
describing the masses in *The Eighteenth Brumaire of Louis Bonaparte*.)
For "in *peace*, the bounds of *civil life* are extended, all its spheres become
firmly established, and in the long run, people become stuck in their
ways. Their particular characteristics [Partikularitaten] become increasingly rigid and ossified" (EPR, § 324).

A nation could fall into backwardness and corporealize: these are not
Kant's evolutionarily circumscribed Africans, whose future shrivels in
a realm of natural indifference. Hegel's nations are complicit in their
stagnation, their future compressed between their own lassitude and
a colonizing threat. The problem is not that Hegel leaves the agency of
political freedom with the enslaved. It is the assumption that popular
sovereignty is the opposite and negation of slavery as it is of tyranny.
Hegel assumes the accoutrements of an already political world into
which the slave must fit, and therefore does not pay attention to what
slavery may hold other than the negativity that should nurture subjectivity. Also problematic is the corollary that a people must subdue others (internally or externally) before another rightfully subdues them,
since the society that has fallen from or failed to rise into legitimate na-
tionhood is likely to run into a state in pursuit of self-realization. Hegel

---

future: "On the order of historical generality that he names as 'civilization,' Du Bois calls
such presumption murder" (*Toward an African Future: Of the Limit of World* [London:
Living Commons Collective, 2013], 101).

4. Hegel goes on in an addition, "the true valor of civilized nations [Völker] is their
readiness for sacrifice in the service of the state ... integration with the universal is
the important factor here. In India, five hundred men defeated twenty thousand who
were not cowards, but who simply lacked the disposition to act in close association with
others" (EPR, § 324).

5. The implicit threat to German-speaking polities—that they shouldn't languish in
disorganization if they don't want to become French—does not similarly capture what
is in store for Africans, nor the reasons why.

supposes a relation that is simultaneously a chain, connection as possibility and connection as coercion. As Enrique Dussel notes, colonialism in Hegel becomes "a condition of the possibility of the constitution of the absolute state, the modern European state,"[6] and the generation of "ossified" societies its collateral effect. Colonialism, in other words, can be represented as a line sent from a state to its fantasy of primitive society, in which its own racial status is the stake. In this version of civilizing mission, the state believes that it doesn't want the society it perceives as ossified to be so anymore;[7] it wants the world to open up to itself. Therefore it produces that society as "particular" and "ossified," lackng its own self-critical self-realization. The supposed isolation, commercial or spiritual, of the society seen as racial(ist) by the metaracialist is an "isolation" ironically kept close at hand, "discouraged from existing beyond its separation from the human," as Marriott remarks of the "grammar of separation" that keeps blackness near humanness.[8]

state

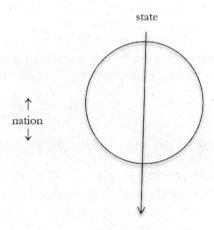

nation

"ossified characteristics"

6. Enrique Dussel, *Politics of Liberation: A Critical World History* [2007], trans. Thia Cooper (London: SCM Press, 2011), 397. See also Dussel, "Beyond Eurocentrism: The World-System and the Limits of Modernity," in *The Cultures of Globalization*, ed. Fredric Jameson and Masao Miyoshi (Durham, NC: Duke University Press, 1998), 3–31 and "Transmodernity and Interculturality: An Interpretation from the Perspective of Philosophy of Liberataion," *Transmodernity: Journal of Peripheral Cultural Production of the Luso-Hispanic World* 1 (2012): 28–59.

7. The second half of this sentence cancels the first: the satisfaction in being nonracial (regulatively) and "racialist" to a lesser degree can't exist without the other society's racialism.

8. David S. Marriott, *Whither Fanon? Studies in the Blackness of Being* (Stanford, CA: Stanford University Press, 2017), 330.

Nation is therefore a middle term that can rise into the state or fall into the racial society, and thereby serves as a reservoir from which the state can draw inspiration without having to grant similar latitude to societies that don't have states—or colonies—of their own. Even at this early date, then, the racial(ist) society is a nonpolitical or subpolitical society *ideationally*, according to its degree of self-awareness or insensibility. Eventually, at another turn, nationalism will come to be seen as racial polity itself. Yet, in statehood it depends on the lesser reality of nonpolitical and subpolitical spaces, too.

This play of force, counterforce, and situation, the conditions of emergence of each contest of power, contextualize Hegel's approach to the agency, and therefore the negativity and emancipation, of slaves. In *Elements of the Philosophy of Right*, Hegel writes

> If we hold firmly to the view that the human being in and for himself is free, we thereby condemn slavery [Sklaverei]. But if someone is a slave, his own will is responsible, just as the responsibility lies with the will of a people if that people is subjugated. Thus the wrong of slavery is the fault not only of those who enslave or subjugate people, but of the slaves and the subjugated themselves. Slavery ... occurs in a world where a wrong is still a right. Here the wrong *is valid*, so that the position it occupies is a necessary one. (EPR, § 57)

Clearly, part of the trouble is the "if" clause. The clause assumes a previous philosophy that justifies slavery on the grounds that human beings are not always in and for themselves, but in countering that view furnishes the complementary justification. Although the literary drama of the *Phenomenology* does not occur in this text, the reader may still discern a distinctly unfree Prussian narrator identifying with a slave. I agree with Nesbitt, who takes the paragraph to refer to chattel slavery, that the passage is telling the "people" to get up and open the door, if possible, while also implying that it really cannot open now.[9]

The reason lies in "those who enslave or subjugate people" and the "world where a wrong is still a right." But it is more complicated as soon as, putting this together with the previous passages of *Philosophy of Right*, those who enslaved and subjugated did so in order to maintain their strength, *in order not to ossify in their particular characteristics* (EPR, § 324), in order not to be enslaved. This slavery is "valid" not only in the minimal sense that it is able to be at all but in the sense that

---

9. For alternative exposition of this passage, see Nesbitt, *Universal Emancipation*, 118–124.

another nation moves to actualize itself through it. Together, these lines imply that that in the course of making the world real, derealization occurs in the colonies as a collateral effect. Integrating slavery into capitalism "inseparabl[y,]" making it the "cornerstone of capitalism's articulation of exploitation, appropriation, and dispossession,"[10] tracks this effect without perceiving it.

Elsewhere, Hegel reflects on derealized zones and entities through the idea of sublation, another form of validity, not for peoples but for history and the species. In the context of slavery, however, sublation looks like a means of retrojecting human resources. Reflecting on the "estrangement" integral to Hegel's process, and the fact that in Hegel there is no alternative to externalization, since every alienation externalizes itself in some way in turn, Ray Brassier concludes that Hegel "requires self-consciously projecting the retrospective preconditions that determine our current possibilities. We must retroject a previous unfreedom, or estrangement, in order to discern our current measure of freedom, not as a positive, substantial attribute, but as the estranging of estrangement."[11] This always "previous" unconsciousness projected from the present, even when it is only a moment ago, and even when it brings only a negative realization of one's own self-contradiction, is now the very resource of enabling action. The contradiction grasped "provides the ground for re-founding the actuality of society" (Brassier, 104). Brassier's "indivisible movement wherein estrangement and de-estrangement, compulsion and freedom, coincide" translates what I have been trying to describe as actualization's derealization of the subpolitical *slave maudit*. After Hegel, this double movement is the spring of springs.

10. Nikhil Pal Singh, "On Race, Violence, and So-called Primitive Accumulation," *Social Text* 128 (2016): 27–50, 43.

11. Ray Brassier, "Strange Sameness: Hegel, Marx, and the Logic of Estrangement," *Angelaki* 24 (2019): 103.

§ 3

Around Political Identity: Master, Slave, Bondsman, Objects

The individual as he appears in this world of prose and every day is not active out of his own self and resources, and he is intelligible not from himself, but from something else.

HEGEL, *Aesthetics*

[Negativity] is also a superior mark of the transformative, insofar as it makes something by cutting through the "pure and simple" of the "undifferentiated."

HORTENSE SPILLERS, *Black, White, and in Color: Essays on American Literature and Culture*

No particular body in the scene incorporates the ontology of racial blackness.

LINDON BARRETT, *Racial Blackness and the Discontinuity of Western Modernity*

Hegel's Slave Protagonist

Hegelian thought continues to generate critical provocations regarding inhabiting a violent totality. These provocations include the involuntary relationality of forces and entities; productive negativity; a mediated reality of disjunction, open-ended historicity, and complicity; and a subjectivity or nonsubjectivity of self-shattering, constitutively broken rather than whole, freeable through its surrender to historicity rather than through subjective sovereignty classically understood.

If the potential of these Hegelian principles is celebrated, there is less consensus about how to hold them together with Atlantic slavery.[1] C. L. R. James's enjoyment of Hegelianism's diagnostic power against Stalinism, Stuart Hall's essays working through "unresolved difficulty (and genuine curiosity) concerning Hegel" and Ferreira da Silva's extensive criticism are cases in point.[2] Yet Hegelians often argue that Hegel "above all" "gives us true risk, gives us hope," "offers a political subjectivity capable of escaping the dominant social order," and "gives an explicit theoretical space to non-western thought."[3] It can seem that because historicity and subjectivity are disjunctive and empty in Hegel, Hegelianism can provide the resources for an antiracist politics that, accepting contradiction, eludes humanism and identity or revises them to such an extent that they become open categories.[4]

1. The extensive literature on this question extends from midcentury Marxist studies of US slavery in various languages and nations to Fanon and his legacy to reassessments of philosophy in Black Studies. For a recent organization of some of the main issues, see Ulrike Kistner, Philippe van Haute, and Robert Bernasconi, eds., *Violence, Slavery and Freedom between Hegel and Fanon* (Johannesburg: Wits University Press, 2020).

2. C. L. R. James, *Notes on Dialectics: Hegel, Marx, Lenin* (Westport, CT: Lawrence, Hill & Co., 1980); Gregor McLennan, "Editor's Discussion of Part I Materials," in *Selected Writings on Marxism*, by Stuart Hall, ed. Gregor McLennan (Durham, NC: Duke University Press, 2021), 158–176, 172.

3. Clayton Crockett and Creston Davis, introduction to *Hegel and the Infinite: Religion, Politics, and Dialectic*, ed. Slavoj Žižek, Clayon Crockett, and Creston Davis (New York: Columbia University Press, 2011); Geoffrey Holsclaw, *Transcending Subjects: Augustine, Hegel, and Theology* (Chichester, UK: John Wiley & Sons, 2016), 27; and Timothy Brennan, "Hegel, Empire, and Anti-Colonial Thought," in *The Oxford Handbook of Postcolonial Studies* (Oxford: Oxford University Press, 2013), 145, respectively. Andy Blunden's *Hegel for Social Movements* (Leiden: Brill, 2019) is a florid case, but atypically undercuts the novelty of Hegelian reality. More typical is McGowan, *Emancipation after Hegel*.

In better balance, David Scott's several interventions explore how "the ethos of [the] internal principle of historical consciousness is that of 'vindication'" ("The Theory of Haiti: The Black Jacobins and the Poetics of Universal History," *Small Axe* 18 [2014]: 42); see also Scott, *Omens of Adversity: Tragedy, Time, Memory, Justice* (Durham, NC: Duke University Press, 2014). Rocío Zambrana deploys Hegel to reflect on colonial ambivalence while observing that "Hegel does not help us with our political task" ("Boundary, Ambivalence, Jaibería, or, How to Appropriate Hegel," in *Creolizing Hegel*, ed. Michael Monahan [New York: Rowman & Littlefield, 2017], 40); see also Zambrana, "Hegel, History, and Race," in *The Oxford Handbook of Philosophy and Race* (Oxford: Oxford University Press, 2017). Étienne Balibar's reexaminations of Hegel in *Citizen Subject: Foundations of Philosophical Anthropology* [2011], trans. Steven Miller (Bronx, NY: Fordham University Press, 2017), face myriad aporias.

4. Cicciarello-Maher, for example, preserves "a separatist moment of dialectics" for the colonized, featuring "resist[ance to] teleology, determinism, linearity," "foregrounding rupture and shunning the lure of unity" (*Decolonizing Dialectics* [Durham, NC: Duke University Press, 2017], 6–7). It's impossible to distinguish these qualities

It turns out, however, that antiracism formed along Hegelian lines remains within Wynter's organization of *homo politicus* and *homo economicus*. It registers the worldly significance of Atlantic slavery, condemns racism, and exhorts self-criticism, all in a way that renovates the beneficiaries of global totality into exemplary political identities. The presumed reader of the *The Phenomenology of Spirit*, the unfree European, "is" the "slave" of the drama, and the problem with the narrative is less the quality of its psychological insight[5] into that reader than the costs of the premise.

Hegel aspires toward a collective that is both "I" and "we"—"IWWI" as readers call it in "a kind of monogram" (Balibar, *Citizen Subject*, 139). The world of involuntary relation that Hegel describes not only promotes open relation in the form of physical access to people across the globe (as I discussed in § 1); open relation also frankly means dependence on them, a generalized bondage labeled as interdependence. As Hegel envisions it, each party striving to understand this world will notice what seems at first to be external in the other—hostility, stupidity, and so on—also within itself, on reflection. The self is continually crushed by this ordeal (as I'll detail especially in § 7), yet also continually regains disavowed parts of itself by understanding its relations with others in this way.[6] As Warren points out, relation is "always already infused with metaphysical presumptions (i.e., it presupposes a relation is comprised of discrete entities that can be differentiated and brought

---

from what Hegel already provides. The resulting "moment" diminishes the complexity of colonization, arguing that it is "upheld more by force than by ideology, 'life and death struggle' simply waiting in the wings to be unleashed" (81). Abigail B. Bakan is similarly satisfied to emphasize "not ... totality as purely universalistic, but as a contradictory totality," when contradictory totality is the issue in the first place (Abigail B. Bakan, "Marxism and Anti-Racism: Rethinking the Politics of Difference." In *Theorizing Anti-Racism: Linkages in Marxism and Critical Race Theories*, edited by Abigail B. Bakan and Enakshi Dua (Toronto: University of Toronto Press, 2015), 98.

5. The psychological insight of Hegelian negativity is almost isomorphic with core principles of European postwar psychoanalysis—both Lacanian and Kleinian. I cannot substantiate the implications in this project, but the limitations of negativity have consequences for that period of psychoanalysis. In other words, it's not just that this psychoanalysis supports Hegel but that its replication of Hegelian effects raises questions for it.

6. D. W. Winnicott writes, "when we need to find the things we disapprove of outside ourselves," "[we] do so at a price, this price being the loss of destructiveness which really belongs to ourselves" ("Aggression, Guilt, and Reparation," in *Deprivation and Delinquency* [London: Routledge, 1990], 117). Winnicott is right about destructiveness (it is a resource), but is it possible for anyone and no one to possess it as a belonging?

together).''[7] Now, the Hegelian left does not rely on metaphysical presence to limn the relationships between positions. Rather, it links them by a "negative universality of being-human," a humanity that is nothing more than an empty placeholder subtracted from every determinate example (Brassier, 103). IWWI, the signature of collectivity in the making, entails that anyone or no one (let's call this "ANNA," a newly minted monogram), *with the emphasis on no one*, may assume this signature, and that complicity is the exemplary and, finally, only possible rite of passage to this valuable realization. Avowing this kind of realization, however, serves more to separate the radical self from the racialist errors of others than to turn it toward the implications of slavery.

In liberal interpretations of Hegel, IWWI is nurtured by the coordinates of civil society. Social relations enable "the incipient realization that I depend on others *as others depend on me*."[8] To shift to a radical and negative construction of the text, we might interpret instead that *The Phenomenology of Spirit* extends these coordinates over ANNA, anyone *or no one*, whom it calls the slave to represent. If slaves cannot be anyone, they can be no one, so the reasoning goes. The dialectic needs, for its radical aspirations, to bring along ANNA, and in its negative openness encloses the slave on whose participation in principle its own hopes depend.[9] Underlining that no one possesses such realization keeps the slave on board, and so learns from Roman errors. Hence the casting of the slave in the lead of the master-slave dialectic: the "slave (that is, the subject)," Balibar rightly calls him (*Citizen Subject*, 214). Readers of the *Phenomenology* imagine themselves slaves imagining their incompleteness and complicity.[10] This will take unfold-

7. Calvin Warren, *Ontological Terror: Blackness, Nihilism, and Emancipation* (Durham, NC: Duke University Press, 2018), 186n.

8. Alfredo Ferrarin, "Hegel on Recognition: Self-Consciousness, Individuality, and Intersubjectivity," in *"I That Is We, We That Is I": Perspectives on Contemporary Hegel*, ed. Italo Testa and Luigi Ruggui (Leiden: Brill, 2016): 268.

9. Is the master-slave dialectic an "amalgamation scheme" at the locked door of revolution? Much of what I have to say grows out of my interest, in a double sense, in a genealogy for Jared Sexton's insight into the left's imaginary of social space as amalgamation (*Amalgamation Schemes*, 87).

10. This is not to limit Black complicity, or Black Hegelianism, but to inquire into the gratifying effects for non-Black readers of emblems of Black complicity.

For thoughtful explorations of Black complicity, see Jerome Dent, "Athazagoraphilia: On the End(s) of Dreaming," *InVisible Culture* 31 (2020): unpaginated, www.invisibleculturejournal.com/pub/athazagoraphilia/release/1?readingCollection=56e19667; Axelle Karera, "Paraontology: Disruption, Inheritance, or a Debt That One Often Regrets," lecture at Cooper Union, November 17, 2020; Fumi Okiji, *Jazz as Critique:*

ing that I must skip for now, but for various reasons, to follow Hegel here is to accept an impoverished and ultimately antiblack account of racial violence, one that will narrow it to "racialism" and the false externalization of enemies.

In *The Phenomenology of Spirit*, Hegel allows for "the incipient realization that I depend on others *as others depend on me*" (Ferrarin, "Hegel on Recognition," 268) to be set in a master-slave scenario where it seems least plausible, and indeed shows it to fail there—for anyone and no one, however. In the fully Hegelian perspective, Hegel is not making the error of overlooking differences by showing this failure, but asserting the human capacity to face *any* antagonist, *any* disproportion, *any* violence, in failure or not, by finding some of its ugliness within and putting the realer self that results to work on a world whose conditions don't yet enable recognition. Hegel must make the ambitious theoretical choice, in his own terms, to both show and override the multiplicity of negativity. If slavery is an insanity exceptional to dialectics, the reader can toss dialectics right away. But if it's not exceptional, then dialectics stands and falls with it.

In what follows, I'll explore how Hegel approaches the slave figure in the master-slave dialectic, but not only the singular slave protagonist. Many readers argue that Hegel's term *Knecht* (serf, servant, laborer; also translated by A. V. Miller as "bondsman") cannot *intend* the chattel slave. I argue that it *includes* the chattel slave and must do so, the slave at the front of the collective body it constitutes. *Notice the assumption that "slave" can metaphorically mean a worker, yet "Knecht" cannot mean a slave,* even metaphorically. Even the word *slave* seems not to own itself, to be all vehicle, such that another word cannot be its metaphor in turn. In the dialectic as a whole, however, Hegel is staging an incomplete reciprocity from its unaccustomed side. Hegel's point about Roman jurisprudence is that the subject of history has to include the slave for the sake of its own existence, but to do that—to allow the not very free German to imagine a collectivity that would include a slave—a blurry term will be needed. The meaning of *Knecht* enacts the amalgamation effect of IWWI–ANNA. The collective entities are not manifest presences, but virtual focal points, whether positive (IWWI) or negative (ANNA). To posit them, Hegel must avoid the mistake of the Romans; he has to bring the Atlantic slave into political life.

Adorno and Black Expression Revisited (Stanford, CA: Stanford University Press, 2018). More polemically: what if afropessimism is the most Hegelian work of the day—the work that advances Hegel's promise in and through being more than dialectical?

The Slave's Objects

While I feel apologetic for returning to the "seemingly interminable question" of the master-slave dialectic (Scott 2010, 152), there seems to be no way around it. This time I'd like to shift the question, over the course of this section, to the derealized "objects" in the productive matrix—to what Jean Hyppolite, for instance, means when "he writes that there can be a master and a slave only when there is animal life, *an existence according to the specific mode of life*."[11] This will be a way of beginning to track the costs of Hegel's slave protagonist for other slaves blurred in the drama, and therefore to think of Hegel's antiblackness as a relay "determined by the capacity to participate in relations of exchange" (Hartman, *Scenes of Subjection*, 124). Put another way, already in Hegel "the slave" *is* another slave. First, however, we need a brief synopsis of Hegel's myth of forms of life.

Because Hegel never presents bodies but figures of processes, Kojève's deliberately reductive summary helps to show how those processes might appear as concrete actions. In Kojève's retelling of the myth, encounters become human social relations when "animal Desire," without recognition or ethical purpose, moves, or is moved, away from "a real, 'positive,' given object" and "toward another Desire."[12] The encounter's "fight to the death," ending in mastery and slavery, is for "pure prestige" (Kojève 1980, 7). The slave then embarks on "the real transformation of the existing World" (190), especially the self, called *work* (59; see also 189), and Hegel leaves the narrative amid ongoing struggle and shifting differentials of creativity, to be resolved only when master and slave are "synthesized," beyond the state, at the horizon of individuality (60).

In this story negativity encompasses both a psychic therapy of self-transformation for a new radical subject and a "real movement of history that abolishes the present state of things"[13] to make actual what consciousness cannot realize. Only historical movement is actuality, but the therapy Hegel offers is "training" in that realization, in turn.

11. Jean Hyppolite, *Genesis and Structure, of Hegel's* Phenomenology of Spirit, trans. Samuel Cherniak and John Heckman (Evanston, IL: Northwestern University Press, 1979), 168.

12. Alexandre Kojève, *Introduction to the Reading of Hegel: Lectures on the Phenomenology of Spirit*, assembled by Raymond Queneau, ed. Allan Bloom, trans. James H. Nichols Jr. (Ithaca, NY: Cornell University Press, 1980), 6.

13. Karl Marx and Friedrich Engels, *The German Ideology*, pt. 1, trans. W. Lough, C. Dutt, and C. P. Magill, ed. Chris [C. J.] Arthur (New York: International Publishers, 1970), 57.

Both first-level, or "abstract," negation and double, "absolute" negation are required. Psychically, the first appearance of negativity is the self's registration of friction in a relation. In the second turn, the self discovers energies of the self in what seemed to be only external negativity. Materially, negativity that seems to ruin something from outside employs forces and conditions from within it, and from the self, as well, as it makes something new. Hegel's radical subject attempts to hold a point of view that finds part of itself within the force of negativity.

In the foreground the master-slave relation concludes in enslavement/unfreedom, a hanging ending, while the slave's political preparation becomes the compensation. In this foreground, then, it is the master who is insufficiently political. As Kojève describes the master, "He is recognized by someone whom he does not recognize ... he can be satisfied only by a recognition from one whom he recognizes as worthy of recognizing him.... The Master's attitude, therefore, is an existential impasse" (19, 25). From Kojève on, the master's situation is commonly referred to as an "impasse." Orlando Patterson's eye roll is refreshing: "I disagree totally with the view that slavery created an existential impasse for the master."[14] Gilroy's influential interpretation of Douglass's *Narrative*, however, both accepts "Kojève's identification of an existential impasse that develops out of the master's dependency on the slave" (Gilroy 1995, 51) and uses "impasse" to describe the prolonged struggle between Douglass and Covey: "the two men were locked together in the Hegelian impasse" (Gilroy 1995, 62). In this way the dead end of domination is seen as entangled with liberation struggle. The literal interval—two hours—when "each was able to contain the strength of the other without vanquishing him" (62), for Douglass, metonymizes the entirety of struggle. The interval itself prefigures his "independence," as does his refusal to subordinate liberation to life (63). Kojève's and Gilroy's responses to *The Phenomenology of Spirit* locate the potential for liberation within destructiveness in a situation of indefinite abstract negativity.[15] And yet Gilroy also describes how the end of slavery is subsumed in political education. Beginning with Douglass's bondage, Gilroy's own narrative will invest in "how Black Atlantic political culture changed as it moved out of the early phases that had been dom-

14. Orlando Patterson, *Slavery and Social Death: A Comparative Study* (Cambridge, MA: Harvard University Press, 1982), 99.

15. See Antonio Gramsci, "Equilibrium with Catastrophic Prospects," in *Selections from the Prison Notebooks*, 2nd ed., ed. and trans. Quentin Hoare and Geoffrey Nowell-Smith (New York: International Publishers, 1997), 221.

inated by the need to escape slavery and various attempts to acquire meaningful citizenship in post-emancipation societies" (x).

Gerard Aching takes a quite different route to a similar association between political growth and emancipation.[16] Aching follows the "impasse" line (Aching, "No Need for an Apology," 28) for unusual reasons: he takes Fanon's clinical studies of torturers and avengers to attest that the conflict does not end with the death of one of the parties (Aching, "No Need for an Apology," 33–34). "Internal grappling with . . . coercion"[17] leads to the decision to "set all of this evidence aside in an all-out struggle for political freedom" (36) corresponding to the "trial by death." But after this, for Aching the slave gains "political freedom" only: a true rather than an "arrested dialectics" (31), "proper binary oppositions" instead of "distorted Manicheanisms" (28). To return from critical readings to the eight pages of the *Phenomenology* that are "Lordship and Bondage" is to stress that any liberation—as opposed to political education—occurs in the scene only if the reader assumes that liberation and the preparation of political identity are the same, as Hegel does not. Explicitly, the episode presents "a life-and-death struggle, after which one becomes the slave"[18] and can be read as showing that "self-consciousness is not a social achievement" (Ferrarin, "Hegel on Recognition," 267). The episode's reward is the birth of the slave's political possibility that he holds in reserve. If the master is the slave's foil, however, and lacks a corresponding possibility, Patterson and Fanon are right to imply that his impasse, if any, is never manifest in their functional relation. This raises the question of how the slave can have changed, through what concrete interactions.

"Independent Objects"

Hegel's answer to how the slave could even begin to actualize negativity as a slave (although this effort is, strictly speaking, barely inside the episode) is work, of course. It matters to take work as more than subsistence activity: it means expression against an object in preparation for the abstraction of the political sphere. This idea about how the slave

---

16. Gerard Aching, "No Need for an Apology: Fanon's Untimely Critique of Political Consciousness," *South Atlantic Quarterly* 112, no. 1 (2013): 23–38, 28. Aching stipulates that "colonialism [is] the originating context" of "asymmetrical binary opposition" (27).

17. Gerard Aching, *Freedom from Liberation: Slavery, Sentiment, and Literature in Cuba* (Bloomington: Indiana University Press, 2015), 18.

18. Denise Ferreira da Silva, *Unpayable Debt* (New York: Sternberg Press, 2022), 43n31.

would develop negativity requires the slave to work on an object, "introducing in him the constituent-element (Moment) of Mastery which he lacked" (Kojève 1980, 231). Hegel argues that emancipation develops in subjugation—both self-subjugation and subjugation of others.[19] Continuously, subjection passes through the slave and on to something or someone else; through the slave's medium realization occurs. Therefore, Hegel shows what the slave must do by introducing a third into the dialectic, the "thing" or "object" on which the slave works. This is a prop, in effect, not involved in political incubation within slavery.

According to Hegel, the two self-consciousnesses that confront one another in the dialectic, which A. V. Miller's translation generally refers to as self and other [Selbst and Andere], are both traumatized by "the object" [Gegenstand: *the relational, grammatical object*] and distinguished by their different relations with the same object(s). Occasionally the other or the "I" is also called "object," as when the subject's "absolute object is 'I' [sein ... absoluter Gegenstand ist ihm *Ich*]"; or when the self's "being-for-self" needs to appear to it as an object; or when both self and other can be, perhaps prehistorically, "for one another *like* ordinary objects [ind sie füreinander in der Weise gemeiner Gegenstände]" (PS, § 186; my italics). But the "ordinary objects" that they stand in relation to are sources of unease and energy,[20] for "the object gave the first impulses to changes in consciousness."[21] Therefore, in Hegel's mythic telling—not to be confused with the archives of labor—the Knecht has been coerced to deal with ordinary objects on the master's behalf. When self and other "are for one another *like* ordinary objects," that's unfortunate because they then appear as "*independent* shapes, individuals submerged in the *being* [or immediacy] *of Life* [*selbständige* Gestalten, in das *Sein des Lebens*]" (PS, § 186; my italics). In their disconcerting self-sufficiency "ordinary objects" offer nonrelation, prerequisite to recognition between human beings. This weakly differentiated, pre-ethical reservoir of "life," in which animate-sounding

19. "Quite arbitrarily, apparently," Chris Arthur remarks, "Hegel assumes everyone must undergo breaking of self-will through subjection to an alien power before being capable of rational freedom" ("Hegel's Master-Slave Dialectic and a Myth of Marxology," *New Left Review* [November–December 1983]: 70).

20. Andrew Cole argues that the objects Hegel intends are plots of land. Cole's reading is limited by his flat conviction that if German feudalism is Hegel's referent, the argument cannot concern slaves (*The Birth of Theory* [Chicago: University of Chicago Press, 2015], 70, 67). Shilliam and others have explained the antiblack framework of Hegel's address to Germany, which intimidates domestic citizens by comparing them to slaves.

21. C. L. R. James, *Notes on Dialectics: Hegel, Marx, Lenin* (Westport, CT: Lawrence, Hill & Co., 1980), 51.

objects intermingle with preindividuals who are "submerged in" them, recalls the precolonial realms of *World History*. It conjures a zone of affectable being as the individualized slave protagonist does not. That zone is a matrix the slave has risen from and its "objects" are not distinguishable from human beings described in a primitivist and distant way. If the Knecht lived among the ordinary objects only and unreflectively, he himself would be something else: a "specific existence," an "individuality common to existence as such [die allgemeine Einzelheit des Daseins überhaupt]" (PS, § 187).

David C. Lloyd has reflected on Hegel's realm of objects as possibly an alternative society. Drawing on Moten's interest in "another idea of nothingness altogether that is given in and as and to things,"[22] Lloyd asks whether

> the thing, as it is conceived and dismissed in the Hegelian dialectic offers equally the means to think back into the definitively multifarious social forms that a process of philosophical subsumption, whose universal claims are the repetition in thought of the material drive to uniformity of production that characterized the colonial capitalism coeval with it, sought to liquidate.[23]

Correspondingly, the whole purpose of the slave from the mistaken perspective of the master is that the slave should be the one to spend time with things, to hazard becoming more thinglike, to approach "consciousness in the form of thinghood [Bewußtsein in der Gestalt der Dingheit]" (PS, § 189). The master, Hegel states, "is a consciousness existing *for itself* which is mediated with itself through another consciousness, i.e. through a consciousness whose nature it is to be bound up with an existence that is independent, or thinghood [Dingheit] in general. The lord puts himself into relation with both of these moments, to a *thing* as such, the object [Gegenstand] of desire, and to the consciousness to which thinghood is essential" (PS, § 190). Since having a "consciousness to which thinghood is essential" appears dangerous, to distance the self-sufficiency of objects the master deals with them through intermediaries: "the lord relates himself mediately to the bondsman

22. Fred Moten, "Blackness and Nothingness (Mysticism in the Flesh)," SAQ 112 (2013): 737–780, 751.

23. David C. Lloyd, "Civil War: Race under Representation," UCHRI Podcast, December 18, 2019. https://www.listennotes.com/podcasts/uchri-podcast/civil-war-race-under-c8xh2QuDMUH/. See also Lloyd, *Under Representation: The Racial Regime of Aesthetics* (Bronx, NY: Fordham University Press, 2019), 74–75.

through a being that is independent [selbständige Sein], for it is just this that holds the bondsman in bondage; it is his chain from which he could not break free in the struggle" (PS, § 190; my italics). The difference between master and slave is predicted by their terms of triangulation with the object, the means of domination's "duplication" (Lloyd, *Under Representation*, 143). The slave is neither subject nor object, but a potential: political material to the extent that he negates the object, and an object of subjects himself to the extent that he doesn't. He works toward absolute negation and realization, unless he attaches to the objects and becomes like one. In that case he too "constitutes a mere prop" (Warren, "Barred Objects," 31) expropriable by someone else. He can be the first slave or the second. Hegel asserts that it is not the master, but "just this" "being that is independent," that is *still* independent of the bondsman, "which holds the bondsman in bondage" (§ 190).[24] Complementarily, the master abolishes the object so much that he overshoots the mark. He has "proved in the struggle" that for him the independent being was "something merely negative," that it was possible to "go the length of being altogether done with it to the point of annihilation [bis zur Vernichtung mit ihm fertig werden; alternatively, deal with it until it was destroyed]" (§ 190), but to be "done with it" is to be done with reality. What is at stake is the ability to realize and derealize, to add and destroy value. Not being eager in this, the Knecht's inadvertent cultivation of his own reluctance to destroy (without annihilating) becomes a factor in his own enslavement, according to this origin myth.

The only point that either Hegel or his most canonical readers make regarding the "annihilation" of the objects per se is that it is *bad for the master's health*. The master's "sheer negative power for whom the thing is nothing [reine negative Macht, der das Ding nichts ist]" (PS, § 191) fails by destroying the object altogether so that *the relation is no longer there to benefit from*. And all that happens after the lord's "unalloyed feeling of self" (§ 195) wears off, and the reader ceases to be involved with him (but, as Patterson implies, isn't he perhaps more dangerous than ever in his disgruntled state?), is a "permanent" ongoing sublation of independent being ("ordinary objects") by the slave. For

24. Reviewing the literature on the symbiotic relationship between political freedom and classical slavery, Rosenberg discerns that the latter's "supply of cheap labor ... acted also as a valve reducing the pressure on the economic independence of the smallholding class which was the precondition of political democracy" (Justin Rosenberg, *Empire of Civil Society: A Critique of the Realist Theory of International Relations* [New York: Verso Books, 1994], 78). He therefore stresses that the benefit, for citizens, was that the system "did not require the *political* subjection of laboring fellow-citizens" (78).

Marx, as Arthur points out, this result depicts "a sphere of estrangement brought to life" and not a potential for anything more without further commentary.[25] Hartman adduces Marx as well—this kind of actor has only "brought his own hide to market,"[26] a market that "induce[s] internal forms of policing" every bit as much through the medium of blackness as ever (Hartman, *Scenes of Subjection*, 120). The continual sublation of independent being to production reflects the natural sublation of retrojected lives into *Science of Logic*'s "process of the genus" in which "isolated singularities of individual life perish" (12.191).[27] In his first critiques of Hegel, Marx responds that "man becomes objective for himself and at the same time becomes a strange and inhuman object for himself ... his realization is his loss of reality, is an *alien* reality."[28] For this to keep happening, independent being must never be extinguished, its naturalness regenerated by the upward mobility of the slave that retrojects it.[29] Its "independence" remains as though amortal, like the fantasied inexhaustibility of the natural world whose extraction is mourned only because it also spells modernity's collapse.

It matters outside the master-slave dyad, then, when Hegel tasks the political slave to learn that the violence of the master is inside him, to avow that he uses it on "objects," and affirm the enabling contradictions of his awareness. It's far from clear that in the *Phenomenology*, culture

25. Chris Arthur, "Hegel, Feuerbach, Marx, and Negativity," *Radical Philosophy* 35 (1983): 14.

26. Karl Marx, *Capital: A Critique of Political Economy*, vol.1, trans. Ben Fowkes (Harmondsworth, UK: Penguin, 1976), 280.

27. G. W. F. Hegel, *Science of Logic. Part One of the Encyclopaedia of the Philosophical Sciences*, trans. William Wallace (Oxford: Clarendon Press, 1975); henceforward *Science of Logic*.

28. Marx, *Economic and Philosophic Manuscripts of 1844*, in *Collected Work of Marx and Engels*, vol. 3, 299, trans. modified. In this passage Marx does not narrate realization in a way that comprehends what happens to human use values—he is a step away, near and yet far, pointing out that the process of realization can only make an object of the *laborer*. At times, Marx demands man's release from property so that he can realize himself against objects in a *less limited* way: "Each of his *human* relations to the world ... are in their objective orientation, or in their *orientation to the object*, the appropriation of the object, the appropriation of *human* reality. Their orientation to the object is the *manifestation of the human reality*" (Marx, *Manuscripts*, 299–300). Yet, the early Marx's analysis of alienation is close to apprehending the realization and derealization that, in Hegel, helps to reproduce slavery.

29. Fanon comments: "For Hegel, the slave turns away from the master and turns toward the object[, h]ere [in colonialism] the slave turns toward the master and *abandons* the object," and "therefore he is less independent than the Hegelian slave" (*Black Skin, White Masks* [1952], trans. Richard Philcox [New York: Grove Press, 2008], 195n; my italics).

depends on avowing externalization in this way. In fact, in parallel to *Lectures on Religion*, Hegel closes the master-slave dialectic by distancing the accomplishments, or what would otherwise look like accomplishments, of being, and even "consciousness," that acts and creates but not with derealizing negativity. "If consciousness fashions the thing without ... initial absolute fear ... *its formative activity* [Formieren] cannot give it a consciousness of itself as essential being" (PS, § 196; my italics). According to Hegel, then, there can be formative activity, fashioning, "consciousness," "skill which is powerful over some things [eine Geschicklichkeit, welche nur über einiges]," without "negativity *per se*" (§ 196). What is negativity that is not "negativity *per se*"? Another negativity, presumably within the merely abstract negativity that simply notices frictions, can accomplish most of culture and yet not be "negativity per se." What it does not engage, apparently, is the target between formative activity and the total violence with which the master destroys his own supports.

This not-negative-enough negativity is an indefinite area potentially corresponding to a whole society (a second society), as Lloyd suggests. Since it's a kind of hallucination inscribed into Hegel's text, however, it cannot be focused without its relation to the brutal foreground. It's Hegel's myth of prehistoric life, misty on the horizon like the little strip of landscape in a Renaissance portrait. It's beautiful only in connection with the portrait, yet looking at it can be a critical way to study the relation between background and foreground. In Hegel, these beings must be there if the slave is to develop, as Hyppolite writes. A long practice of *making a resource*—not the inevitable result of any creativity, as Hegel points out—begins to consolidate Hegel's slave protagonist into *homo politicus* out of the innumerable cuts it makes between its work and its resources. Directing destruction to self-realization, which for Hegel just is realization of contradiction and one's own object status in the real movement, rather than *no particular reason* such as needing to eat, creates a prop for the slave protagonist.[30] Again, nothing says what kind of beings are the objects being used. So the situation here repeats that negativity needs to be practiced, if not in confrontation with antagonists, then on others as a preparation for, and in that sense part of, that struggle.

This threshold is indeed one of radical complicity, for better and worse, with making beings into resources. Various readers get off at

30. Hegel's recommendation to the use of a prop is followed by readers who think the dialectic is fake or incomplete but want it to be real. What if the more real it gets, the more decreated a nearby prop must be?

the stop where the violence of totality is ritually consumed as political education.[31] Marx points out that Hegel's philosophy mythologizes as necessity the violence without which Hegel's own work could not be produced. Adorno declares—not just in one place, but across his work—that if Hegel is right about this, there's something more important than being right.[32] Derrida "insist[s] much and without ceasing on the necessity" of nondialectical negation, the logically earlier "phase of overturning [renversement], which one perhaps too quickly attempts to discredit."[33] Chandler cites this passage of Derrida to observe that complicity, "if not accompanied by a simultaneous elaboration of the distantiation of the hegemon, can function principally to resituate tradition, or the given, as hegemon or authority" (*X*, 187). It is in their commitments to unsettling or reinforcing the hegemon that "not all inhabitation of such a limit is the same" (187). And Fanon shows, in passages Marriott has unfolded, that the *"colonisé … fail[s] to own or possess"*[34] its work and expression, even if the self's ownness in Hegel is itself only its own contradiction. Contradiction too can fail to be wielded and possessed.[35] Fanon indicates that domination of another nearby—the gambit of Antillean society, according to him—does not demonstrate the colonized self's participation in realization since it remains assigned to him as a strategy.[36]

Fanon has the least moral argument and so the one least anticipated by Hegel's criticism; namely, that to follow Hegel, the reader must assume that the *colonisé* possesses the internal and external means to arrive at even the dialectic's incomplete realization of negativity. Marriott

31. It's the moment when Žižek gets on: "in order for this transposition from the immediate biological reality of the body to the symbolic space to take place, it has to leave a mark of torture on the body in the guise of its mutilation" (Slavoj Žižek, "Hegel versus Heidegger," *e-flux* 32 [February 2012]: unpaginated, https://www.e-flux.com/journal/32/68252/hegel-versus-heidegger/).

32. T. W. Adorno, *History and Freedom: Lectures 1964–1965* (Cambridge, UK: Polity, 2006).

33. Jacques Derrida, *Positions*, trans. Alan Bass (Chicago: University of Chicago Press, 1982), 56–58.

34. David S. Marriott, "En Moi: Frantz Fanon and René Maran," in *Frantz Fanon's Black Skin, White Masks: New Interdisciplinary Essays*, ed. Max Silverman (Manchester, UK: University of Manchester Press, 2005), 151.

35. "The Hegelian subject is *nothing but* the very movement of unilateral self-deception, of the *hubris* of positing oneself in one's exclusive particularity, which necessarily turns against itself and ends in self-negation," Žižek contends. The opposite happens in Fanon: the hubris of positing himself in universality only returns him to his starting line, or behind it.

36. Fanon, *Black Skin, White Masks*, 167–171.

rephrases the problem regarding Lacan's Hegelianism, where (I add) awareness of constitutive human lack occupies a function parallel to acceptance of complicity in Hegel,

> Fanon discovers what seems to him the Lacanian mystification: not everyone posits the infinite as the unity, or identity of the object, and not everyone shares the presumption by which infinite division is the true meaning of deception.... In brief, lack for some is upsetting precisely because it makes real a certain being in the world. With respect to the black subject, in short, *manque-à-être* means repudiating the flaw that makes blackness one with its own infinite incommensurability to the world. For to *be* black is to live the truth of one's own monstrous disunity without alibi. To put one's hopes in the amputated necessity of such disunity is to be returned, as it were, not to the world, but to the nonreferential reality of martyrdom and massacre—a reality, moreover, from which one is repeatedly *cut* and nothing can be done to stop this severing.[37]

It doesn't matter whether Hegel's self coheres or shatters.[38] Marriott writes about Lacan: "at bottom, or its end, the x that is not-all remains absolute, it is only conceivable as absolute negation ... all that Lacan is doing here is inverting Hegel's point about the identity of difference" (Marriott, *Lacan Noir*, 33). Indeed, all *Hegel* is doing is inverting what could be a normative-Hegelian point about the identity of difference into a radical self-difference, the nonspace of *no one* and therefore of ANNA, that remains the prerequisite for Hegelian radical activity. This vision of negativity, like the former one, sees the slave practice for realization on or against a split-off slave figure that becomes as though a natural form of existence as a consequence.

Within the mythic landscape, which evokes something like agricultural fields surrounded by an uncultivated area, something less than political activity is everywhere. At the moment, there's only the nonpolitical self-destruction of the master (because it's only domination); the insufficiently negative practice of the Knecht with regard to the objects; and the not even nonpolitical existence beyond them, absorbable into history without scars, formless, nourishing. The latter evokes what the sublation of "specific" life looks like from the perspective of the dialec-

---

37. David S. Marriott, *Lacan Noir: Lacan and Afro-Pessimism* (Cham, Switzerland: Palgrave Macmillan, 2021), 20.

38. For Winnicott, as well, recovered negativity refreshes the self in *un*integration, freeing it from its limited envelope of a personality (*Playing and Reality*, 78).

tic, its suffusion out of reach of difference and identity, consciousness and memory. This is what the ground of the *Phenomenology* evokes, a soil permeated with organic matter *made* organic by social reality. In this landscape the slave protagonist is depicted working and waiting, learning from negativity, an exemplary figure to be continued, to realize, and from there his image gives succor to unfree political subjects awaiting their moment. What makes it possible to believe that anyone or no one can be this slave, if not the confidence that the only person who can play *anyone or no one* is the white beneficiary of enslavement?

PART 2

Romanticism and the Impossibility of Slavery

Slavery is null and void, not only as being illegitimate, but also because it is absurd and meaningless.

ROUSSEAU, *On the Social Contract, or Principles of Political Right*

As with the Negroes on the Sugar Islands ... [a slave] will in fact have given himself away, as property, to his master, which is impossible.

KANT, *The Metaphysics of Morals*

Suppose that Hegelianism executes a turn from transcendental frame to historico-material ontology, from limit to transgression, from critical to absolutely mediated reality. In the process it shifts from racial hierarchy to metaracial logic and introduces a Hegelian radical who carries an untheorized attachment to the slave. In part 2, I consider some of the romantic and transcendental ideas that Hegel "overcomes" as a way of taking a measure of this shift. Part 2 addresses Rousseau, Kant, and Shelley chronologically to complicate the idea of a rationalistic early enlightenment made dynamic by a later emphasis on historical contingency. My question is not whether or not pre-Hegelian lines of thought are primitivist; they are. Instead, we can question the contemporary eagerness to have left this primitivism behind, to make it a matter of stances and worldviews inconsistent with a newly contingent actuality.

Rousseau's *Discourse on Inequality* (Second Discourse, 1755) and *Social Contract* (1762) present an overt account of slavery that cannot distinguish racial slavery and, I argue, an unconscious counternarrative. Overtly, Rousseau repeats the idea that any slavery materializes a contradiction, and so cannot be realized for long. He derives a material genealogy of society from the circulation of social status incentives; in this way, he arrives at an explanation of property in which enslavement is simply the trailing ill effect of property. Rousseau hypothesizes—sounding like contemporary genealogies of race—that race arises to assist accumulation.[1] Race, he guesses, is an instrumental ideology of difference that justifies expropriation. His *Discourse on Inequality* en-

---

1. Howard Winant, for example, asserts that "because the occupying powers had to be able to distinguish native from settler, enslaved from 'free,' they gravitated toward 'optical' or phenomic criteria to organize their regimes.... So race developed as a highly

tails a radically indeterminate vision of history—a vast production of social relation that can't be limited by modern concepts—which he leverages against property. Speculation on prehistory, and the socially constructivist ontology that it brings him, allows Rousseau to unsettle the givenness of property and the state.

At the same time, Rousseau's use of a generic, neither classical nor modern reference to slavery[2] becomes the vehicle of a fragmentary counternarrative. In his work, the generic slave does not seem to transfer energy from the chattel slave to the laborer, as it has often been seen to do—the laborer barely appears. Instead, the generic slave projects "slavish"-ness upon a second chattel slave in the background in order to attack "slavish" pursuers of capital in the foreground. Ultimately, Rousseau's notion of property itself is split between inanimate commodity and slave commodity, a difference in kind and register that destabilizes his overt account of property and popular sovereignty.

Kant responds to Rousseau's indeterminate and abyssal prehistory by ordering beings in time, seeking to reconcile contingency with the appearance of a world and with cause and effect. Again, many have analyzed Kant's distress about the "purpose" of Africans whose lives he believes are empty of reward. In § 5, Kant's "Analogies of Experience" in *The Critique of Pure Reason* (1787) is reconsidered in this context to show how Kant's grounding of perception in temporally understood cause and effect establishes subjective and nonsubjective beings in a cause and effect relation that is also a consecutive relation in time. This part of Kant's project helps to institutionalize a syntax subordinating past to present beings that continues through Hegel and today.

Shelley's *Frankenstein* (1818)—set in Rousseau's progressive home

---

practical political technology of oppression and resistance" ("The Dark Matter: Race and Racism in the 21st Century," *Critical Sociology* 41 [2015]: 317).

2. On the controversy of the servitude-slavery relationship, both the practice of conflating the positions and the interpellation of slavery to the benefit of servitude, see, for example, Walter Johnson, "The Pedestal and the Veil: Rethinking the Capitalism/Slavery Question," *Journal of the Early Republic* 24 (2004): 299–308; Williams, *Capitalism and Slavery*, 18. Losurdo argues that wage labor at its extremities troubles the worker/slave border in *A Brief History of Liberalism* [2006], trans. Gregory Elliott (New York; Verso Books, 2011), as does Massimiliano Tomba, who supposes that "the slave's health was kept in a condition sufficient to allow continuing work" when he describes the consumed body of the laborer (*Marx's Temporalities* [Leiden: Brill, 2013], 155).

Sara-Maria Sorentino and Tapji Garba address metaphoricity in its own materiality: when slavery travels through culture to circulate and manage meanings, "slavery is only ever available as a semantic displacement" ("Slavery Is a Metaphor: A Critical Commentary on Eve Tuck and K. Wayne Yang's 'Decolonization Is Not a Metaphor,'" *Antipode* 52 [2020]: 1–19, 11).

city of Geneva—was interpreted by its contemporary readers as imagining an escaped or free Black who is neither political subject nor chattel slave. Shelley implies that this being can have no appearance because civil society cannot conceive of him; she attempts to imagine his impossible *existence* regardless. In doing so Shelley wanders, inadvertently and surely, into the racial blackness of racial slavery. Instead of Rousseau's impossibility that cannot exist, and Kant's impossibility that cannot be knowledge, Shelley registers an impossibility that exists nevertheless. *Frankenstein* is an immanent satire on the radical's struggle to think a free Black, performing his impossible manifestation in the society Shelley describes. As the novel layers several first-person narratives concentrically around the first-person narrative of the Creature, *Frankenstein* externalizes a stitched-together discursive composite, like a parody of Hegel's IWWI (or ANNA). Shelley inverts the roles of Hegel's dialectic, in which political subject readers imagine themselves as Hegel's slave imagining himself complicit in slavery. She imagines herself as several European men, similar to her problematic radical father and husband, tasked with conveying the words of and sometimes speaking as the Creature. Another case of blurred protagonism, then, laboring to render the dense medium of history and association that makes it impossible to render a free Black, Shelley's novel reflects on the generation of a phobic figure while generating one itself. To notice this is not to condemn Shelley morally, but it suggests a legacy of antiblack repetition that is not yet optional.

§ 4

After the Final Limit:
Rousseau, Prehistory,
and Slavery

For according to the axiom of the wise Locke, "where there is no property, there is no injury."

—ROUSSEAU, *Discourse on the Origin of Inequality*

Although Hegel does not believe that just any relation is valuable, he does believe that the potential of relation is inscribed in political organization broadly construed. Relation is realized not in consciousness but in history and for history. Realization remains unavailable in individual consciousness and robust only in and as Idea. However, realization as a value does appear to consciousness, and consciousness can appreciate the reality of the Idea and attempt to live by it. Because of this, the world can be a "discipline," and for some a "training," in which consciousness's affirmation of reality shows in its awareness of its inability to coincide with itself. In part 1, I explored the costs in derealization of a reality of actualization that occurs through the discipline of the world alone. Promoting "interdependent" access to a reality process that gathers and produces differences, I argued, obscures the movement of antiblack violence and shifts emphasis from former distinctions to a metaracial level of stances. Given slavery's challenge to the centrality of political organization as a reality principle, I argued that Hegel needs a political slave to affirm the process. By splitting "good" slaves from "bad" slaves, this overinvestment can only discern indefinite, alternative forms of life in the vicinity of an exemplary slave who is bound for politics.

In his account of a process that converts what had been "boring difference" into political distinction, Hegel overturns Rousseau's critique of relation in *Discourse on the Origin of Inequality*. Hegel embraces the development of society and property that Rousseau had described as misfortune. The Second Discourse, then, can help us start exploring contemporary criticism's attachment to the idea that enlightenment racism is "overcome" by Hegelian history. Rousseau had hypothesized that exchange relation, and increasingly comparative, increasingly networked awareness generally, had been responsible for unfreedom and the invention of property. While Hegel and Marx imagine emancipation building on modernity's development for better and worse, Rousseau agrees that it is not a matter of "returning to the forest to live with bears," and yet insists that the development of abstract relation was not auspicious, asking that the reader speculate on alternatives to co-constitutive individuality and relation. To do this, he mobilizes exercises of social constructivist imagination. By unsettling relation as a given of human nature, and understanding nonrelation as something other than "individuality," Rousseau hopes to leverage an attack on property *on behalf of unfree political subjects*. In doing so, however, he splits off property as slavery.

Rousseau practices radical philosophy in something other than a relational mode, and his writing might still spark further lines of radical thought. I'll take note of Althusser's *Lessons on Rousseau* in this context. Rousseau's attack on property hints, however, that slavery may be just as corrosive of the notion of property as it is of the notion of labor. Explicitly, Rousseau hypothesizes that race arises to justify property accumulation, and that slavery follows as an effect. But in practice, Rousseau's writing becomes unstable in the midst of these hypotheses. Rousseau's interjections about an underdetermined "slavery" and "slavishness" interrupt his analysis of property at pressured moments. His references to slavery open on to problems of desire, suggesting that chattel slavery is more than an effect of property and enclosure. Ultimately, Rousseau's notion of property shows a rift between commodity manufacture and slave commodity.

So contemporary Atlantic slavery does enter Rousseau's political theory, although he does not consciously pursue it. Rather, Rousseau briefly presents conscious theories of race and slavery, and throughout, *unconscious theories of racial slavery*. One of the techniques by which Rousseau leaves the impression that evanished slavery is present—a problematic of sublation that he discusses in various examples—is his use of a generic "slavery," the technique that in itself gives away the slave's function as medium of political amalgamations. Instead of transferring affects from slavery to labor, generic references to slavery interrupt Rousseau's argument when anxiety about chattel slavery hovers. In the explicit argument, slavery disappears into property. In the shadow one, slavery splits property apart.

Imagine No Relation

In Rousseau's *Discourse on the Origin of Inequality* (Second Discourse, 1755) and *Social Contract* (1762), the rise of property depends on modernity's creation of relation and nonrelation. A system of relation is implied by "amour-propre [self-regard]," the notion that so many political theory readers of Rousseau focus on.[1] *Amour-propre* is Rousseau's term of art for modern individuals' demand for recognition over and against others—the "petulant activity" (Second Discourse, 74) of relative status and honor. For Rousseau, modern individuals "know how to live only in the opinion of others" (Second Discourse, 91), as self-images passed through status mediation. Jimmy Casas Klausen, whose interesting anarchist reconstruction of Rousseau I'll discuss later, emphasizes that amour-propre depends on spatialized relation that is both material and abstract. As Casas Klausen argues, "Rousseau's hyperbolic references to the total global absence or presence of a thing or relation"[2] frame the discussion at all times. To ask whether relation has literally totalized misses their force. Casas Klausen points out that the issue is the *horizon* of globalization and pressure toward "'closure of the map,' the total global dominion of territorial states and the regime of private property" (35)—the implications of that threat even when it is only a threat. Rousseau argues that the specter of relation and nonrelation that hyperbolically conditions all existence arises from exchange spaces. In exchange, people are "forced to make comparisons among

1. This emphasis has been spread by the influential reading of John Rawls. See Rawls, *Lectures on the History of Political Philosophy* (Cambridge, MA: Harvard University Press, 2007). See also Robert Jubb, "Rawls and Rousseau: Amour-Propre and the Strains of Commitment," *Res Publica* 17, no. 3 (2011): 245–260; Michael Locke McLendon, "Rousseau and the Minimal Self: A Solution to the Problem of Amour-Propre," *European Journal of Political Theory* 13.3 (2014): 341–361; and Niko Kolodny, "The Explanation of Amour-Propre," *Philosophical Review* 119.2 (2010): 165–200. Charles Mills describes his work as mobilizing Rousseau against Rawls's Rousseau, correcting Rawls's methodological exclusion of slavery "by (following Rousseau) representing the actual 'contract' as a domination contract, a racial contract" ("Rousseau, the Master's Tools, and Anti-Contractarian Contractarianism," in *Creolizing Rousseau*, ed. Gordon and Roberts [New York: Rowman & Littlefield, 2014], 177). Mills's theory is interesting to consider alongside Hegel's realization by derealization.

2. Jimmy Casas Klausen, *Fugitive Rousseau: Slavery, Primitivism, and Political Freedom* (Bronx, NY: Fordham University Press, 2014), 35; my italics.

themselves and to take into account the differences they discover in the continual use they have to make of each other" (Second Discourse, 88).[3] For Rousseau, exchange comparisons lead to property and finally slavery.

The interest of prehistory for Rousseau, and the source of its ability to place pressure on modernity's relational reality, is that its practices' meanings are entirely unavailable.[4] Whether modern concepts would no longer be intelligible thirty thousand years ago or a hundred thousand years ago is not the question: at some point they would be, and it is the implication of that point that deranges modernity. Since it's difficult for modern individuals to experience relation as anything but given, Rousseau invokes this prehistory "that no longer exists, that perhaps never existed, that probably never will exist" (Second Discourse, 40). *Why* is it important to imagine? In contrast to Hegel, it allows for *relation itself*, not just this or that social relation, to be a product of contingencies. It allows that relation too, like "sex," is an impermanent abstraction. Therefore, when Rousseau promises that everything he's writing has nothing to do with "facts," he specifies that "comparative anatomy" isn't outside the problem of human origin and cannot solve it: "I will not stop to investigate in the animal kingdom what [man] might have been at the beginning so as eventually to become what he is. I will not examine whether, as Aristotle thinks, man's elongated nails were not at first hooked claws ... I will suppose him to have been formed from all time as I see him today" (Second Discourse, 47).[5] Rousseau is not invoking Wynter's standard enlightenment monohuman: he has dug under its quasi-transcendental description and presents in the same body—he doesn't know what, but proposes that it's radically different. The point of Rousseau's supposition is that no empirical variation can form an organic basis for social distinction or automatically rep-

---

3. I disagree with a large part of Rousseau's readership that decides to treat amour-propre itself as a natural human need.

4. Unlike Kant's noumena, which are inaccessible to knowledge but bring relief because then he doesn't need to try to know them, Rousseau's prehistory can't be dismissed in that way because it can't be irrelevant to present conditions and possibilities.

5. Critics since Rousseau's day have pointed out that the Second Discourse's distance from fact allows readers to interpret it as nothing but thought experiments, with no actual or intended impact. Fayçal Falaky discusses Rousseau's invitation of this effect thoughtfully in "Reading Rousseau in the Colonies: Theory, Practice, and the Question of Slavery," *Small Axe* 46 (2015): 5–19, e.g., 14. In closing, however, Falaky argues that the "supposed virtues of distinguishing the practical from the theoretical" themselves contributed to creating a "vacuum" in which "the freedom of African slaves [was] an inconceivable chimera" (46).

resent improvement in the social condition. Disconnected from modern norms, there's no imperative to invent language (Second Discourse, 56), to notice death (Second Discourse, 50), and so on. Rousseau rejects the very notion of objectively worse and better conditions as opposed to conditions that come with different qualities. Another way to phrase this is that the heterogeneous practices that appear not negative (self-aware) enough to Hegel appear to Rousseau as artifacts of processes immeasurably far beyond his own conception.

A lot of the first part of the Second Discourse is therefore taken up with pedagogical exercises of redescription that are meant to defamiliarize modern norms until the reader sees that they're not natural. For example, Rousseau refers to "these relationships which *we express by the words* 'large,' 'small,' 'strong,' 'weak' [Ces relations que *nous exprimons par les mots* de grand, de petit, de fort, de foible]."[6] He supposes that these "perceptions of certain relations" between people and elements of their practices had to have arisen earlier than the social relations with which his home city of Geneva understands them. At a time that Rousseau calls "earlier" but that he also states occurs in its own unknown medium different from time (which at some point did not yet exist), "large" and "small" did not exist. It's impossible to say what prehistoric peoples thought instead, and impossible—because prehistory is an *infinite* problem—that it could have been any eighteenth-century concept. Likewise with relation and nonrelation: at some point, they need not have existed at all.

Louis Althusser's lectures on Rousseau connect his radicalism to his commitment to this limit of prehistory.[7] According to Althusser the unknowability of prehistory leads Rousseau to speculate on virtual reservoirs of possibility and radical separation as a clue to revolution (Althusser, *Lessons*, 71). Althusser suggests helpfully that Rousseau's fictional prehistoric era is the first of four epistemes: (1) prehistory, the "pure state of nature"; (2) the "youth of the world," or early "savage" society; (3) the period from agriculture to private property and the "state of war"; and (4) civilization, the social contract yet to come (75). The four scenarios, Althusser continues, are organized by two unimaginable discontinuities: the first between prehistory and history (eras 1 and 2), and the second between modern immiseration and the social contract.

---

6. Jean-Jacques Rousseau, *Discours sur L'Origine et les Fondemens de L'inegalite parmi les Hommes*, in *Oeuvres Completes*, 3 vols. (Paris: Éditions Gallimard, 1964), 3:111–223, 165; my italics.

7. Louis Althusser, *Lessons on Rousseau*, trans. G. M. Goshgarian (New York: Verso Books, 2019).

"The isolation of the state of pure nature" to which Rousseau refers does not mean primarily the isolation of prehistoric people from one another that Rousseau sketches but their real isolation, however they lived, from the modernity that they nonetheless continue to affect:

> Rousseau thus opposes another, pure form of origin, one not compromised in its result, one so absolutely separate from its own result that we may even wonder whether it has a result that we can call its result. Rousseau opposes an origin as a different world, separated from our world by something like a distance or an abyss, an insurmountable distance: an origin whose purity and separation are reflected, or would be reflected, precisely in this abyss. (Althusser, *Lessons*, 70)

Responses to the Second Discourse that assert that, against Rousseau, human beings are inherently relational,[8] then, do not connect with his framework, in which relation cannot be a natural given. Rousseau refuses to unseal the question of what a human being is because interlocutors for whom humanity is always relational would then try to claim that the nonrelational being is definitionally nonhuman. To break this circuit, Rousseau wants to preserve the terms in asymmetry: human beings that are not relational. Alternatively, it might be possible to avoid patrolling the border of the human by claiming instead, metaphysically, that reality is relational, often down to the laws of physics, a tactic that Tyrone Palmer analyzes as "the coerciveness of the World's underlying logic of relation(ality)."[9] As soon as this claim is made, to differ on the status of relation is to be at odds on reality altogether. For Rousseau, though, physicality separated from conceptuality and practice is inherently nonexplanatory. Rather, relation can only relate for specific beings in specific material circumstances who have organized

8. Jane Anna Gordon cites Anna Julia Cooper, who argues that "the ideal of independence that lay at the core of political doctrines of republican self-governance ... cloaked the ongoing dependence of all human beings on one another" ("Unmasking the *Big Bluff* of Legitimate Governance and So-Called Independence: Creolizing Rousseau through the Reflections of Anna Julia Cooper," *Critical Philosophy of Race* 6 [2018]: 1–25, 3; thanks to James Bliss for this reference). Gordon's stress that "*no one* was actually independent" (9) occupies a more metaphysical register than another phrase of Cooper's: "exploitation means using your neighbor as yourself" (quoted in Gordon, 10).

9. Palmer goes on to "broach the possibility of a nonrelational conception of affect by thinking [its] problems through an attention and fidelity to Blackness as the limit case of relation(ality)." See "Otherwise Than Blackness: Feeling, World, Sublimation," *Qui Parle* 29 (2020): 247–283, 260 and 249.

chemical reactions, astronomical patterns, and so on into a specific reality of relation. To dislodge the naturalism that he targets, then, Rousseau depicts prehistory while insisting that nothing at all can be grasped
about the prehistoric.

Looking back on his tale, Rousseau observes that he has been dealing with unnarratable possibilities: "In discovering and following thus
the forgotten and lost routes that must have led man from the natural
state to the civil state; in reestablishing along with the intermediate positions I have just outlined, those which pressure of time have made
me suppress *or that my imagination has not suggested to me*, no attentive
reader can fail to be struck by the immense space that separates these
two states" (Second Discourse, 90; my italics).

Readers may "reestablish" what Rousseau never thought of; readers may think whatever they like, but in the process, they'll realize that
they, too, cannot begin to diminish the immensity of the space. The
"time pressure" that makes Rousseau leave things he did think of out of
the book sounds trivial, comically juxtaposing time-to-press to time-
to-civilization, but the joke is a glimpse into the nontrivially impossible
task of narrating the emergence of society. In another small example of
temporal insuperability, philosophers cannot account for the millennia
"even if they were able to occupy themselves with that thorny problem
for whole centuries without interruption" (Second Discourse, 37). To
take one more example from outside the text, the exigent support of
mother for infant for the infant's very survival, mobilized by Gordon's
(9–10) essay on Rousseau and Cooper, leaves aside the radical isolation
of infantile life from the time of memory and thus from time at all—
the *incredible separation* of the infant from society to which maternal
support has to respond, and which it does not entirely repair.[10] These
instances support what Althusser suggests, that the image of dispersed
prehistoric people reflects radical separations *in the now*. More than any
content, the reader is asked to absorb the sensation of "immense space"
(Second Discourse, 57, 90) from Rousseau's flight over the eons (Second Discourse, 71). It is a sensation of possibility's immensity for the
better and the worse.

10. Winnicott uses the term *relation* to theorize an era that *follows* that of immemorial maternal support psychoanalytically. "Relation," entailing the interaction of separate entities, doesn't capture the nonindividual. Then relation, when it develops, exists
in opposition to the "feeling of real" that comes only with the aggressivity against which
"relation" defends (*Playing and Reality* [1971] [New York: Routledge, 1991]). The feeling
of real corresponds to negativity in Hegel. For a counterpoint on involuntary attachment
from the maternal object's perspective, see Joy James, "The Womb of Western Theory:
Trauma, Time Theft, and the Captive Maternal," *Carceral Notebooks* 12 [2016]: 253–296.

The Second Discourse leaves the epistemology of relation with a problem, a need to do something about the relation that Rousseau renders materially contingent. As I'll go on to argue in the next section, following Rousseau, Kant stabilizes the contingency by dividing the past and the dead from the present and the living, conflating unknowability with irrelevance. As much as "comparative anatomy," and indeed in explicit parallel to the comparative anatomy of Kant's "Teleological Principles," Kant's division between past and present, object and subject, draws the line of the modern *between every cause and effect*, as I'll go on to in the next section. Here in the Second Discourse, the pressure of abyssal history, an unknown that cannot be unrelated to the present, compels a "separation" (Althusser, *Lessons*, 90)[11] that is relevant in a way that cannot be known and is not dialectically recuperable.

Althusser finds the abyss separating eras (1) and (2) returning in the revolutionary abyss in front of modernity: "It would be a question, this time, of a new necessity that hinges on human will. What is interesting, but obviously very hard to conceptualize, is Rousseau's acute awareness of the extraordinarily precarious character of the social contract. It is, literally, a leap into the void.... It is something which is not without affinities with the events that proceed from contingency" (101).

By "events that proceed from contingency," Althusser means society as is.[12] Rousseau remarks that the social contract amounts "so to speak" to "chang[ing] human nature [de changer, pour ainsi dire, la nature humaine]" (*Social Contract*, 181; OC 3:381); Althusser uses this to enjoin human nature to change again, as prehistory unfolds in the present. Unknown capacity holds potential for the better and for the worse, and from the perspective of European revolutionaries who always seem to need a miracle, it stands in for the total resources available.

Relating with the Wild

All of this comprises the context in which Rousseau brings up "wild" (*sauvage*) society. All in all, Rousseau's recourse to the "wild" in Althusser's era (2) shows him unable to hold on to radical separation—and perhaps nobody could. Making the turn from prehistory to "savage" mo-

11. While Hegel resolves societies into sublation, and Kant into teleological principle, in Rousseau modern values are disoriented by a limit that prehistory, but noy only prehistory, exposes to them.

12. Althusser develops this idea in his late work. See *Philosophy of the Encounter: Later Writings, 1978–1987*, ed. François Matheron, trans. G. M. Goshgarian (London: Verso Books, 2006).

dernity, the "nascent stage" of premodernity ends for good in the third paragraph of part two of the *Discourse on Inequality* (Second Discourse, 69). Early "savage" societies find themselves "learn[ing]," "spread[ing]," and having more "difficulties" (Second Discourse, 70). In fictionalizing these epochs, Rousseau calls on archaeo-anthropological images of sparsely populated forests, nomadism, temporary settlement, early agriculture, setbacks, and eventually rising populations (which he does not treat uncritically as a happy ending). These fictions depict modern societies: they have amour-propre and the symbolism on which it depends, they have materially conditioned social relations, and to various degrees they are status unequal without being class societies. As "reciprocal needs" accumulate, individual existence lives for the first time in and against a social mean. "Each one began to look at the others and to want to be looked at himself"; "as soon as men had begun mutually to value one another, and the idea of esteem was formed in their minds ... it was no longer possible for anyone to be lacking it with impunity" (Second Discourse, 73). These early societies may also have something like ethnicity in the form of regional practices, since "along the seashore" they were one way, "in the forests" another (Second Discourse, 70). What they don't have is property, and Rousseau convenes them to apply pressure to property relations.

Now, in Rousseau's telling, it's crucial that early "savage" societies, being descended in Rousseau's story from prehistoric peoples of whom *nothing* is known, are literally the ancestors of all people on earth: they are, for him, a common denominator of anyone and no one. But obviously the circularity to which Rousseau objects in other writers on the prehistoric (they use the modern human to define the human) dominates his own argument about the "wild." *Sauvage* is a transhistorical word in the Second Discourse, stretching over prehistoric non-societies, early societies, *and eighteenth-century societies*. This is where Rousseau transgresses his own limit, anchors unrepresentable wildness in contemporary reference points—and so reveals his inevitable starting place. To refer to early hunter-gatherers, he has worked backward from given notions of eighteenth-century "Caribs" (Second Discourse, 55), "Negroes" (Second Discourse, 49), and "savages of America" (52). As *slave* names a hardest-case scenario with the greatest payoff for Hegel when it is offered to the reader as an identificatory device, *sauvage* bids to name the most encompassing humanity inside society. It joins the absolutely unimaginable prehistoric human to still distant but not completely unknown peoples and then finally contemporary "Caribs" and "Negroes," such that wildness constitutes an interiorized collective resource in the present. Rousseau recruits contemporary people to testify to the persistence of possibilities that were "inscribed in the origin ... for later" (Althusser, *Lessons*, 136), for societies to come, not so much to evidence the virtues of specific practices as to stand for *any* as-yet undisclosed possibilities of human being. To this end, Rousseau finds it helpful to underline that early "savages" invented civil society, property, and relation so that wildness may invent again. It is this convocation that Rousseau hopes to leverage into the general will, his edition of ANNA or IWWI.

"Savages" provide Rousseau with an outline[13] in which to place prehistoric activity and make the gesture of relating to possibilities expressly beyond the knowable. They are vehicles for "carrying one's entire self, as it were, with one" (Second Discourse, 48). They are the only possible device "in terms that suit all nations, or rather, *forgetting times and places in order to think only of the men* [i.e., other free thinkers] *to whom I am speaking*" (Second Discourse, 46; my italics). Rousseau's readership of political identities is invited to use the Second Discourse to form a collective, on the strength of IWWI's undetermined wildness, heading toward Althusser's fourth stage. This constitutes Rousseau's education for radical identity: reference to "savage" societies invokes free thinkers who identify with them to grasp the contingency that speculating on prehistory brings home. This is a pedagogical fantasy of multicultural basis, predicated on progressive tenets: the universality of "savage" societies in their indeterminacy and potential; the possibility for language to hold the place of possibility; the possibility to argue from socially constructed facts to voluntary social reassembly (*Social Contract*, 224). Whoever is the necessarily undifferentiated "savage" thus bears the burden of exemplifying untellable possibility. Another way to put this is that the transhistorical, multicultural figure of the wild human is the only thread that connects otherwise disjunct parts of the narrative of unfreedom and liberation. Without it, there is no modern conception of either time or history, and no vessel to fly through them.

After the Final Limit

Working through property and prepared with both an acidic, dissolutive history and capacity for social construction of future realities, Rousseau does not foreground chattel slavery, as his readers note, and does not mention racial slavery. Part of Rousseau's reception argues

13. This is how Kant treats Jesus: as "*a schematism of analogy*" ("Religion within the Boundaries of Mere Reason," in *Religion and Rational Theology*, ed. and trans. Allen W. Wood and George di Giovani [Cambridge, UK: Cambridge University Press, 1996], 106).

that his philosophy reverses the polarities of prehistory and history to reproduce the fundamental repressive categories of history and race, modernity and premodernity. In this view, Rousseau stands Hobbes on his head only to create a mirror image of Hobbes. In Charles Mills's formulation, "the praise for nonwhite savages is a limited paternalistic praise, tantamount to admiration for healthy animals, and in no way to be taken to imply their equality, let alone superiority."[14] Mills, however, objects that Rousseau's "primitive beings" "are not actually part of civil society" (Mills, *Racial Contract*, 69), thereby assuming that civil society furnishes the right standard. But in the *Discourse on Inequality*, Rousseau questions civil society's ability to do that.[15]

Alternatively, Louis Sala-Molins's 1992 study of the French enlightenment focuses on the inability of chattel slavery—either classical or racial—to "rais[e] a philosophical problem"[16] for Rousseau. If Sala-Molins is right that Rousseau finds slavery loathsome but intellectually uninteresting, this points to the fact that Rousseau is uninterested because he can't discern in slavery the causes and effects that he expects. In the *Discourse on Inequality* and *Social Contract*, these questions arise abstractly. Rousseau rarely provides any specific setting for classical slavery and, as Neil Roberts remarks, "racial slavery is the institutional form of enslavement Rousseau fails to comment on" altogether.[17] In fact Rousseau often presents "slavery" so thinly that the reader has no idea which slavery he means. Rousseau himself seems to assume that his attack on private property *covers* slavery. Further, he takes racism to refer to no substance but concludes that it therefore has nothing to add to the understanding of property. Nonetheless, his attempts to locate this generic slavery's relations to property and sovereignty, if

14. Charles Mills, *The Racial Contract* (Ithaca, NY: Cornell University Press, 2014), 69.

15. According to Gordon and Roberts, in the Caribbean "no other text [of Rousseau's] is engaged more substantially than the Second Discourse" (*Creolizing Rousseau*, 16). They link their project to C. L. R. James's criticism of "the superficial ways" in which Rousseau's arguments "were often summarily dismissed" ("Rousseau and the Idea of the General Will," in *You Don't Play with Revolution: Montreal Lectures*, ed. David Austin [Chico, CA: AK Press, 2009]). James implies that for many, interest in alternatives to European polity cannot be taken seriously.

16. Louis Sala-Molins, *Dark Side of the Light: Slavery and the French Enlightenment* [1992], trans. John Conteh-Morgan (Minneapolis: University of Minnesota Press, 2006). Rousseau's objection to slavery subsumes Atlantic chattel slavery, Sala-Molins points out. His work "does not deviate toward the juxtaposition of what could be considerably different" between Atlantic chattel slaves, Greek and Roman slaves, and European subjects of unfreedom (74).

17. Neil Roberts, "Rousseau, Flight, and the Fall into Slavery," 220n6. Roberts reflects that an analysis of racial slavery by Rousseau "would have been invaluable" (220n6). See also Roberts, *Freedom as Marronage* (Chicago: University of Chicago Press, 2015).

we stay with them, do reveal their own active connection to Atlantic slavery. First, Rousseau gives separate accounts of race and slavery that need to be excavated before considering why and how, in the end, he relegates slavery to a subset of property. In fact, Rousseau not only elaborates conscious theories of race and slavery separately but also scatters fragmentary, *unconscious theories of racial slavery* throughout the Second Discourse and *Social Contract*. In the conscious argument property accounts for slavery, not completely but almost; at the same time, slavery overspills property and its limits.

First, the conscious approaches, first to race, then to slavery, through property. As I've mentioned, Rousseau imagines modern social relations becoming totalized without attributing them to a developmental principle. His stance is neither mechanical nor organic in Hegel's specifically dialectical way. Rather, relation consists in the "chance coming together of several unconnected causes that might never have come into being" (Second Discourse, 68). The "youth of the world" could have gone on forever, or *homo sapiens* could have been wiped out at any time, as it almost was during the ice age. But bullets get dodged, and occupation grows denser and more stationary. With the onset of agriculture for surplus, "one man" could not do it all and "needed" "the help of another" (Second Discourse, 74), a condition that incentivized institutions of servitude. Rousseau argues that accumulation then begins to turn already-concentrating unevenness into vicious ontologized difference:

> The farmer had a greater need for iron, or the blacksmith had a greater need for wheat; and in laboring equally, the one earned a great deal while the other barely had enough to live. Thus it is that natural inequality imperceptibly manifests itself together with *inequality occasioned by the socialization process*. Thus it is that differences among men, developed by those of circumstances, make themselves more noticeable, *more permanent in their effects*, and begin to influence the fate of private individuals in the same proportion. (Second Discourse, 67; my italics)

This is effectively Rousseau's theory of race. There are happenstance differences, not originally economic, that economic motives seize on and render "more permanent." Rousseau's account matches contemporary historical ones;[18] the intent to accumulate brings along a desire to be able to justify accumulation by discriminating between kinds of people

18. For a similar procedure in which the motive is extraction, see Abigail B. Bakan, "Marxism and Anti-Racism," in *Theorizing Anti-Racism*, ed. Abigail B. Bakan and Enakshi

and so desires standards of legibility (not necessarily physiognomic), even if legibility in practice remains a problem. Schematically, this approach to race envisions it as various performances of "mark[ing]" "as a way to distribute positions and powers differentially," as in Geraldine Heng's nonunified study of medieval race(s).[19] Social incentives also account for the materialization of the norm being marked. Alongside the ontologization wreaked by the "socialization process," and in theoretically loose relationship to it, modern difference in Rousseau can also appear less malignantly as "nations" (e.g., Second Discourse, 80), "peoples" (Second Discourse, 65), "lifestyles" (Second Discourse, 70), and "the imaginary barriers that separate peoples" (Second Discourse, 80).

Rousseau goes on to stress that without economic consequences even a hierarchized ontologization of differences would not have "much reality and influence" (Second Discourse, 67). These unmonetized differences are what he means by the confusing phrase "natural inequality"—that is, *differences that have not been formally incentivized.*[20] (Hegel also posits such a stage before legality.) In conditions of, for example, foraging, "it would be difficult even to explain ... what servitude and domination are ... what can be the chains of dependence among men who possess nothing?" (Second Discourse, 67). Disaster arrives only "as soon as one man realized that it was useful" to accumulate more than his share (Second Discourse, 74) and acts on his realization by enclosing land. The implications for others of this intensification of accumulation meant that "property came into existence, labor became necessary" for everyone (Second Discourse, 74). As Rousseau locates transformation and world construction at property relation, he imagines it bringing slavery. This slavery is socially omnibus—classical

---

Dua, 97–122, and Nikhal Pal Singh, "On Race, Violence, and So-Called Primitive Accumulation," 27–50.

19. Heng's medieval Jews and Christians are "marked" by badges, dress, names, or "color and physiognomy" (Geraldine Heng, *The Invention of Race in the European Middle Ages* [Cambridge, UK: Cambridge University Press, 2018], 12, 76, 51n36, 27, 227, respectively). See also Thomas C. Holt, "Marking: Race, Race-Making, and the Writing of History," *American Historical Review* 100 (1995): 1–20. The metaphor of superficiality can make it sound as though there were a natural substrate, Wynter's monist human, being marked. For Anthony Farley, for example, "before the mark, the skin we are in holds all of us in common and all is common ... the mark splits the first commons" and "the inaugural dispossession is occasioned by the violence of the mark" ("The Colorline as Capitalist Accumulation," *Buffalo Law Review* 56 [2008]: 953–963, 953, 955).

20. Differences that are not yet invidious appear in every long genealogy of race; in them, race is the name for the degradation that afflicts them as a later development. This pattern suggests the recurrence of "primitivism" unconnected to essentialist beliefs and inherent in even relativized notions of origin.

slavery, war slavery, chattel slavery, racial slavery?—and an effect of property. It will turn out that the cause/effect distinction between property and slavery won't be unproblematic. Nonetheless, *property becomes cause and slavery becomes effect.* As property *creates* an incentive to coerce labor in "smiling fields that had to be watered with men's sweat...[,] slavery and misery were soon seen to *germinate*" (Second Discourse, 75; my italics).

This causal arrangement recurs in Rousseau's iconic depiction of primal theft by "the first person who, having enclosed a plot of land, took it into his head to say 'This is mine,' and found people simple enough to believe him" (Second Discourse, 69). The bystanders who sustain the "impostor" (69), not owners of anything themselves, are vital players. Their attendance indicates property's contingency and the potential for future action. But their inaction reflects their fears and dependencies, showing "that by then things had *already* reached the point where they could no longer continue as they were" (Second Discourse, 69; my italics). Although the impostor's theft may seem *ex nihilo*, its "perfection of the individual" in the crystallization "mine" (Second Discourse, 74) is rather the "*final* limit" (69; my italics) of human being entangled in "chains of dependency." It is the last time the human being is seen. And slavery takes place after all this, "after *the final* limit" of dependency. After private agriculture, chattel slaves and racial chattel slaves remain undifferentiated among the "new slaves" that wealthy landowners "us[e] their old slaves to subdue" (Second Discourse, 78). In this "chain" in which every link is one kind of slave or another, slavery does not require anything more than readers have learned from the analysis of property as such. Therefore, radical collectivity will do for slaves as well. While the natural law theories that Rousseau disdains add racial science to explain slavery, Rousseau assumes that no explanation needs to be added, because the whole outrage is presaged in the appearance of property.

That was the explicit theory. Now the unconscious imaginary of slavery, that travels through the blurred word *slave*. What relation does the blurring obscure? Some arguments, such as that "slavery and misery... germinate" from property (Second Discourse, 75) assume a common root of slavery and labor in property, from which they speak. Other statements of Rousseau's attempt a specific and almost total substitution of meanings, and these are more disruptive and introduce questions of desire. Rousseau often uses *slave* to mean someone immersed in naturalized relations of amour-propre and exchange dependency— someone who internalizes and perpetuates coercion because they stand to gain or lose. "Slaves" in Rousseau are paradigmatically good citizens of business: "the word *finance* is a slave's word" (*Social Contract*, 218).

To excoriate the activities of financial citizens, Rousseau pulls out all the stops of a moral language of degradation, since what they threaten to degrade is the indelible wildness within. Therefore—to take the substitution to its hyperbolic peak—for Rousseau chattel slaves are usually not what he means by "slaves" *because they are forced* to live and die as slaves.

If the financier is called slavelike, decadence is a clue to what *slave* means to Rousseau. It's possible to see here that Rousseau's generic use of *slave* is often immersed in the image-repertoire of Atlantic slavery, as though the generic term were the means to write about Atlantic slavery without saying so. This mirrorland in which the slaveowners are slave-like prefigures the spendthrift destructiveness of the master in Hegel's dialectic.

Rousseau gets to his strange usage of *slave* through the academic riddle of whether persons can legitimately sell themselves. The conundrum usually takes shape as debates about possessive individuality—Locke's bourgeois idea of the "proprietor of his own person, and the actions of labor in it."[21] Rousseau's intervention in this rather perverse debate redefines slavery as attempted self-sale. Thus he can reinforce the degradation of buying and selling property and reinforce the wildness of human being by finding it ineliminable in (even) the chattel slave. To this end he cites Jean Barbeyrac,[22] the French editor and translator of natural law theorist Samuel Pudendorf, to support an ethos of nonpossessive life. A person's consent to slavery "would be selling his own life, of which he is not the master" (Barbeyrac, note to Pudendorf, quoted in Second Discourse, 84).[23] "Life," a "gift" rather than "goods," cannot be sold even when the person agrees to do so (Second Discourse, 84). "In giving up life one annihilates that being *insofar as one can*" (Second Discourse, 84): the slave owner lacks capacity to possess "that be-

21. John Locke, *Treatise of Civil Government [Treatise Concerning the True Original and Extent of Civil Government]*, ed. Andrew Bailey (Peterborough, ON: Broadview Press, 2015), 52.

22. Jean Barbeyrac's editorial notes to Samuel Pudendorf's *Of the Law of Nature and Nations: Eight Books* [1672] are incorporated and translated by Basil Kennett and George Carew in their edition of Pudendorf (London: Walthoe & Wilkin, 1729).

23. Pudendorf (vs. Barbeyrac), writing of war slaves, believes that "equality" is derived as a result of the very mutual obligation of civil society that, Rousseau claims, enables inequality. Therefore, for Pudendorf, even hereditary war slavery is acceptable as long as it's a matter of legal arrangement and not immediate physical force. Slavery's legitimacy is "built on [the slave's] exemption from chains and imprisonment" (Pudendorf, 617). Pudendorf's accepted, chainless slavery *is Rousseau's model of civil society as such*. It attempts to trade away its wildness but cannot fully do it.

ing," natural law lacks the capacity to encompass it, and the self lacks "the right to divest" it (Second Discourse, 84). So Rousseau insists on a space within the juridical and practical acts that comprise slavery where the wildness of unrealized potential still resides. Indeed no one can or should know potential. The problem is that Rousseau does know it. Since slavery tries to destroy a constitutive wildness that can finally only be destroyed "insofar as one can," it becomes delusion not to be taken fully seriously. Rousseau expects that as contradictions of life's impropriety and wildness, slavery and tyranny will run themselves into the ground.

When Rousseau calls buyers and sellers slaves, however, he revives the slaveness of the slave in the circuit:

> Give money and soon you'll be in chains. The word *finance* is a slave's word ... In a truly free state the citizens do everything with their own hands and nothing with money. Far from paying to be exempted from their duties, they would pay to fulfill them themselves. Far be it from me to be sharing commonly held ideas; I believe that forced labor is less opposed to liberty than are taxes. (*Social Contract*, 218; OC 3:429)

The desire to buy, here, is a depravity that Rousseau wouldn't mind suppressing by force—forced shared labor. Moreover, citizens who purchase labor and those who appoint representatives to make their decisions for them work in parallel. They do not, as in the liberal tradition, strengthen their grasp of relation through abstraction and exchange: they are training in capitalism, not community. The sudden appearance of the consumer-as-slave collapses buyers and their objects of consumption in an unlicensed desire[24]—consumers' horrifying desire,

---

24. In this context it matters that, against his own constructivist current, Rousseau allows sex to exist in prehistory in its "physical aspects" apart from the "moral aspect of love" (Second Discourse, 65), as though it alone were a natural need without a social ontology and a historical meaning. If sex were not built in the image of need, it could suggest a broader range of motives for possession and slavery. Across Rousseau's other work, obviously so in his *Confessions*, he has things to say about excessive desire. Carole Pateman discusses the sexual contract, including marriage and prostitution law, as "a repressed dimension of contract theory." She observes that "for Rousseau ... no contract theory that creates a relationship of subordination is valid—except the sexual contract" (*The Sexual Contract* [1988] [Cambridge, UK: Polity, 2018], xiii, 76). See also Nalini Persram, "Pacha Mama, Rousseau, and the Feminine: How Nature Can Revive Politics," in *Creolizing Rousseau*, ed. Jane Anna Gordon and Neil Roberts (New York: Rowman & Littlefield, 2014), 225–251.

also, to flee what should be satisfying, direct democracy and creative subsistence. In the Second Discourse, Rousseau had imagined how different it would be to have desires if everything were free: satisfaction would be possible and pleasure could precede desire (see also Casas Klausen, *Fugitive Rousseau*, 86). Calling the buyer "slave," however, models his damage on that of an earlier slave, and here Rousseau draws from the antiblack imaginary that makes "slave" pejorative by way of illicit desire.

Writing about the perceived decadence of Black consumption, Marriott remarks that it is as though "black property becomes identified with a pleasure that enslaves itself."[25] He goes on to address the perceived "slavishness" of the master:

> Even with the death of the slave, the endless expenditure of mastery remains the truth of a supernumerary economy, rather than the sign of lasting sovereign power. This would also mean that all racial mastery is necessarily servile. But this conclusion is immediately impaired by another: such social death meets its necessary limit in a kind of decadence that cannot finally be captured by the moral legacy of humanism, and whose pleasure cannot be said to be located either exclusively in language (whether or nouns or names) *or in a sovereignty that is slavishly perverse.* ("On Decadence," unpaginated)

In fact in Hegel we have seen a master who cannot control his expenditure; it annihilates his resources, including his relations as resources. Marriott's comment on the antiblack desire that names the master's pleasure "slavish" raises the question of what the pejorative "slave" (the reappearance of the "bad" slave) displaces when it distributes slaveness over the slavish owner *and* the slave as commodity. Manifestly, Rousseau's economy of social coercion and incentive, a "chain" in which every link is, to him, some kind of slave or other, finds the "slavish" all along civil society itself. If slavishness is endemic to society, not only figuratively but also as a cause of slavery, this suggests a crisis in sovereignty whose perception is deferred by rendering blackness as "unsovereign life."[26] The slave's relay of anxiety about expenditure reappears in Rousseau's sense that popular sovereignty is being degraded: it's slavish to throw oneself away politically, in representation, as citizens do.

25. David S. Marriott, "On Decadence: *Bling Bling,*" *e-flux* 79 (February 2017): unpaginated, https://www.e-flux.com/journal/79/94430/on-decadence-bling-bling/.
26. Jared Sexton, "Affirmation in the Dark," *Comparatist* 43 (2019): 90–111, 101.

A political anxiety irrupts repeatedly just where Rousseau vents his desire to degrade a political corrupter. In the middle of *Social Contract*'s discussion of the labor of governance, direct democracy, and the structural function of slave classes in Greece that, so the myth goes, existed to give citizens the leisure to attend to government, Rousseau obliterates contemporary slavery:

> There are some unfortunate circumstances where one's liberty can be preserved only at the expense of someone else's, and where the citizen can be perfectly free only if the slave is completely enslaved. Such was the situation in Sparta.[27] As for you, modern peoples, you do not have slaves, but you yourselves are slaves. You pay for their liberty with your own. It is in vain that you crow about that preference. I find more cowardice in it than humanity. (*Social Contract*, 220)

The parting shot at contemporary liberals, in and through a spectacular moment of blindness, implies certain relationships. It has at least three phases: first, slavery supports democracy; unlike the slavery in the Second Discourse, which is only an unfolding effect, this slavery—distinguishable as classical by its political character and implying that the for-profit slavery of the Second Discourse is primarily modern—has a structural function serving a status quo. This point immediately gives way to another, that moral outrage against slavery screens readers from their degradation of self-government. "You crow about that preference [vous avez beau vanter cette préférence]" (OC 3:431) is radical-to-liberal language to antagonize a complacent "you."[28] Rousseau's self-consciousness drops during his confrontation with the liberal, however, and third and finally releases its own hostility—misrecognizable as radical bravery—on the slave.

Borrowing the pejorative association of slave from somewhere, Rousseau activates the second-degree of "mention" common in antiracist discourse. He relies on a second slave, out of the frame, whose slaveness remains the standard for political slavishness. This liminal figure of a "bad" slave lends its badness to the unfree, insufficiently political subject. The insult to petty, propertied slavishness through this

27. Such was not the situation in Sparta. Aristocratic and military elites symbolically presided over a representative democracy that institutionalized a slave class. But Sparta's population of 40,000–50,000 was small enough that, according to Rousseau—who was in the midst of advocating direct democracy in small states—it should not have had this "use" for slavery.

28. On uses of "you," see Philip Brian Harper, "Nationalism and Social Division in Black Arts Poetry of the 1960s," *Critical Inquiry* 19 (1993): 234–255.

moment's deletion of contemporary slavery is the one moment and mode in which Rousseau explicitly involves the Black Atlantic slave. So, while in explicit explanation Rousseau proposes that property accumulation created incentives for invidious racial distinction, in implicit explanation Rousseau stresses the desire to spend, to throw oneself and others away, to depreciate, to sell for no good reason. In the first version, property explains slavery. In the second, the figure of the slave stands where the theory has difficulty explaining itself.

Null and Void

Sora Han analyzes the legal affair of Betty, a slave who was declared free in the North, where she had traveled with her owners, but returned with them to Tennessee (where her husband lived), to the disappointment of abolitionists who had brought her case. Han argues that "personal sovereignty... is haunted materially at the level of formal legal reasoning by a notion of 'free will' that is free precisely because this freedom can be given away."[29] Now, explicitly Rousseau defines self-sale out of existence—he would argue that it could not have been what Betty did. He is not invested in liberal self-possession; he is invested in involuntary wildness. He is left with the problem of accounting for why people act as though involuntary wildness did not exist. Civil society's circulation of coercion and benefit is his technological answer: but it's not, *and is never*, much of an answer, being only a technique. As a result, in Rousseau's social ontology, standing institutions have a quality of irreality reminiscent of derealized entities in Hegel. For Rousseau *hegemonic* entities radiate this effect. Rousseau does lend positive force to property, even while demonstrating the incredulity with which he thinks it should be regarded. Yet this positivity is secondary, there because he needs property acquisition as a motive that wards off still more difficult, perhaps unanswerable, questions about why proponents of slavery "have not been afraid to debase themselves to this degree" (Second Discourse, 84). He wouldn't have this problem if he thought that accumulation, or attraction to power, was somehow natural; he has it because he does not. So property stays put, slavery stays impossible, the social contract remains possible, and the institutions remain irreal—a kind of bargain that holds Rousseau's text together. A derealized world is both the cost (because Rousseau's explanations of its existence can only go so far) and the gain (because it seems unjustified and liable to collapse at any moment).

29. "Slavery as Contract: *Betty's Case* and the Question of Freedom," *Law and Literature* 27 (2015): 395–416, 400.

Derealization is the effect when something survives its self-contradiction untransformed. During the self-sale debate, for example, Rousseau hopes that those who can't agree that life is not something anyone "possesses" may still agree that "subjecting [war slaves'] posterity," separate persons, to the "degrad[ing]" arrangements that Lockean liberals make for themselves (Second Discourse, 84) is contradictory: "Just as violence had to be done to nature in order to establish slavery, nature had to be changed in order to perpetuate this right [of heredity]. And the jurists, who have gravely pronounced that the child of a slave woman is born a slave, have decided, in other words, that a man is not born a man"[30] (Second Discourse, 84).

Rousseau might have remembered here that the constructivism of the Second Discourse argues that man is not *born* anything, leaving space for a slave society to make it so that he is born a slave *in actuality*, in Hegel's sense of actuality. That would be more consistent with Rousseau's earlier argument. Instead, the *Social Contract* rejects any possibility that the liberal polities proposed in natural law actually exist, as opposed to tyrannies whose subjects don't really consent to be ruled at all. To suppose they "give [themselves] gratuitously" to an external sovereign "is to suppose a populace composed of madmen" (*Social Contract*, 160). To the extent that such a populace exists, it is "incompatible with the nature of man" (*Social Contract*, 160). Likewise, "[arbitrary] power, *being illegitimate by its nature, could not have served* as a foundation for the rights of society, nor, as a consequence, for the inequality occasioned by social institutions" (Second Discourse, 84; my italics). Rousseau proceeds (reasonably) to the conclusion that slavery and tyranny can only exist as part of a social totality of property, and that that totality can exist because civil society circulates coerced incentives.

In practice though, society does not play by the rules, creating problems for the social ontology Rousseau elaborates in the Second Discourse. In the Second Discourse nothing exists without social agreements; social relations, though, may or may not be agreements. Therefore, Rousseau wants explicit agreements: since territories, rules, and buildings don't make a civil state, by the time of *Social Contract* Rousseau is moved to ask what makes "a people a people"[31] and to answer that it requires "unanimity on at least one occasion," the occasion of its

---

30. The slavery "contradiction" contains the anxiety "a man is not a man"; phrased in other words, man singularly "succeeds in preserving error in the very heart of reality" (Kojève, *Introduction*, 187).

31. On the paradoxes of Rousseau's "people," which is not an essentialist "nation" and yet still uses "confrontation with its boundary" to provoke its "political awareness," see Gillian Rose, *The Broken Middle: Out of Our Ancient Society* (Oxford: Blackwell, 1992), 242.

constitution (*Social Contract*, 163). The members' "total alienation" of any private concern or property when they join the community (*Social Contract*, 164) expresses the spirit of their unanimity. All or nothing: since the collective exists only as public good, "by the mere fact that it exists, it is always all that it should be" (*Social Contract*, 166), and yet by the same token, *it can become clear at any moment that it no longer exists.* It becomes buildings and regulations, but not a state.

The fragility of social agreement and the difficulty of telling what an agreement looks like—a difficulty that Hegel evades when he focuses on ontological process instead—leads Rousseau to set up various partitions to protect agreement. He must separate police power from state right and authority over persons from authority over laws (*Social Contract*, 182), for example. Enforcements of particular cases can never be acts of general will (*Social Contract*, 175), but mere demonstrations of police power (*magistrat*) that must be carefully limited. As David Wootton notes in his annotation to Cress's translation, *magistrat* can be anyone "responsible for what the French call *police*—a term that covers all measures to order a society" (*Social Contract*, 175n43). Police power, encompassing "sovereign decrees concerning a particular object" (179) and elections of particular leaders (*Social Contract*, 175), expresses the unvanquished privateness of civil society inside the state. The state is always on the brink of becoming private, and once it declines into mostly private arrangements, "it falls apart and exists no longer" (*Social Contract*, 184).

Not only does the state have no legitimate autonomous being, the general will that justifies it also has no primary, autonomous being but is merely the "result from the large number of small differences" among the people(s) involved (*Social Contract*, 173). Just as it depends on "the labor of its members" economically (*Social Contract*, 209), the state depends on the population politically for the substance of differences that it mediates.[32] The very existence of the state then is not distinct from its authorized performance, and a political form is never an end in itself in the way that the living persons within it are. Its legitimacy consists in the fact that it can cease to exist at any moment and for any reason, and if for any reason it does not disband when no longer authorized it is no longer legitimate and not a state.

The state is a tyranny when its lack of legitimacy annuls and voids it.

---

32. "The accord of all the interests is found in the opposition to that of each. If there were no different interests, the common interest, which would never encounter any obstacle, would scarcely be felt" (*Social Contract*, 172–173n38). Through Marx, I'll return to the state's dependence on this mediation in § 9.

But its persistence in illegitimacy becomes a problem that Rousseau can only account for and solve by force. The null and void polity has a name: tyranny. But if slavery is also void, "absurd and meaningless," what is it while it is null and void? On what does its persistence run?

Having proposed that without accumulation, prehistoric people would have no reason to enslave one another, Rousseau entertains another prehistoric hypothesis:

> Is there a man with strength sufficiently superior to mine and who is, moreover, depraved enough, lazy enough, and ferocious enough to force me to provide for his subsistence while he remains idle? He would have to resolve not to take his eyes off me for a single instant, to keep me very carefully tied down while he sleeps, for fear that I escape or kill him. In other words, he is obliged to expose himself voluntarily to a much greater hardship than the one he wants to avoid and gives me. After all that, if his vigilance relaxes for an instant? If an unforeseen noise makes him turn his head? I take twenty steps into the forest, my chains are broken, and he never sees me again for the rest of his life. (Second Discourse, 68, trans. modified)

Rousseau's thought problem sidesteps another question embedded in it: What would slavery be and imply if someone were "sufficiently depraved" in this way? Alternatively, and even less "reasonably," what would it be if it needed no one to be depraved? This is a moment that opens and immediately closes a line of thought. Rousseau reasons that it doesn't matter what it would mean, because before settlement the captive can just run away, and afterward he could "just" be imprisoned. In this way, focusing on the technologies of bondage, "the how and not the why,"[33] limits Rousseau's discussions of both wildness and property.

Splitting Property

What if property, the solid, understandable form of illegitimacy that accounts for both unfreedom and slavery, contains an unhinging difference between unfreedom and slavery, the difference that generic "slavery" constantly elides? Almost singularly in the secondary literature, Casas Klausen's very helpful *Fugitive Rousseau* makes a case for Rousseau's active contributions to thought about Atlantic racial slavery, and

33. Wendy Hui Kyong Chun, introduction to the special issue "Race and/as Technology; or How to Do Things to Race," *Camera Obscura* 70 (2009): 7–35.

he and I cover a great deal of similar ground. (I came to many similar conclusions independently, maybe because of the shared anarchist orientation that makes both of us interested in Rousseau.) I would like to attend to it here to examine further the difficulty of containing slavery in property. Because of our common ground, attention to Casas Klausen's argument can also help to summarize what has happened so far.

In addition to assessing notions of marronage and contiguous land use drawn from Rousseau for their suggestions toward anarchist collectivity, Casas Klausen reconstructs Rousseau's criticism of civil society and analyzes his generalization of slavery as a work of ambivalent condensation and displacement (*Fugitive Rousseau*, 85) that reflects the relationship between property and slave *as* property:

> In situating Rousseau alongside Douglass, Du Bois, or Wright, I do not mean to suggest that Rousseau's big-bang theory of the global effects of uttering *"this is mine"* should *replace* the Middle Passage as constitutive of modernity. Rather, I am suggesting that reading from our perspective and with its globality in mind, Rousseau's presentation of the triangulation of landed private property, slavery, and the territorial state offers a critical counterhistory ... political modernity might, counterfactually but truthfully, trace itself to the moment that *"this is mine"* becomes regnant globally (which is nearly the moment it is first pronounced). (Casas Klausen, *Fugitive Rousseau*, 37)

Casas Klausen's reconstruction underlines that Rousseau develops the conditions of chattel slavery: "property generates both the global and the local displacements that bring chattel slavery into being"; "self-enslavement ... brings in its train chattel enslavement of others" (*Fugitive Rousseau*, 62, 86). Rousseau's metaphor of seeds germinating recurs in Casas Klausen's language for property's generativity, as does the asymmetrical attribution of causality to property on the understanding that it is not unilateral. In Rousseau, the alternative to property's fecundity appears as "force." Because he eviscerates natural law, he "leav[es] us only with force" to account for slavery *or* tyranny even while he insists that force is unable "to sustain an institution on its own" (40). Rousseau also views circular convention—the technologies of social regulation—as nothing but "underlying brutality" (45), prompting the same need for a stronger explanation, for positive motives to sustain slavery. So, Casas Klausen goes on, "Rousseau must then supply a supplement to force that can account for slavery *qua institution*. For this supplement we must go back to the Second Discourse to the account of the origin of territorial property" (40; my italics).

Property brings the required endurance and motive to the analysis of slavery because its development can be understood as a spatial consequence of globalized relation, the "structural truth" of political modernity (Casas Klausen, *Fugitive Rousseau*, 35). It is not *ex nihilo*: it occurs along the way of migration and tenancy. In Rousseau's counternarrative, remember, "new spatial relationships" (54) emerge as land is occupied, and these contingent relationships constitute the social relations ripe for property before the words *this is mine* are uttered. The formalization of property, momentous as it is, is only the "*second* closure" of space (63), the first being the emergence of relation through inhabitation of land. Casas Klausen phrases this circumstance eloquently: "'this is mine' addresses a captive audience: its audience cannot in fact flee" (55). In Rousseau's texts, slavery's origins are not as deep as these roots of property. Rather, enslavement is the end point of global exchange: "Slavery follows this final closure (of the regime of property) almost trivially as a universal institution—an institution made universal by the infinite substitutability of the position of slave" (70).

Everything must be the result of something. But isn't this a case of a place where the roots are "never touching the soil" (Derrida, *Of Grammatology*, 101), so that "property" is called to represent slavery's origin, lest origin collapse altogether? It seems remarkable that *property is both effect and cause*,[34] autopoetically self-sustaining once it comes to be, while slavery "*follow[s] the final.*" On the heels of his attack on hereditary war slavery in Pudendorf, Rousseau offers "the necessity of this progression": "The condition of rich and poor was authorized by the first epoch, that of the strong and the weak by the second, and that of master and slave by the third: the ultimate degree of inequality and the limit to which all the others finally lead, until new revolutions dissolve the government or bring it nearer to a legitimate institution" (Second Discourse, 87). "Issu[ing] from the global order of things" (Casas Klausen, *Fugitive Rousseau*, 70), slavery is its last instance, and the best name of contemporary disaster. Slavery completely coincides with modernity understood as a downslope between a wild past and a possible future of social being.

Slavery belongs, then, to the Second Discourse's era of present-day barbarism. Yet this dangling, secondary status does not fully stabilize property itself, which never sounds like merely an understandable supersession of nomads' use of the earth. It remains incredible, as Rousseau

---

34. For reflections on entanglements of cause and effect in arguments about slavery, see Patrice Douglass, "The Claim of Right to Property: Social Violence and Political Right," *Zeitschrift für Anglistik und Amerikanistik* 65.2 (2017): 145–159.

has said; it's from its advent that people whose only reality is social reality begin to act as though they were under a spell and cannot do anything. Meanwhile, the sequence property-slavery maintains a deep rift within property that unsettles relation in a way that Rousseau's own prehistoric speculation might have understood. Casas Klausen presents the dehiscence of property powerfully: "*This is mine*' is not yet '*you are mine*'" (*Fugitive Rousseau*, 62). Supposedly, property's generative capacity extends itself across this difference with time: "However, private property generates both the global and the local displacements that *bring* chattel slavery into being" (62; my italics). The *difference* between possessing an inanimate property and a slave is represented as a *temporal development*. Alternatively, and in illumination, the figure of the slave is stretched between ownership ("This is mine") and the register called "love" ("you are mine"). The space of the "not yet," filled in Rousseau's explicit argument by property, again sounds as though it were reaching for something else, a kind of possession and self-abandonment for which "property" is only a substitute, displacing other problematic transformations such as "I am this" and "I am yours."

What if the break between "this is mine" and "you are mine" re-expresses the breaks that Althusser finds between prehistory and history, and history and its beyond, as a break within property? Slavery, this language implies, cannot tolerate a speculative memory of love, love in a violent register indistinguishable from its experience as separation. Can this need be managed by the political subject's reach for the slave? Rousseau's gulf between prehistory and history reads as though he'd been there: "the more one meditates on this subject, the more the distance ... increases before our eyes; and it is *impossible* to conceive how a man could have crossed such a wide gap" (Second Discourse, 55; my italics). "Shocked by the unending difficulties" of his position, and finding himself no longer "in a situation in which two facts have been acknowledged as real, but need to be connected by a series of intermediate facts" (the situation of "history," Second Discourse, 69)—could Rousseau have written, "convinced of the almost demonstrable impossibility that slavery could have arisen and been established by merely human means, I leave to anyone who would undertake it the discussion of the following difficult problem: which was the more necessary, an already formed society for the invention of slavery, or already invented slavery for the establishment of society?" (Second Discourse, 60, amended).

§ 5

The Racial Grammar of Kantian Time

Discontented with your present state, for reasons which threaten your unfortunate descendants with still greater discontent, you might wish to be able to go backward; and this feeling should be a panegyric on your first ancestors, a criticism of your contemporaries, and a terror to the unfortunates who will come after you.

ROUSSEAU, *Discourse on the Origin of Inequality*

Objects are destined for me; they are for me. Desire as a relationship with the world involves both a distance between me and the desirable, and consequently a time ahead of me, and also a possession of the desirable which is prior to the desire.

EMMANUEL LEVINAS, *Existence and Existents*

The Kant-Hegel dichotomy, a momentous passage from transcendental to historical reality, also shows systems interlocking to form something more intractable than either system by itself. The contrast is genuine, with innumerable consequences, yet reception of the Kant-Hegel dynamic as a whole, when understood as flowing away from racist rigidity, makes it more difficult to notice antiblackness.

Chains of relation in nonrelation involve not only subject-object relations but also object-object relations, object-subject relations, and temporal relations. Sublation in Hegel opens the past, maintaining its present and future existence as a lasting resource for the benefit of the living.[1] In the passage from *Discourse on Inequality* that I've chosen as

---

1. Further, "being left behind" is the elevated purpose of the sublated being, which "comes to be only by being left behind; its immediacy is sublated immediacy" (*Science of Logic* 11.252).

an epigraph above,[2] Rousseau indicates the well-known uses of locating a past/present threshold anywhere: placing something in the past may in itself be an act of praise, derogation, or terror. In the second epigraph above, Levinas ventriloquizes a voice issuing from the space-time of modern intentionality. For this "me," not only the temporal direction but also the very existence of objects is "for me." The spatial distance between the "me" and the object creates both "a time ahead" and "a possession of the desirable which is prior to the desire" (21). Interestingly, Levinas's phrasing is stronger than reason. Not only is the possessability of the desirable prior to the desire but also the distance has already been crossed. The spatiotemporal structure of desire—distance, consequence, time—rationalizes a possession that has already happened.

The past/present threshold is not only an instrument of this or that interest, as Rousseau writes, but also a frontier of the political altogether, as Sexton remarks. To the extent that the past lies "behind" intention, it disappears from subjectivity.[3] In his own construction of space-time Kant complements Hegel: rather than opening the past to continual consumption, Kant makes the past the domain of objects that can no longer be subjects, and relation the domain of subject-subject dealings in the present only. In Kant's case, the distinction of present and past beings orders and separates them; in Hegel's, a present demand for unending access to past beings preserves them *as resources*.

In the following discussion, I hope to show how Kant's construction of the conditions of possibility for telling the past from the present reflects an existing global violence—prior to the argument, prior to Kant altogether—determining what can count as relevant and therefore political, political and therefore relevant. While not any possible notion of pastness is necessarily tendentious, Kant's is, and despite dialecticization, its logic continues in common use. Kant's notion of a nonsubjective past is complicated but not improved by Hegel. Rather, in the Kant-Hegel sequence, philosophy shifts from a racial to a metaracial plane.

2. Jean-Jacques Rousseau, *Discourse on the Origin of Inequality*, in *The Discourses and Other Early Political Writings*, ed. and trans. Victor Gourevitch (Cambridge, UK: Cambridge University Press, 1997), 133.

3. Donna Jones has argued that Bergson writes in such a mode, rendering the past into an accessible reservoir of objects of desire. See Jones, *The Racial Discourses of Life Philosophy: Negritude, Vitalism, and Modernity* (New York: Columbia University Press, 2010).

Why Nonreciprocal Relations Do Not Coexist in Time, or, Two Moving Images

In the First Critique, time is known through causality. Establishing the enabling limits of any possible community[4] in its space and time, Kant also embeds political strictures on community in the conditions of space and time that explain them—as in Levinas's satire on the perspective of teleological space-time.[5] I could as easily say that Kant's human space-time consists in anthropolitical strictures. In "Teleological Principles," he imagines Black Africans as consummate sufferers of hardship and meaninglessness. That discussion echoes in the First Critique's design of time. To get there, however, I first have to reconstruct Kant's proof of causality in the First Critique, and this will take a while.

In *The Critique of Pure Reason* two sets of relations—between entities or forces that are present at the same time and those that are not—with their subsets, organize the field of possible space-time configurations.[6] Some of these options are lose/lose situations, like "forks" in chess. Kant positions such a fork here: to be available to cause and effect, or else not be in the present. The fork appears in the two illustrations that Kant uses in the "Analogies of Experience" section of the First Critique to secure the two kinds of temporal relations, "coexistence" and "succession." In the "Analogies of Experience" Kant sets himself the task of grounding both successive and coexisting states not through their subjective appearance in one's sensory field but through their connections to cause and effect in the reasoning that he believes one must use to grasp them.[7] Kant starts with succession and provides two sup-

4. Social arena, I would say, but *community* is Kant's preferred term.

5. Grasping this reciprocity must depart from a reconstruction of what Kant thinks he's doing, in that its territory is much larger than Kant's own; it is not "in" his text alone.

6. Moten's discussion of Kant's emphasis on "containment" and the challenge to Kant posed by "irruptions on the surface of the event" are helpful here (Fred Moten, "Knowledge of Freedom," *CR: The New Centennial Review* 4 [2004]: 269–310, esp. 272–273).

7. Kant observes that it's noncontroversial to ascribe permanence to substance: "the permanent ... is substance in the [field of] appearance" (*Critique of Pure Reason*, trans. Norman Kemp Smith [New York: St. Martin's Press, 1965], A182/B225; henceforward CPR). This truism suggests that at one pole, wherever time exceeds the imagination of *activity*, it appears congealed as substance. Seeking a temporal analogue to the permanence of substance, Kant makes "time itself" a container for various kinds of relations (CPR, A183/B226).

Derrida notices that time can be used in this way, as an analogue to fantasmatic substance. He points out that in Husserl, *hylē*, literally "matter," means material that is

posedly contrasting prompts from the visual field. He does this while making the point that visuality is not responsible for the insight and must be abstracted.

The first image is "the apprehension of the manifold in the appearance of a house which stands before me" (CPR, A190/B236):

> I have to show what sort of connection in time belongs to the manifold in the appearances themselves. For instance, the apprehension of the manifold in the appearance of a house which stands before me is successive. The question then arises, whether the manifold of the house is also in itself successive. This, however, is what no one will grant.... That something happens, *i.e.*, that *something, or some state which did not previously exist, comes to be,* cannot be perceived unless it is preceded by an appearance which does not contain in itself this state. For an event which should follow upon an empty time, that is, a coming to be preceded by no state of things, is as little capable of being apprehended as empty time itself. (CPR, 191–192/B236–237; my italics)[8]

Kant evokes a moving image; the example is cinematic. He's striving to explain how he uses cause and effect to decide that one state of things necessarily follows another without access to an appearance "that does not in itself contain this [new] state." For Kant, what he has here is the apprehension of a successive flow of motion and time—it feels like time passes—without authority to assign cause and effect. Time is a sensation, showing nothing yet. Kant's shot of the house is brief and undeveloped, as if there were nothing to it. He implies that it doesn't lead anywhere cognitively. This implication is deliberately misleading—he'll

---

perceived but not yet conceptualized and grasped by intention: unmarked, undamaged substance. For Husserl "the sensuous hylē, as such and in its purity, that is to say, before being animated by intentionality, would *already* be a piece of lived experience" (Jacques Derrida, *The Problem of Genesis in Husserl's Philosophy*, trans. Marian Hobson [Chicago: University of Chicago Press, 2003], 86). Implicitly, *hylē* is to perception the fantasy of transparency and primacy that suspension of identification is in the realm of ethics. In his introduction to Husserl's *Origin of Geometry*, Derrida further notes that to propose spatio-perceptual hylē, Husserl needs temporal hylē.

In some unpublished material [Husserl] seems to go much further: "Urhylē," i.e., *temporal hylē* (my italics), is defined there as "the core of the other of the ego's own" ... "*alien to my Ego,*" "*the intrinsically first other,*" or of "the first 'non-ego'" in the constitution of the *alter ego* (*Edmund Husserl's "Origin of Geometry": An Introduction*, trans. John P. Leavey Jr. [Lincoln: University of Nebraska Press, 1978], 86–87n90).

8. See *Kritik der reinen Vernunft*, in *Gesammelte Schriften* [Akademie-Ausgabe], I–XXIII, Electronic Edition, vols. 3–4.

propose later that the example shows *grounded simultaneity* instead of grounded succession. In a moment, Kant will actually prefer this kind of image, like an image in a New Wave film in which "nothing happens." It will turn out to be the image of *rampant* reciprocity.[9] But it's not Kant's rhetorical tactic to begin there. At the moment, he needs a clear determination of cause in succession "to secure the fiction of being through time," as Warren phrases philosophy's connection to freedom (*Ontological Terror*, 97), and the moving image of the house doesn't provoke that.

In contrast is the kind of successive appearance that only occurrences, or "happenings" [*Geschehen*],[10] have:

> I see a ship move downstream. My perception of its lower position follows upon the perception of its position higher up in the stream, and it is impossible that in the apprehension of this appearance the ship should first be perceived lower down in the stream and afterwards higher up. The order in which the perceptions succeed one another in apprehension is in this instance determined, and to this order apprehension is bound down. In the previous example of a house my perceptions could begin with the apprehension of the roof and end with the basement, or could begin from below and end above; and I could similarly apprehend the manifold of the empirical intuition either from right to left or from left to right. In the series of these perceptions there was thus no determinate order specifying at what point I must begin in order to connect the manifold empirically. But in the perception of what is happening [was geschieht] there is always a rule that makes the order in which the perceptions ... follow upon one another a *necessary* order. (CPR, A192–193/B237–238; trans. modified)

Kant now asks the reader to work with the comparison between the examples. For him, again, the house image shows only the succession "common to all apprehensions," in which "nothing is distinguished from anything else" (CPR, A198/B243).[11] It seems to contain merely the subjective sense of time passing, whereas Kant wants a line of rea-

---

9. Reminiscent of Derrida's multiplication of distinctions that destabilize humans and animals in *The Animal That Therefore I Am* (Bronx, NY: Fordham University Press, 2008).

10. *Kritik der reinen Vernunft*, Electronic Edition, vols. 3–4.

11. Lack of distinction here recalls the "boring" or "indifferent diversity" in *The Phenomenology of Spirit* § 18 and the image of a noninvidious primitive state that recurs throughout philosophy.

soning that "necessitates some one particular mode of connection of the manifold" (CPR, A191/B236) and through that particular necessity plants itself in general necessity. Thinking about the appearance of the ship's movement does the trick when Kant locates his reasoning's law-like constraint: the fact that he cannot conceive of the locations happening in the opposite order.

If Kant were substituting perception of movements for understanding of causality, that would be the mistake he calls "subreption" *par excellence*—"tak[ing] his inferences from perceptions as experiences."[12] But Kant's move here has been easily defended from that charge, since he refers explicitly not to his visual experiences but to the reasoning around them.[13] Kant insists that the fact that the shot of the house is experienced by him as having duration—"the apprehension ... is successive"—does not mean that it could only be that way. A cinematic way of getting at the point might be to say that if some Antonioni shots ran in reverse—for example, of leaves rustling in a wind—it's possible that no causal impossibility would be implied. What is going on in this kind of apprehension that prevents Kant from penetrating to necessary cause and effect? Relations between weather conditions, changes of light, and fluttering leaves, as well as changes in the observer, for example, retinal adjustments, are part of the scene. Each of these is microcausal. Chained and meshed, however, they are potentially successive in multiple directions in a way that proliferates what it means to be successive. In fact, this kind of image contains too many reciprocal cause-and-effect relations. The proliferation of relations seems to mean to Kant that they don't necessarily have to be thought of as successive overall— that is, they don't have to be thought of as adding up to a change in which some state that "did not previously exist, comes to be."

But is that so? Kant does make a substitution here, not a substitution of perception for reason but of one idealization of succession for all succession. Kant is presupposing a standard for tense that he is supposed to be grounding. A static shot of nearly stationary objects turns up the kinds of dynamics that nonlinear partial differential equations express, and that often lead to singularities when followed out. In setting aside the static-seeming image that is too dynamic, Kant leaves the impression that nothing in the image must be thought of as having happened successively, but that is true only in a certain *already constructed*

12. Immanuel Kant, *Lectures on Metaphysics*, trans. and ed. Karl Ameriks and Steve Naragon (Cambridge, UK: Cambridge University Press, 1997), 374.

13. Kant stresses that the issue is not "making the representation of objects distinct, but in making the representation of an object possible at all" (CPR, A199/B244).

sense of "happening" located back at his definition of *Geschehen*. Henry Allison, making note of the need to be precise about a specific kind of succession that Kant is looking for, "propose[s] to translate Kant's term *Wechsel* (both 'change' and 'exchange') as '*replacement change*.'"[14] But it is what counts as "happening" that Kant is supposed to be constructing now, and not already using. Instead, the house image's kind of spatiotemporality appears as different in kind from succession because *succession is already "replacement change."* That it has to be, reflects Kant's exclusion of a middle between past and present in the first place. This, finally, allows us to consider the conditions and effects of Kant's argument for past-present political relations.

When at the beginning of the section, he writes that he needs a way to tell at any juncture "whether this manifold, as object of experience, is coexistent or in sequence" (CPR, A182/B226), the elision of a possible "and," "coexistent *and* in sequence," divides *coexistence—which is now confined to relations in the present*—from sequence. The exclusion of coexistence with the past is a particular figuration of the past that expresses the supersession of the past by the present. In the context of life and death, "replacement change" conflates the difference between the living and the dead with the difference between existence and non-existence in any form whatsoever; it apprehends the dead only as the formerly alive, and the past as a former and no longer present. This is a view of the world that precedes Kant's analysis and dodges his critique. Conversations about tensed and "detensed" time in analytic philosophy confess as much. They freely opine that "human freedom" is the stake of understanding time in this way or that. Time's organization must be settled in order to secure the possibility of the human being's "autonomous control over what does or does not exist."[15]

The Critique of Pure Reason maintains an idealized difference in kind between (1) consecutive ("replacement") states that are not reciprocal, their replacement indicating the difference between the past and other tenses and (2) the reciprocity of objects in the world that is and any community that ought to be. Unlike the latter, "an object A that belongs to past time ... can no longer be an object of apprehension at all" (CPR, B258).[16] Coexistence is coexistence only against the backdrop of this

14. Henry Allison, *Kant's Transcendental Idealism: An Interpretation and Defense*, 2nd ed. (New Haven, CT: Yale University Press, 1983), 204.

15. L. Nathan Oaklander, *The Ontology of Time* (New York: Prometheus Books, 2004), 347, 336.

16. Michelle Wright discusses time schemes' relevance to community boundaries yet identifies "Middle Passage Epistemology" as a "linear spacetime that dominates the academic canon on Black diasporic identities" (*Physics of Blackness*, 14). The phenomenon

nothingness. Similar effects of positioning a past on the other side of a threshold influence debates about historical "transition"; the afterlives of slavery; subaltern studies critiques of anthropology and history; environmental policy; psychoanalytic theory; and transitional justice and reparations. Meister, whose book *After Evil* analyzes the many eschatological and psychoanalytic mechanisms of transitional justice, goes beyond the point that it's convenient to decide that the time of atrocity has passed and proposes that "justice itself is an intertemporal problem (the supersession of one time by another)."[17] These assumptions of the past's lesser relevance recall a joke of Meister's about the limits of historical justice—that no one wants to calculate "the present value of the damages to the Carthaginians or the Albigensians" (247).[18] But if Meister is right that justice per se is an intertemporal problem, and if the Carthaginians can be excluded from relevance because they are too far in the past, all determinations of position in time will appear as assertions of relevance or irrelevance. In discussions of slavery, "freedom becomes a mode of temporalizing, and the human being must activate existence in the present to have any intelligibility in a metaphysical world" (Warren, *Ontological Terror*, 97).

Because critical philosophy is formal rather than essential, at first it seems antithetical to the racial science of the period as it "shifts in the late eighteenth century from being a system of arbitrary marks that distinguish between humanity to being 'an ascription of natural signs' written on the body."[19] Determined to prevent sensation from recommending itself as knowledge, Kant insists that he cannot see or experience laws of cause and effect as though they were exposed to him directly

---

of trauma in itself renders this judgment reductive. Wright does not take up the substantial thread of scholarship that studies the Middle Passage otherwise, for example as "always an event too soon and too late.... The existence and recognition of the historical void is the second or retrospective blow that makes the time of trauma continuous and discontinuous" (Rinaldo Walcott, "Middle Passage: In the Absence of Detail, Presenting and Representing a Historical Void," *Kronos* 44 [2018]: 59–68, 44–45). See also Stephanie E. Smallwood, *Saltwater Slavery* (Cambridge, MA: Harvard University Press, 2008), and Sean Capener, "Time in the Middle Passage: Race, Religion, and the Making of Modernity's 'Second Moment' in Kant and Hegel" (University of Toronto, Feb. 10, 2022).

17. *After Evil: A Politics of Human Rights* (New York: Columbia University Press, 2011), 19.

18. The Albigensians, called after the city of Albi, were eleventh- and twelfth-century heretics who were systematically massacred in the tens of thousands. Historians debate whether their persecution can be called a genocide.

19. Peter Kitson, "'Bales of Living Anguish': Representations of Race and the Slave in Romantic Writing," *ELH* 2 (2000): 515–537, 518. Kitson is citing David C. Lloyd, "Race under Representation," *Oxford Literary Review* 13 (1991): 62–94, 69.

by objects. But if the Kantian system rejects any authority of traits, its potential antiracism is confined to rejecting a rac(ial)ism of traits that was never comprehensive as an account of racism, nor probed the limits of racism as a paradigm.[20] Further, the "shift" from unsystematic marks to systematic and internalized marks that recurs in historical accounts of race brings effects of limitation and gratification, implying an undamaged difference ruined by racial science and regressive politics. The emphasis on racial science and naive naturalization suggests that de-essentialization and political organization vanquish race. My point is that versions of this suggestion can be found preceding contemporary antiracist work on its behalf, in enlightenment styles of antiracism that are consistent with antiblackness. Kant's refusal of inherence in "Analogies" is such an instance of anti-essentialism.

Up till now, it seems as though Kant wants the reader to see simultaneous relations as less useful philosophically than successive relations. The latter seem clearer and more criterial. As I mentioned earlier, though, Kant has set this impression up only so that he can turn it around. Out of the failure to determine succession in the house image as opposed to that of the ship, "a difficulty arises with which we must at once deal" (CPR, A202/B247), that of *necessary simultaneity* [Zugleichseins], which must also be known through cause and effect. For Kant, if indetermination is subordinate philosophically to necessary succession, only in necessary simultaneity do "states" perform the interlocking, interdependent relations that Kant favors ethically (for instance in *Perpetual Peace*, his theory of international relations). "Zugleichseins"—"coexistence" in the interesting translation of Norman Kemp Smith—relies on *reciprocal* cause and effect. On one hand, as Kant points out, even "when cause and effect are simultaneous" in experience, as when "the stove, as cause, is simultaneous with its effect, the heat of the room" (CPR, A202/B248), their necessity remains successive—since, he goes on, their relation too can only be grasped in one causal order. On the other, it's peculiar to simultaneous relations that they coexist causally, and therefore necessarily, only when they follow the "law of reciprocity [Wechselwirkung]" (CPR, B257; my italics) "immediately or mediately" ["oder mittelbar," CPR, A213/B259], which, as above, proliferates cause and effect toward maximum complexity.

By the time that necessary reciprocity introduces the kind of realm

---

20. On Kantian formalism and teleology, see R. A. Judy, *(Dis)forming the American Canon: African Arabic Slave Narrative and the Vernacular* (Minneapolis: University of Minnesota Press, 1993); and Lloyd, *Under Representation*, 128–30.

that Kant prefers ethically, the social implications of the whole discussion lie on the surface. These have been developed in recent romanticist work by Kevin McLaughlin, as I'll address in a moment. First, though, as is clear from the functions assigned to Kant's object, the following conclusions have emerged so far:

1. Time of any kind, successive or simultaneous, *reflects forces and states that are in the grammatical position of subjects* (CPR, A204–205/B249–250). To condense: time takes its character from causal subjects. Succession can be established as necessarily happening only when a force acts transitively to produce an effect; and *coexistence, therefore and complementarily, can only occur between two causal subjects*. That's the remarkable punchline of the "Analogies of Experience." Relevant to the relationship to Kant's view of justice, in Kant's world, temporal coexistence *does not exist without reciprocity* and implies ("arcs toward," so to speak) equality, these demands being characteristics of the only necessary apprehensions of perceptions of coexistence that can be known. This is a recognizably liberal humanist view, with the disadvantages thereof; it is the transcendentalized version of liberal humanist coexistence. Kant's assertion of what is here follows his preference regarding what should be.
2. The negative corollary of this conclusion, taken back to the social realm, is that any relation *lacking* in causal reciprocity can only be critically verified as to its temporal orientation if it is successive.
3. Moreover, states in subject/object cause and effect do not coexist in time.

Why Coexistence in Space and Time Is Not "Ethical"

Making the social stakes still more explicit, Kant goes on to specify weaker and stronger versions of reciprocity, the stronger only achieving commutation, or community. When and only when forces not only can be reciprocal but also each grounds the determination of the other, the relation is "of community [Gemeinschaft]," to which the Third Analogy of Experience is devoted. But Kant has been reverse-engineering community into the structure of time all along.

Kant knows that a causal standard for reciprocity is infra-thin to the point of triviality. Bullet against flesh, flesh against bullet can only be "reciprocal" in an academic sense. Therefore, there's one more twist that McLaughlin emphasizes. In the Third Analogy commutation splits once again into "*communio* or *commercium*."[21] The dynamic coexistence

---

21. Kevin McLaughlin, *Poetic Force: Poetry after Kant* (Stanford, CA: Stanford University Press, 2014), 5.

of commutation above is bare *commercium*—and *communio* fascinatingly goes missing, never ruled out logically and never to be referred to again. *Commercium*, translatable as "trade," names the chains of causal reciprocity that "lead our senses from one object to another" (CPR, A213/B260). Kant portrays this space as the infrastructure of positions: "the light, which plays between our eye and the celestial bodies, produces a mediate community between us and them, and thereby shows us that they coexist" (CPR, A213/B260).[22] But *communio*, community, would be something other than this "mediate community" of mere copresence. McLaughlin goes through the implications of this last distinction between commerce and community, and writes, "On this point Kant is unambiguous: when it comes to the cognition of community, what we perceive is a *commercium*. Temporal simultaneity is a matter of a community of entities interacting on one another at the same time. Empirical community, in other words, is commercial interaction. Kant does not speculate about nonempirical simultaneity in this section of the *Critique of Pure Reason*. However, he is explicit about not refuting its existence" (5). Actually existing coexistence is a realm of economy whose brutality Kant acknowledges (it needs supplementation by the utopian *communio*). *Commercium* is not much—which is to say that for Kant, it's everything knowable. Its space is necessary for Kant not for the historical characteristics and uses it enables, but in its *boundedness*, separating the knowable from matters of faith. Again, it looks at first as though the universality of this space might be supposed to distinguish it from the spaces of racial science. Standing beyond characteristics in its formalism, it can be used only as a grammar. But it is not less powerful than racial science. No other grammars can be used now to produce reciprocity.

Although the discontenting thinness of the sociality that spatiotemporal laws can authorize is evident, establishing the transcendental security of a single system for "exchange" is no small move. On either side of Kant's invocation of the mediating light are these passages:

> It is therefore necessary that all substances in the [field of] appearance, *so far as they coexist*, should stand in *thoroughgoing community [Gemeinschaft] of mutual interaction*.
>
> We cannot empirically change our position, and perceive the

22. "Mediate community" grounded by the infrastructure of transcendental laws will be remodeled by Hegel into "mediation"—that is, in another anti-essentialism, the social relation from which alone all qualities come. Social relation from this perspective is infrastructure generated by global historical drive. Kant, in contrast, treats the economic mobilization of mediate community as though it were still *latent*.

change, unless matter in *all parts of space* makes perception of our
position possible to us. For only thus by means of their reciprocal
influence can the parts of matter establish their simultaneous existence, and thereby, though only mediately, their coexistence, *even to
the most remote objects* ... I do not by this argument at all profess
to disprove void space, for it may exist where perceptions cannot
reach, and where there is, therefore, no empirical knowledge of coexistence. But such a space is not for us an object of any possible experience ...

    This is a reciprocal influence, a *real community* [commercium] *of
substances*; without it the empirical relation of coexistence could not
be met with in experience. (CPR, A214–215/B261; my italics)

Like Levinas's desiring subject, Kant's argument starts with a condition
that has already been "met with." The "thoroughgoing community of
mutual interaction" that connects Kant's body, quite frighteningly, to
"matter in all parts of space" (CPR, A213/B260) lives on in theses of in-
escapable relation. In social relation construed as thin but omnipresent,
all bodies take part in a lawfully inevitable mesh in which each in principle can reach any other, "insofar as they coexist." Hegel redescribes this
result as the historical unfolding of the "world [a]s a *cosmos*" in "essential and reciprocal relation" (LPR, 177).

    Relation that is real and philosophically secure in this way is often
celebrated in liberal discourse, as if connection in principle to all things
were necessarily good, and even inherently ethical—keeping "everyone" in check, or constituting the very possibility of communication.[23]
But it doesn't keep everyone in check. The "thoroughgoing community of mutual interaction" that connects Kant's body to "matter in all
parts of space" makes connection merely a logistical challenge, and this
suggests that what's at stake in "coexistence" and "relation" is as much
access as communicability and reciprocity: Why has finding their principle become urgent at Kant's time of writing? To his credit Kant registers an *ethical* problem of his epistemological arguments: if there is
"thoroughgoing community," it must be curbed by the complete exemption of the "human" from the instrumental. But that Kant adds the

---

23. Axelle Karera shows that "social antagonisms, and more specifically those enacted
along racial lines ... are smoothed over and displaced in the name of an ethics of futu-
rity grounded on a deeply naturalized variation of relationality—namely that all beings,
insofar as they are earthly at least, are fundamentally interconnected and can (or must)
only be perceived as such" ("Blackness and the Pitfalls of Anthropocene Ethics," *Critical
Philosophy of Race* 7 [2019]: 32–56, 43). See also Palmer, "Otherwise Than Blackness."

qualification shows that he knows what's already been done: it's access to persons and regions, already occurring, that the lawfulness of causality describes. Kant does not give the instrumentalization of the human the status of an impossibility. He cannot, because he knows it has already happened.

Thus Kant's Doctrine of Right attempts to articulate the business opportunity of "thoroughgoing community" by maximizing its mutuality. It is filled with containment gestures, like the quick braking above. Hegel unbinds each one, pointing out that they try to prevent what has already happened anyway. Peter Fenves notes Walter Benjamin's objection to Kant's effort, in the Doctrine of Right,

> to expand the concept of right ... on the basis of the postulate that every nonpossessed thing must be available for my use under the condition that I be able to bring it "under my control" ... [A]t the outset of the Doctrine of Right, then, is the following thesis: Gewalt [power] in all its troubling ambiguity prepares the ground for right, *which should eventually extend to every part of the globe* under the sign of "eternal peace."[24]

As Fenves describes, Kant's "dozens and dozens of drafts of a solution" (192) show his lengthy struggle to integrate *Critique of Pure Reason*'s conclusion that causality undergirds globality with any argument that existing globality ought to exist. Kant hunts for a rightness that he can accord global commerce "by analogy with presenting the possibility of bodies moving freely under the law of the equality of action and reaction."[25] But as Fenves notes, the gap between *is* and *ought* will not close. Barely avoiding the conclusion that causal law has *no* connection to right, Kant effectively throws in his lot with the legal system—as though sending the police and lawyers after in hopes of enforcing the already transgressed ethical limit.

Finally, then, what does it mean that, in the context of global violence above, Kant reserves the possibility of a nonempirical community that would be neither succession nor "commerce"—the absent possibility? To the a, b, and c ending the section above I need to add: (d) there are states of coexistence without relation and nonrelation, but not in time.

24. Peter Fenves, *The Messianic Reduction: Walter Benjamin and the Shape of Time* (Stanford, CA: Stanford University Press, 2011), 13–14.

25. *The Metaphysics of Morals* [1785], ed. Lara Denis, trans. Mary Gregor (Cambridge, UK: Cambridge University Press, 2017), Part I, § E, 233. This hope does not end with Kant.

This coexistence is *no longer spatiotemporal*. But it's still coexistence. For Kant, space (d) *still can only be reciprocal*, since it's a subset of community. The symmetry to which Kant always returns is, and is meant to be, a guardrail for what interaction can be—in contrast, for example, to revolutionary violence. McLaughlin argues that Kant's utopian preservation of community partakes of his presentation of "a shared and sharing ability" (5): "Reason after Kant, in this sense, dictates a vision of community as a matter, not of a common possession of a thing like a parcel of land or sea, but of a communicability shared by all rational beings" who share reason's limits and inabilities (6). Kant's movement away from the substantive is antipossessive and antinationalist. But it is antiracist only in a mode that supports a protagonist of reciprocity. Its communicability for "all" comes at the expense of anyone else.

Over the course of this passage a categorical ability that is also an inability—an "a priori principle of community," a "communability"—becomes more important than "common experience," which is reductively exemplified by "a parcel of land or sea." McLaughlin continues, "the commonness of this community derives from an a priori sense of the common—a commonality that is independent of common experience" (113). But an *a priori* sense of the common justifies seizure of land and sea in the first place. These statements extend a Kantian ethical tradition in which unknowable commonality and areas that no one can possess or represent are seen as void of both dangerous specificity and coercive unity. This "void space," as Kant calls it, passes from Kant to Laclau, to nonsubstantive sovereignty and open dialectics, and perhaps to the Real. Yet upgrading to mediation and abstraction leverages common void space into the colonial "parcel of land and sea."[26] We might suppose instead that the basis and terms of exchange make land and sea seem, to a colonial perspective, to have been merely literal and experiential to their residents.

After Kant, relation is called on to erect a political threshold and to render the racial(ist) primitivist "resistant" to movement-affirming open relation. When, beyond liberalism, political institutions are no longer imagined to be emancipatory, the pattern continues into the radical beyond of formal politics, still using the radical enlightenment's avowal of undetermined openness, negativity, and emptiness. A reality of these features is thought to ground antiracism. Where exemplary radical identity must be able to free itself from racism, entities and activities will appear irreal, unmodern, and racial(ist) wherever the be-

26. For a nonidentitarian vision of indigenous settlement, see Victor Masayesva Jr.'s brilliant film *Itam Hakim, Hopiit* (1984).

ginning and ending of racism cannot be found in an originary "truth of race."[27] Racial blackness, Parisa Vaziri argues, is that crisis, failing "to release slavery to a transparent and objective historiographical account of itself" ("No One's Memory," 17).

Kant's causal temporality forms the minimal spine of historical accounting. Kant's infrastructural claims for causal time, and therefore kinds and bounds of community, relieve society of the burden of inventing the *means* for relation. Kant's architectonic offering is to create spatiotemporal conditions that hierarchize positions by their causal standing. This opens a path to colonial resources—a situation that, in Kant, needs to be politically and ethically managed; shows no signs of being actually managed; and can never be entirely illegitimate.[28] Kant's arrangements negotiate a world where epistemology and metaphysics work overtime to explain destruction that has already happened.

27. Parisa Vaziri, "No One's Memory: Blackness at the Limits of Comparative Slavery," *Racial Formations in Africa and the Middle East: A Transregional Approach* 44 (2021): 14.

28. In an interview, Timothy Morton rehearses from the diametrically opposite position what I've been trying to show—Kant's apprehensive and yet compelled architectonic of thresholds between succession and coexistence, commerce and community. Only, Morton urges Kant to completely enjoy the "access": "if you ... take the anthropocentric block, inhibition, away, what you get is that everything in the universe gets to access everything else, and the way that everything accesses everything is such that nothing is ever exhausted ... actually at bottom everything is playful, like everything is a toy, including political systems" (Timothy Morton and Hans Ulrich Olbrist, "[C]onversation held on the occasion of the Serpentine Galleries' Extinction Marathon: Visions of the Future," *Dis Magazine* [October 2014]: unpaginated, http://dismagazine.com /disillusioned/discussion-disillusioned/68280/hans-ulrich-obrist-timothy-morton/).

Kant's "nervous restriction on what access means" lies in his acknowledgment that "coexistence" is an ethical and economic problem. Kantian limits already grant the infrastructure that universal exchange uses, while failing to paint them in bright colors. Because he can't think of anything to be afraid of in the "access" of everything to everything else, Morton removes even Kantian limits and winds up with an epistemology of "playful" unlimited colonialism.

§ 6

Frankenstein and the "Free Black"

> In a very real sense, a full century and a half after "the fact," "slavery"
> is primarily discursive, as we search vainly for a point of absolute and
> indisputable origin, for a moment of plenitude that would restore us
> to the real, rich "thing" itself before discourse touched it.
>
> HORTENSE SPILLERS, *Black, White, and in Color:*
> *Essays on American Literature and Culture*

Coming Up Empty

While Rousseau renders slavery impossible given human resources of
possibility, Mary Shelley's *Frankenstein* (1818) has been understood in
its own generation and ever after as the imagination of an existing impossibility. *Frankenstein* was immediately taken up in abolitionist and
proslavery circles that read the "Creature"[1] as a maroon slave or enraged
free Black. Since her white supremacist readers have acted as though the
Creature were Black, openly reading through antiblack tropes to do so,
literary critics exploring what Shelley might be saying about Atlantic
slavery tend to leave the problem of blackness to these previous readers.
Uneasy about working with previous antiblack associations, responses
to the novel haven't quite let go of the earlier assumption that leads

---

1. It's a question what to call him: "the monster," "the Creature," and "Frankenstein"
have so far been the options. He could be called "the Being" or "the nameless character."
I'm going along with the currently popular choice "the Creature," not because I think it's
best but because all are problematic: Shelley is right not to name him at all (What does
it mean that she gives him a gendered pronoun and not a name?). On the whole, most
Shelley criticism refers to other characters by first or last names that echo the reader's
assigned proximity to the characters: "Victor" and "Elizabeth," "Walton" and "Clerval."
I call Victor by his first name to condescend to him, as I think Shelley constructs this
character throughout as a parody of masculinist oblivion, and the rest by their surnames.

there, that the Creature's blackness is ultimately a problem of attribution, an instance that must be verified (but how?) and properly labeled before it's explored.[2] Reflecting on the periodized containment of the antebellum free Black, Warren observes that "historiography proceeds as if the problem of existence has been resolved. It has not" (Warren, *Ontological Terror*, 19).

The power of *Frankenstein* is that no one can treat the Creature's problem of existence as "resolved," and yet even that has not lead critics to explore further. In 1993, H. R. Malchow began the scholarly discussion of blackness in *Frankenstein* by interweaving Shelley's portrayals of the Creature and stereotypical images of Black men in nineteenth-century British culture, images "that drew on fears and hopes of the abolition of slavery in the West Indies."[3] These antiblack stereotypes are seen to be energized when white British liberals' progressivism came under pressure from the prospect of Black political agency, as in news of slave rebellions. Stereotypes, in turn, help to generate material conditions, actions, and words. Much of Malchow's article carefully presents the texture of "'Race' in the Napoleonic Era" on the assumptions that racism is grounded in ideology (thus the quotation marks around "race") and organized through racial stereotypes (92). So consistency in stereotyping can be read in reverse as evidence that *Frankenstein* engages the Black Atlantic slave.

Malchow therefore comments that "a reading of this text which attempts to draw out an embedded racial message must begin where racism itself begins, with physiognomy" (102). A review of the Creature's physical descriptions follows, correlated to "the standard description of the Black man in both the literature of the West Indies and that of African exploration" (102). Malchow reflects that "on the level of physiognomy at least, a racial reading seems ... nearer the mark than a Marxist [reading]" that would locate the novel's horror in class unrest (139). I've found no essay on race, slavery, or blackness in *Frankenstein* that does not include Shelley's physical descriptions of the Creature, and every

2. It isn't that most criticism believes blackness to be merely a matter of bearing a label but that even though it does not hold such a belief, critics still express the desire to connect blackness in literature to a literal statement or a prior referent. Shelley Fisher Fishkin's *Was Huck Black? Mark Twain and African-American Voices* (Oxford: Oxford University Press, 1994), which located, or perhaps playfully pretended to locate, a single actual African American boy who lent Twain Huck's voice, was discussed in these terms at the time.

3. H. L. Malchow, "*Frankenstein*'s Monster and Images of 'Race' in Nineteenth-Century Britain," *Past and Present* 139 (1993): 90–130, esp. 90.

essay on race, slavery, or blackness in *Frankenstein* mentions that Shelley's symbolization is not stable. Her narrative evocations of certain circumstances of slavery are taken to be more definitive. All in all, the correlation is thought not perfect but a "near" preponderance, "parallels" (92) that also entail gaps. A contextual-ideological argument such as his, Malchow observes, "necessarily rests on 'evidence' that is indirect, circumstantial, and speculative. There is no clear proof that Mary Shelley consciously set out to create a monster which suggested, explicitly, the Jamaican escaped slave or maroon" (92).

Not only is Shelley's symbolization unstable, but critics who deal with it don't want it to be stable, nor should they. Conditions of slavery can be described, but what would correlation with the "escaped slave" look like?[4] A novel that was completely stereotypical? Completely historical? The problem is the worry, not invested in other abstractions in the same way, that there is no way to talk about blackness unless it is something or nothing, in a specific location or nonexistent.[5] Taking a cue from Shelley's preoccupation with the "human frame,"[6] the Creature's blackness can instead be posited speculatively to frame the novel in these excluded middles. *Frankenstein* is absorbed by the question that, as Chandler writes, had arisen with regard to "the discourse concerning the humanity of the Negro slaves": "on what basis and in what manner can one decide a being, and its character of existence, as one kind or another?" (Chandler, *X*, 21–22). So why is it that *Frankenstein*

---

4. Malchow is already using a hegemonic account to produce what counts and doesn't count as Black when he selects and deselects categories of relevance. For example, he notes that Shelley did not "[intend] to create a specifically Negro monster" because "she writes of the monster's yellow skin" (103), and then overrides Shelley's intention: although she gave him yellow skin, he is still Black. That is possible, not, apparently, because one can be "yellow" and Black at the same time, but because epidermal criteria are not conclusive in academic practice in 1993.

5. Christian dualisms echo in constructions of race as biological or otherwise material, as Biddick, Carter, and Wynter variously explain. See Kathleen Biddick, *Make and Let Die: Untimely Sovereignties* (New York: Punctum Books, 2016); J. Kameron Carter, *Race: A Theological Account* (Oxford: Oxford University Press, 2008); Sylvia Wynter, "Unsettling," 257–337. On Wynter's counterhistory, and so her own reworked humanism, see David S. Marriott, *Whither Fanon? Studies in the Blackness of Being* (Stanford, CA: Stanford University Press, 2018).

6. Victor repeats his concern with the notion of "human frame": "One of the phenomena which had peculiarly attracted my attention was the structure of the human frame... Although I possessed the capacity of bestowing animation, yet to prepare a frame for the reception of it ... still remained a work of inconceivable difficulty and labor" (Mary Shelley, *Frankenstein; or, The Modern Prometheus* [1818], ed. Marilyn Butler [Oxford: Oxford University Press, 1993], 33, 35).

has been studied for its interest in human constitution and its interest in racial slavery, but not for its interest in what happens between them?[7]

If social death charges the bounds of any political identity with life and death implications, then blackness here seems to take on the tension that can be neither managed nor entirely repressed in the absent origins and ends of slavery.[8] Thus the free Black appears as though they presented an ontometaphysical question, presented civil society's interposition of the Black "as a metaphysical form for thinking formlessness" and nothing (Warren, *Ontological Terror*, 119). Manumission clarifies that the end of slavery is unclear—and so, in the same realization, is its origin. If blackness is, with Warren and Edelman,[9] a catachresis

7. Elizabeth Young's *Black Frankenstein: The Making of an American Metaphor* (New York: NYU Press, 2008) transfers the entire investigation to the "tradition" and citation of a Black *Frankenstein*, while asserting that the novel itself is "manifestly unfocused on either blackness or whiteness" (8). Although the references run to sixty pages, almost no Black Studies appears, if that means research that includes blackness as a framing question.

8. Distinguishing indetermination from overdetermination, Zakiyyah Iman Jackson remarks that conflicting oppositions that can't be simultaneously embodied "are in fact varying dimensions of a racializing demand that the slave be all dimensions at once," "coerced formlessness" as "a mode of domination" ("Losing Manhood: Animality and Plasticity in the (Neo)Slave Narrative," *Qui Parle* 25 [2016]: 95–136, 117–118). Jackson refers to proliferating demands that push to eliminate indetermination.

Margo Crawford argues that "when the BAM [Black Arts Movement] mobilized the word 'black' in the most radical manner, it was a way of naming the unknown dimensions of freedom and self-determination... 'Black' signaled excess, the power of the *unthought*" (*Black Post-Blackness: The Black Arts Movement and the Twenty-First Century* [Champaign: University of Illinois Press, 2017]). The different emphases of Jackson and Crawford inquire whether "blackness can be claimed outside of racial slavery"—that is, the relationship of indetermination to antiblack political ontology. See Sorentino, "Natural Slavery," 655; and the questions at the end of David C. Lloyd, "The Social Life of Black Things: Fred Moten's *Consent Not to Be a Single Being*," *Radical Philosophy* 2 (Spring 2020): unpaginated, https://www.radicalphilosophy.com/article /the-social-life-of-black-things.

9. In an outstanding exchange with Warren, Lee Edelman suggests that ontological and historical approaches to blackness are at odds, yet currently combined in discourses of Atlantic slavery. Wilderson's remark, "Africans went into the ships and came out as Blacks" comes to mind (Wilderson, *Red, White & Black*, 38). If these approaches are embedded in relationships between history and ontology, which, Warren replies, "can't be held apart," then neither history nor ontology will be able to be the origin of the other (Lee Edelman and Calvin Warren, "Conversation," Department of Women's, Gender, and Sexuality Studies, Emory University, October 30, 2020). It may be helpful to emphasize culture's substitution of blackness for the origin of racial slavery. Further, since slavery is the limit of the political, the indistinction of slavery will be seen to threaten the integrity of the political by throwing its own bounds into question.

for this necessary unclarity, this allows us to understand that *Franken-stein* criticism's inability to crystallize the Creature's blackness with a direct reference couldn't have been averted: What could a direct refer-ence to blackness be? How could it avoid being one more moment in which blackness is made concrete or abstract, only to fall apart again? The nineteen-year-old Shelley draws acidic vignettes of these struggles, which nevertheless constitute her own and perhaps any literary prac-tice. I think this tension explains why her novel comes across as myth and satire simultaneously. Reading *Frankenstein* through this tension suggests that blackness in the novel might be analyzed, not only by at-tempted correlation to the historical archive of slavery, which winds up stereotypical or allegorical, but also through the interplay between the Creature's ironic prompting of limit questions and the social frames that maintain his impossible actuality.

Romanticism reflects on these questions as long as they are not explicitly connected to Black people, so that the essays that are most helpful on *Frankenstein*'s implications for blackness do not thematize what they are doing as related to blackness. Denise Gigante's approach through aesthesis, beauty, and ugliness, notably, points out without apology that "aesthetic theory comes up empty" when addressing its limit, which in connection to the Creature, is phrased here as "ugliness." She presses home that in aesthetics, the supposed ugliness, or ugliness (since the question whether there is anything that ugliness could be that is not suppositional is part of the topic) of the Creature would be "treated as a negative form," one that "simply lacks," that cannot appear at the table setting across from Beauty, that "emerges as a mere tautol-ogy"[10] or, as in Kant, does not exist at all (Gigante, "Facing the Ugly," 576)—and yet also, as she emphasizes, "functions more positively than lack," is "too real," "exceeding representation" (566). Real fantasy is Gi-gante's psychoanalytic frame, and she pushes it to the existential con-clusion, "not sufficiently accounted for in aesthetic discourse," that the Creature's "radically uninscribed existence" (567)—"existence" makes it more than a question of his appearance, and "uninscribed" pushes it beyond a set of norms—makes encounter in *Frankenstein* "less of an aesthetic experience than a question of survival" (566). Now, if this ar-ticle were talking about blackness in *Frankenstein*, there would be a lot to debate: But is there a way to be sure it's not? Whether Gigante's prov-

10. Denise Gigante, "Facing the Ugly: The Case of *Frankenstein*," *ELH* 67 (2000): 565. Kant "swerves from Burke's empiricist aesthetics by dismissing the 'real existence' of the object: 'All one wants to know is whether the mere representation of the object is to my liking, no matter how indifferent I may be to the real existence of the object of this representation'" (Gigante, 576).

ocations transpose to blackness or have already been transposed, not by Gigante but by the larger system of cultural reference, does not have to be the question. Questions are already possible, as long as blackness isn't expected in the form of an empirical encounter, to be located before it can be discussed.

Geneva Defends Itself

The Creature's question, "What was I?" (97), inquires into "the repertoire of exceeded boundaries—human/social, geopolitical/historical, literary/discursive" (Spillers, *Black, White, and in Color*, 44)—to which the novel belongs, as various phrasings describe Black Studies' recurrent questions: "the position of the unthought" (Hartman and Wilderson); a "critique of Western Civilization" (Moten, citing Robinson); a disassembly and reassembly of the "human project" (Wynter); "a self-critical questioning of the method involved in not only seeing human being, but also making human being" (Gordon).[11] The atopicality of the Creature's "dimension" is striking not as argumentative flaw but as the transindividual pattern of "the relation between transcendental frame and the body, or nobody, that occupies, or is banished from, its confines and powers of orientation."[12]

Staging constitutive questions in the era of their renewal by Atlantic slavery, Shelley summons the Creature to embody a space—neither merely negative nor self-subsisting, as the secondary literature finds— that progressive Geneva maintains, as the novel reflects on the habits of its republican citizenry.[13] Spivak concludes that "Shelley's text is in an aporetic relationship with the narrative support of philosophical resources it must use."[14] Despite its "incidental imperialist sentiment," Spivak finds that "it does not deploy the axiomatics of imperialism" as though they were unproblematic (133). Rather, Shelley "*cannot make the monster identical with the proper recipient of these les-*

11. Barrett, *Racial Blackness*, 2; Hartman and Wilderson, "Position of the Unthought," 183–201; Dylan Rodriguez, "Black Studies in Impasse," *Black Scholar* 44 (2014): 37–40, 40; Fred Moten, *Stolen Life* (Durham, NC: Duke University Press, 2018); Sylvia Wynter, "On How We Mistook the Map"; Lewis R. Gordon, *Fanon and the Crisis of European Man: An Essay on Philosophy and the Human Sciences* (New York and London: Routledge, 1995).

12. Moten, "Blackness and Nothingness," 739.

13. I use *Geneva* as a metonym for the novel's portrait of progressive western Europe: the characters foray into Scotland and France, but the narrative remains "based," as artists say today, in its Genevan family circle, as Shelley was during its composition.

14. Gayatri Chakravorty Spivak, *A Critique of Postcolonial Reason: Toward a History of the Vanishing Present* (New York: Columbia University Press, 1999), 135.

sons" (138).[15] Spivak's observation that parts of the novel pull away
from an axiomatics that it is not capable of dissolving appears in Shelley's mockery of Victor's "philosophical resources" (135). As I'll explore
later, building on Spivak's point about the persistence of the philosophy
under strain, these same passages are also a miniature eschatology that
clings to Shelley (and to me) despite Shelley's mockery.

One way of exploring Spivak's emphatic limit—Shelley "*cannot* make
the monster identical" with a reader—has always been to track it narratively. The novel's structure as a series of frame tales in which the
Creature's own voice is enclosed at length exposes the "impossibility"
of the narrative. Various critics have thought about its similarity to a
slave narrative edited by a white editor. It does read as a parody of ed-
itorship and of the genre's investment in collaborative authorial presence, itself a fantasy investment in the merger of positions into one
political act. Ambiguously, the novel baits the reader into thinking
thoughts parallel to the antiblack thoughts that readers of slave narratives uttered when the Creature appears unaccountably educated and
possessed of good taste in art. Clark meditates on the logical violations
within the narrative structure: we have the Creature's narrative in English without mention of a translator, when we are told that he is mono-
lingual in French; although he only speaks French, toward the end of
the novel he has a very hostile exchange with a narrator (a character
who is by then the narrator) who only speaks English, and yet they understand each other transparently—and so on. Clark concludes of this
narrator, Walton, "the voice that he claims and needs to claim is the
spectral double of a human voice, when his own voice is itself its own
other."[16] When *Frankenstein* is taken as Shelley's meditation on this kind
of anxiety, these effects simulate the moments in slave narratives that
remind the reader of all that remains withheld from the reader's and the
narrator's grasp.

If these contradictions compose society's texture, Geneva defends
itself in *Frankenstein*: What kind of positive substance does this society
have? Shelley depicts civic rituals in which people are often mistaken
for the sake of civility, especially men who are intuitively sure they are
right. They also easily set aside knowledge that they themselves claim is

15. On cognitive limits of the ability to recognize a human figure, see Patrice D. Douglass, "On (Being) Fear: Utah v. Strieff and the Ontology of Affect," *Journal of Visual
Culture* (December 17, 2018).

16. David L. Clark, "Last Words: Voice, Gesture, and the Remains of *Frankenstein*,"
in *Frankenstein in Theory: A Critical Anatomy*, ed. Orrin Wang (New York: Bloomsbury,
2020), 13–32, 19.

correct. Victor Frankenstein's certainties and eternal passions are especially poorly observed and ephemeral, but across the board, conviction is ungrounded. In the throes of his crush on Victor, for example, Robert Walton knows that "no one can feel more deeply" than Victor "the beauties of nature" (17), just as Victor is positive that "none ever conceived of the misery" that he has endured (68) and is sure that Justine, "the poor victim" about to be executed, "felt not as I did, such deep and bitter agony" (67). Walton finds his affection for Victor, intense when he is a total stranger, "excite[d] ... to an astonishing degree" (15), yet never wonders what his attraction is based on.[17] Everyone persists in forming and expressing wildly intuitive convictions and attachments.

At the same time, the characters constantly observe themselves and others abandoning what they know to act on what they "hear ... continually spoken of" (162). Disavowal gets them to the next day. Not only Victor Frankenstein but also Walton and Elizabeth Lavenza confess with abandon that they are aware of what they don't have the wherewithal to think about ("I was unable to pursue the train of thought" [Victor, 155 and elsewhere]; "I cannot bear to look at the reverse side of the picture" [Walton, 11]; "I cannot bear to think of the other side of the question" [Elizabeth, 48]). Some of these intuitions and collapses of conviction turn up in contexts of legal judgment, as when authorities begin to presume guilt (147) or when a magistrate listens with some interest to Victor's story, "but when he was called upon to act officially in consequence, the whole tide of his incredulity returned" (169). On such occasions, the characters can neither defend their intuitions nor mobilize them against petty interests.

Thinking with Gigante, this too is a matter of "survival"—at least of the survival of the self "as is." Among the many occasions when Victor explains why he does not tell his friends that they are in mortal danger, only one sentence, sounding like a slip, indicates his possible calculation: "if I returned, it was to be sacrificed, or to see those whom I most

17. In the 1831 edition, the irony is compounded in that Walton praises Victor for his discernment:

> Sometimes I have endeavored to discover what quality it is which he possesses, that elevates him so immeasurably above any other person I ever knew. I believe it to be an intuitive discernment; a quick but never-failing power of judgment; a penetration into the causes of things, unequalled for clearness and precision. (Appendix B, 203)

"I could not rank myself with the herd of common projectors," Victor avers (180). I agree with Marilyn Butler that Shelley's target here is the solipsism sustained in circles of middle-class white men (*Frankenstein*, xli).

loved die" (141). "Or" wants to mean that two catastrophes could happen, one just as well as the other; it also suggests that if he returned, he would be making a choice between the two that he does not have to make if he "pass[es] [his] life on that barren rock" (an island on the Orkneys) (141). In practice, Victor chooses again and again between endangering his life, at most—part of his reputation, more likely— and one of his loved ones'. He endangers Elizabeth because he wants to marry her before telling her who he is. Shelley presents calculations of major and minor self-interest side by side, tart juxtapositions of life-and-death situations with the revelation that often what counts as survival is the continuation of the self "as is." "Timorous" neighbors decline to get involved in Justine's murder trial (63); "impracticable" obstacles deter police protection (170). Victor makes the Creature eight feet tall only for the convenient magnification, "as the minuteness of the parts formed a great hindrance to my speed" (35).[18]

Into this society of everyday violence that Shelley satirizes, in which intuition has a dubious reputation and knowledge is sacrificed to self-interest "in so deadly a manner" (60), the nameless Creature is forced to life. As Nancy Yousef has emphasized, his difference is a difference of production against differences of degree. The most relevant contrast is the difference of ethnicity over and against its lack: Safie, the "Christianized 'Arabian'" (Spivak, *Critique of Postcolonial Reason*, 137) woman who is also learning a language, delivers "a reminder that the creature is essentially unlike the human, stranger than the foreign."[19] Indeed, his otherness is immeasurable, "'like no one in the whole world,' and the fantastic quality of his existence consists in the literal truth of the statement, the fact that it is true of him in a way that it cannot be true of any other character in the novel" (Yousef, "Monster in a Dark Room," 257).

It is "literal truth" that he is like no one in the whole world—and, as Yousef writes, this literal truth is literally impossible—a fact beyond telling, that arrives only in the envelope of its exclusion from any possible reality. As Yousef details, the Creature's socialization into sensibility and linguistic fluency without any society whatever is Shelley's great lunatic touch. Thus, "an important paradox that readers of *Frankenstein* confront is that a monstrosity that the novel cannot, and does not try very hard to, illustrate is central to the narrative" (258).

18. He knows it is a bad idea: the scale is "contrary to [his] first intention" but easier (35).

19. Nancy Yousef, "The Monster in a Dark Room: *Frankenstein*, Feminism, and Philosophy," *MLQ* 63 (2002): 197–226, 255. I've also consulted her revision of this material in *Isolated Cases: Anxieties of Autonomy in Enlightenment Philosophy and Romantic Literature* (Ithaca, NY: Cornell University Press, 2018), 149–169.

Literal truth and impossibility prove to be codependent, impossibility calling for an emphatic factuality to make it unmistakable. As Safie's ethnic difference measures the Creature's uncategorizable difference, the cheap confidence that the characters espouse and easily abandon highlights the difference in kind of their odd certainty that the Creature is absolutely different. He is not only literally but infinitely legible-as-illegible. Of course, according to Victor, he is eight feet tall; still, he is not apprehended in the way that eight-foot human beings would be, and have been, apprehended. As Elizabeth Young points out, Charles Byrne, a celebrity for his gigantism in the 1780s, was seven feet, seven inches tall and the toast of London.[20] There is something else, another reason for characters to act as though they knew the story: to act as though the story was the Creature's body.[21]

Unmistakable

Finally, with the help of Yousef, it will be possible to explore how the novel stages the conflation between bodily form and the historical itineraries of bodies. The impossible Creature is easier to accept than that these itineraries do not themselves appear.

The general idea is that the Creature is unmistakable and his memory "indelible" (38). But the near contradiction between monstrosity and unmistakability—avowed incomprehension becoming certitude—plays out in different logics running concurrently. Walton records his first description of the Creature before he has heard Victor's tale: "a being which had the shape of a man, but apparently of gigantic stature" (12). It's a strange description, but it lacks the quality of absoluteness that later ones have. "A being which had the shape of a man" is not granted humanness and not denied it. The being's "shape," per se, is here excluded from the criteria of nonhumanity, while his face cannot be seen "at the distance of half a mile," and the crew does not interact with him in any way. So, what is there to keep Walton from writing that, amazingly, he has seen a very large man? Walton's "but" phrase is equivocal over again. "Gigantic stature" qualifies the male shape. On the other hand, this qualification makes it sound as though right now, gigantic stature is the only problem: a minor problem, compared to the ones the reader knows the Creature has. This qualification is fur-

20. Not without cost, but he was hardly attacked on sight.

21. Readers tend to explain the terror the Creature inspires by referring to Victor Frankenstein's sketch of his appearance, which also figures in every reading of the Creature's blackness, along with Frankenstein's testimony, "I had selected his features as beautiful" (39). The reader has already encountered it not adding up, however.

ther qualified with "apparently," making it a kind of double negative. It sounds very odd to be unsure about gigantism; so, it sounds as though Walton is sure of the being's stature, but unsure that human gigantism is the cause of it. It remains opaque what makes him unsure of that. Finally, there is an inverse relationship between all the qualification and the crew's reaction: "this appearance excited...unqualified wonder" (12). The sighting affects them; the appearance of someone, not only surviving but also driving along the frozen sea "many hundred miles from any land...seemed to denote that it was not, in reality, as distant as we supposed" (12). By morning, after they have rescued Victor, things have settled down: he "seemed to be, a savage inhabitant" (13).

Victor Frankenstein is more than familiar with the Creature's form, of course, yet early on, at a time when he has encouraged himself to believe that maybe the Creature no longer exists, even he does not recognize him instantly: "I suddenly beheld the figure of a man, at some distance, advancing toward me with superhuman speed. He bounded over the crevices in the ice, among which I had walked with caution; his stature also, as he approached, seemed to exceed that of a man...I perceived, as the shape came near (sight tremendous and abhorred!) that it was the wretch whom I had created" (76).

Shelley hints that Victor's difficulty shows his resistance to giving up his hope that the Creature no longer exists or at any rate is of no account: with the assistance of the wish that nothing momentous has yet happened, Victor can perceive the figure of a man. Victor has not only seen the Creature but also constructed him, and still he can experience a "first" time when he is not sure.

In later scenes, however, which repeat aspects of Walton's account, Victor Frankenstein is overwhelmed with ungrounded certainty and an influx of orientation when he identifies the Creature. As Victor roams the mountains near his home, mourning for William, he recalls, "I perceived in the gloom a figure which stole from behind a clump of trees near me; I stood fixed, gazing intently: I could not be mistaken" (56). Victor recognizes the Creature without indicating how he does so. It's not clear what exactly he gazes at intently, or whether he is gazing to make a decision or just out of fascination. It is an intransitive, infinite, and yet conclusive gaze, and nothing is on the other side of it; no object is given. Nothing is explained as a matter of sense data to be processed or indeed as any thought. Unlike the implication that monstrousness needs processing as illegible, there is no friction now, and finally, a "full" unmistakability. Victor's phrase "I could not be mistaken" is terser than his endless other protestations of certitude and singularity ("No one can conceive the anguish I suffered during the remainder of the night, which I spent, cold and wet, in the open air" [57]). His intentness here exceeds the strength of his intensions elsewhere, as though he were more able to identify the Creature than his own feelings. Being unable not to recognize him brings satisfaction; everything else disappears. The Creature's unmistakability is his guilt: "He was the murderer! I could not doubt it" (56; "I did not for a minute doubt" [64]).

Victor is infallible one more time, almost as strongly, as Frankenstein and the Creature track one another across the far North: "I viewed the expanse before me with anguish, when suddenly my eye caught a dark speck upon the dusky plain. I strained my sight to discover what it could be, and uttered a wild cry of ecstasy when I distinguished a sledge, and the distorted proportions of a well-known form within. Oh! with what a burning gush did hope revisit my heart! warm tears filled my eyes, which I hastily wiped away, that they might not intercept the view I had of the demon" (176).

Victor's visual strain, replaying his intent gaze in the forest, indicates that he is not content with mere possibility. But why did his eye catch "a dark speck" against a "dusky plain" in the first place? It sounds as though Victor already sees something—some telling quality. By the time that he discerns the "well-known form," he has verified the implications of whatever he saw. But as in the early shot of the Creature half a mile away, the dark speck makes it seem as though there is something other than the sum of the parts to discern. The body that he built to eight feet so that minute parts wouldn't slow him down is recognizable when it is only a speck. How could that be? Far from being overly material, here the Creature is almost without body, a pixel, an embryo, a microorganism, and still has signature, is verified as the same "well-known" being, in spite and because of the fact that what there is for him to be known as is as unthinkable as ever. Further, recalling the critical position in which blackness needs to be found and then thought, in that order, Victor prefers to notice the Creature's existence when it is in front of him. He is unable to notice that the Creature is the invisible "spirit" that seems to follow his travels and "extricate [him] from seemingly insurmountable difficulties," for instance leaving food for him in the wild: "I may not doubt that it was set there by the spirits that I had invoked to aid me" (173). Victor's confidence still indicates mainly what he can't stand not to think. He orients himself by the Creature's singularity, so much so that he can't bear a diminished view of it for a moment.[22] Walton's mariners' orientation becomes Victor's entire orientation. He reenacts the

---

22. The "indelible trace" the Creature leaves extends this orientation in memory, the scar that allows Victor Frankenstein's impulsive life to feel real (58).

Creature's animation, delivering his form from dimness; he wants to do this again and again, to never not be doing it.

More than the inconsistency that all critics querying race in the novel observe in Shelley's physical descriptions (including Victor's bitter remark, "I had selected his features as beautiful" [39]), inconsistency attends the Creature's unmistakability, such that it becomes full only when it is completely empty. Noting the contrast between this treatment and the consistency of the Creature's historical deprivation, Yousef remarks firmly, "I cannot offer so straightforward a reading... of the creature's face" (223). Indeed, the Creature's problem is not having been ripped from a homeland but rather not having one—not an ethnic origin associated with him, but not being able to have any, as Yousef argues. As she points out, the Creature develops everything that he can from a vestibular world, the "low hovel, quite bare" (83) from which he watches social life through "a small and almost imperceptible chink" (85). If his talents seem supernatural, he implies that they are hypertrophic by necessity, "while my friends"—the family who is entirely unaware of his existence—"were employed in their ordinary occupations" (103). When the Creature imagines what it would be like to have a female partner, he depicts a "veiled" life—Du Bois's metaphor for an internally organized Black society, however complex, divided from the world by "a veil so thick, that they shall not even think of breaking through."[23]

Various counterfactuals and hypotheticals—this sketch of what "shall" happen, Victor Frankenstein's attempt to imagine their future situation, and other instances—help to fill in, beyond the social death of the Creature, the range of possibilities of his existence as imagined by Shelley. The Creature's counterfactual statements set up these possibilities and then say what would have happened to them, had they existed. The logic is repeatedly that circumstances of slaves' lives that, in the larger society, produce human history, produce something else in slavery: "No father had watched my infant days, no mother had blessed me with smiles and caresses; *or if they had*, all my past was now a blot, a blind vacancy in which I distinguished nothing" (97; my italics). In the same mode, the Creature's argument for a "companion" expresses the best case scenario of veiled life in the novel: "*we shall be monsters, cut off from the world*; but on that account we shall be more attached to one another" (120; my italics). Returning from hypothetical time, the

23. W. E. B. Du Bois, *The Souls of Black Folk* [1903] (New York: Pocket Books, 2005), 90.

present is more abstracted: no relation among slaves, no sexual relation; but what would companionship be, "cut off from the world" on pain of death?[24]

It is as though Shelley, familiar with slave narratives and her mother's review of Equiano's,[25] thinks what slavery would be without captivity and without toil. The Creature steals and gathers but doesn't work, nor is he "property."[26] Far from being confined, he and the other masculine protagonists of the novel crisscross national borders as though they had Eurail Passes. His narrative renders captivity atopic, bursts the categories of freedom and bondage, and distinguishes freedom from the absence of both forced and waged labor. After Shelley is done stripping away characteristics of slavery, what is left of it?[27] Her abstraction reproduces the quandary of the free Black; not only the Black laborer of Du Bois's *Black Reconstruction*, "compelled to wander" the postbellum minefield,[28] but also the "eternal captive" "never at rest"[29] from exposure to antiblack violence, whether confined or not.

Yousef has written thoughtfully about Shelley's abstraction, emphasizing its literal impossibility. The impossibility is best exemplified for

24. From this perspective there is a double edge to Chris Washington's sense that the scenario "expands what a relationship between a male and female can be" (Washington, "Non-Binary Frankenstein?" in *Frankenstein in Theory*, ed. Orrin N. C. Wan [New York: Bloomsbury, 2020], 79).

25. Mary Wollstonecraft, review of *Narrative of the Interesting Life of Olaudah Equiano* [1789]; in Wollstonecraft, *The Vindications: The Rights of Men* and *The Rights of Woman*, ed. D. L. MacDonald and Kathleen Scherf (Peterborough: Broadview, 1997), appendix A.

26. John Bugg, "'Master of Their Language': Education and Exile in Mary Shelley's *Frankenstein*," *Huntington Library Quarterly* 68 (2005): 655–666, 663. Bugg calls the Creature "property" because his exposure to violence recalls "the race-specific laws governing homicide on Caribbean plantations" (663).

27. As Victor Frankenstein lays out the problem of the free Black for the non-Black, he anticipates that the Creature, and even more so the female Creature, will want more power if they live at all, "mak[ing] the very existence of the species of man a condition precarious and filled with terror" (138).

28. W. E. B. Du Bois, *Black Reconstruction in America: An Essay Toward a History of the Part Which Black Folk Played in the Attempt to Reconstruct Democracy in America, 1860–1888* [1935] (Oxford: Oxford University Press, 2014).

29. Linette Park, "The Eternal Captive in Contemporary 'Lynching' Arrests: On the Uncanny and the Complex of Law's Perversion," *Theory & Event* (2019), 674–698, 692. On "Social death as a permanent legal category" enshrined in the Thirteenth Amendment, see Joy James, "Introduction: Democracy and Captivity," in *The New Abolitionists: (Neo)Slave Narratives and Contemporary Prison Writings*, ed. Joy James (Albany, NY: SUNY Press, 2005), xxvii–xxix.

Yousef by the Creature's socialization without society—the idea that without any nurturing or exchange whatsoever, he could get the point of social life at all, as he does in the novel. In Yousef's original interpretation, privation is maximized so that the Creature can be a thought experiment: What if the radically individual masculine human of Locke and Rousseau escaped from the pages of their books? Contrary to their hypotheses about human nature, she argues, if that being could exist, he would not seem human at all; he would be monstrous.[30]

For Yousef, then, the Creature's "radical autonomy" (220) explains his impossible singularity. There are two passages of Yousef's essay it will be helpful to juxtapose. After drawing out how Victor Frankenstein "is first, finally, and throughout the object of human sympathies from which the creature is first, finally and throughout excluded" (223), she goes on: "In arguing for a more precise sense of what the novel is allegorizing as monstrous... I have suggested that his giantism exposes the monstrousness of leaving out the roles of infancy, childhood, dependence, and relation in human formation... *Frankenstein* does not present us with a monstrous body, only with testimonies to its monstrousness that are so unvaried and unrelenting as to amount to the proposition that it cannot be seen as human" (224).

Yet the creature is not a figure for the failure of sympathy, because insofar as the novel insists that he can never be looked on without horror, it equally insists that the human form and countenance (however miserable, however badly shattered or wrecked) will never excite such horror. It is never a matter of choice or avoidance in the imagination of this novel that the human attitude toward the human face will be an "attitude toward a soul ... the demand [the creature] makes of Frankenstein arises from his realization that the 'human senses are insurmountable barriers to our union'" (119). This is so not because he is cursed with a hideous body veiling a nonmonstrous person but because to wear the human form in this novel is to bear a human history (224–225).

I agree with Yousef that Shelley's treatment of the Creature goes deeper than misunderstanding and a "nonmonstrous" self beneath that can be uncovered. (*Nonmonstrous* is an interestingly vast word.) In *Frankenstein* "it is never a matter of choice." Yousef decides that the Creature's underdetermined but apparently rivening presence allego-

---

30. As I would or did phrase it, the most monstrous thing that could exist is a subject, the impossible being whose nearest approach to fulfillment is the aspirational sovereignty of a state: "if I saw one coming, I too would run away": the last sentence of *Feeling in Theory: Emotion after the "Death of the Subject"* (Cambridge, MA: Harvard University Press, 2001).

rizes his nonrelational existence, bare of the social connections that other characters introduce themselves with. In so doing, she hypothesizes that in Shelley's conceit, historicity forms or is inscribed onto the body, which is therefore understood as human, or as not, if there has been none. Yousef means (I think) that for Shelley, everybody has a human history, and the fact that everybody has a human history cannot be missed. Therefore, if it could be missing, as Shelley explores counterfactually, that too would necessarily be obvious. To grasp this obviousness, it's hard not to involve the phenomenal in some way—thus the ambiguity I tried to phrase above, "forms or is inscribed onto the body." Human beings would encounter monstrosity, nonmemberment—something other than a body. From this ultimately phenomenal perspective, this "culturally unmade" (Spillers, *Black, White, and in Color*, 215) entity would *appear* as having lacked relation while recalling in form the outline of a possible history (that can then be perceived as missing).[31]

The "female creature," most of all, appears as this nonmemberment, for this entity without pronoun exists without ever being born, or in Victor's terms, finished. The female creature reaches the status only of "as if . . . mangled . . . living flesh" (142), and so is not "female" in any usual sense, but "as if" flesh slated to be female. In two of the most violent paragraphs of the novel, Victor, "trembling with passion, t[ears] to pieces the thing on which [he] was engaged" (139) and waits until the next night to dispose of the remains. Her remains are not only unmournable but as though below the level of the disposable. Victor makes clear that he wouldn't have returned to them except that he wanted to "pack [his] chemical instruments" and, once in the room, decided "not to leave the relics of my work to excite the horror and suspicion of the peasants" (142): "The remains of the half-finished creature, whom I had destroyed, lay scattered on the floor, and I almost felt as if I had mangled the living flesh of a human being . . . [I] put them into a basket, with a great quantity of stones, and laying them up, deter-

---

31. Representational theories of race argue that aesthetic and scientific theories, and their institutional extensions across culture, have a major role to play in inculcating the criteria for humanity with hegemonic forms, values, and rules. Shelley represents this criterial outline, the schematic human, when the Creature appears as "the figure of a man," "a being that had the shape of a man." "Figure" phrases and "being" phrases dodge blackness twice, splitting it into generic form and enigmatic content. Victor fully grasps the role of outline when he thinks that the Creature "might . . . conceive a greater abhorrence for [his own deformity] when it came before his eyes in the female form" (138).

Yousef, again, takes a more constitutional approach: what matters *causally* is not conformance to a set of norms, physical or mental. What matters is what has and hasn't happened to the Creature.

mined to throw them into the sea that very night; and in the mean time I sat upon the beach, employed in cleaning and arranging my chemical apparatus" (142).

For Victor, who is, as ever, evading a thought in danger of entering his mind, the horror lies only in the contracted likeness of the female creature to "the fiend I had first made" (143). The various phases of destruction (mangling, abandoning, sinking—and, of course, cultivation and assembly are forms of destruction as well) exist independently of memberment. Missing body, parts, name, pronoun, form, detail, life, death, and more, the creature-not-to-be appears only as matter in the hands of others' intention to shape and sexuate it.

When "to wear" is "to bear" for all human beings, when dualism has been rejected and political ontology is all surface and reality, corporeality is not a base, and history, defined here as minimal nurture, is the ability to appear as a body. The human body is realized in and as an itinerary and a basic social agreement that in the instance of the female creature literally falls apart. The next question is: What, then, is minimal nurture?

In pursuit of this next question, let's go on to Yousef's contrast between Walton and the Creature: "Whatever the brother may mean when he says [to his sister], 'I have no friend,' it cannot be what the creature means when he says, 'Where were my friends and relations?'" (Yousef, "Monster in a Dark Room," 222).

If it's important to notice the difference between what Walton means and what the Creature means, it's also important to ask for the difference between what Walton means and what the Atlantic slave means, and what the Creature means and what the Atlantic slave means and what the prisoner in solitary confinement means. Scholarship debating the ontological implications of chattel slavery might intervene exactly here, where various thresholds are pressing. Gigante's and Yousef's theories about what enables the Creature's difference are responding to the question put by slavery. Chandler points out that taking "the problem of the Negro," in its exorbitance, "as a problem for thought" would be the only possible way to produce a general account that did not "[presuppose] the status of a European, Euro-American, or 'White' identity, subject, or mode of identification as coherent" (X, 23, 22). In the case of Frankenstein, Shelley's approach to the question "What is Man?" relies in no way on establishing a racial referent for the Creature.

From here it's not just allegorically possible but necessary to ask after Frankenstein's implications for blackness. Reading through blackness is not allegorical because blackness is not a set of objects that can be taken for granted to reside within the historical and metaphysical frames to which allegory belongs. Confidence about what Black allegory could be falls away from *Frankenstein* as soon as it brings up the prerequisites and bounds of identity. What is a history that might be begun only to be abducted into a "blind vacancy," or cultivated only "cut off from the world"? What happens now that the Creature's blackness is not the implication of a racial identity but the phenomenalization of a fear of the impossibility of accounting for its origin?

With all the above in mind, Yousef's line of thought suggests the unusable space of that part of slavery not reparable within the frame of the political. It interrupts the Creature's speculations through the illegibility of the Creature's origin—hypostatized in the novel as literal impossibility—and, therefore, end. Yousef argues that for Shelley, (a) sympathy cannot fail among humans (224), and (b) everyone who exists is human, so (c) there can be no "failure of sympathy." Therefore, Yousef does not interpret Shelley as intending "the monster as a figure for cultural constructions for the other as outsider, deviant" (224). To turn this around, one reading of this sentence is the conclusion that Shelley does not elaborate the free Black as merely an outsider or deviant. Warren discusses how "the act of manumission places the free black" at a remove from temporal horizon: the free Black exists in a legal suspension, an undecidable being in a "temporal caesura created by the law" (*Ontological Terror*, 97). That law creates the caesura suggests that this suspension cannot be said to be simply outside the law. Similarly, the Creature is not without political identity in the sense of being outside of its reality; he is rather the inside-out of it within its Genevan delineation. For its part, this progressive society struggles with a debordered intimation of slavery that in turn threatens its own political security.

Boreal Eschatology

The casual sequencing of the Creature's materialization, not once but recurrently, and the sense that something other than spontaneity is occurring at the brinks of "first" and "second" instances of animation, comes to bear on the end of the novel, where the lastness of the last time reflects the first and vice versa. End time contains *Frankenstein*'s various counterfactual and negative possibilities without completely organizing them.

As Shelley prepares for the ending of the narrative, the landscape buckles, wears away, and freezes. The area in which the characters travel

is limited, the restriction of Europe is felt,[32] but within it, a phantasma-
goria of elided borders and jutting landscapes threatens to return the
geography to a kind of hyletic condition.[33] The Creature's and Victor's
descriptions of it are seamless—as though to stress that underneath
them lies the same world, however turbulent and unknowable. Mont
Blanc and the "stupendous" Jura range, as the Creature calls it (116),
which rises vertically while diminishing laterally, are called on to set
the symbolic world askew, only to imply another, mysterious but fundamental, the origin of the symbolic one. The sense of hylē, Husserl's
term for perceived and yet unconceptualized matter, summons entities
not yet encountered and named, troubled only by winds and tides. As
the landscape flattens, worn down at the poles, the novel shifts to one of
the parts of the globe that "had been held to be uninhabitable" in a former era (Wynter, "Unsettling the Coloniality," 275). The landscape void
of the spatial orientation that allows time to be measured, the eroded
poles, summon the possibility of a "temporal hylē,"[34] a phenomenolog-

32. On the Creature's restriction to Europe, see Maureen N. McLane, *Romanticism
and the Human Sciences* (Cambridge, UK: Cambridge University Press, 2000), 92.

33. Shane Denson argues that *Frankenstein* films "[make] certain demands on their
human users, at times altogether *unreasonable* demands that challenge the very coherence and stability of viewing subjects and pressure them to submit to a disorienting
affective experience" (*Postnaturalism: Frankenstein, Film, and the Anthropotechnical Interface* [Bielefeld: Transcript Verlag, 2014], 26). For Denson, however, the "impact of
cinematic technology" that they reveal is "direct, non-cognitive and pre-personal" (26).
Rather than a hyletic, unmarked plenum before the world, he posits a technologically
broken and reorganized sensory field that offers the chance to work toward species being
for the first time. On my reading, this echoes the technophilia disparaged in *Frankenstein*.

34. Shelley is interested in something like *hylē* (as I mentioned in § 5, *hylē*, literally
"matter," means material that is perceived but not yet conceptualized: unmarked, undamaged substance as in Derrida, *Problem of Genesis in Husserl's Philosophy*, 86). The
Creature relies on a hyletic idea when he describes his prelinguistic world: "I started up,
and beheld a radiant form rise from among the trees. I gazed with a kind of wonder. It
moved slowly, but it enlightened my path" (80). He implies that the radiant form grad-
ually becomes the concept sun (without the word *soleil*) as he understands its relevance
to him; agreeing with Husserl, it had to be something before. Episodes like Walton's pro-
visional descriptions of the Creature, while they are not nonconceptual, share with *hylē*
a smaller degree of suspended intention. Commenting on Husserl, Moten remarks: "to
engage the phenomenality of the nation on the level of its *original constitution* is, in some
sense, what occurs in the illuminative relay between self and world. However, what is
for some a pathway is, for others, a dislocation" (*The Universal Machine* [Durham, NC:
Duke University Press, 2018], 106; my italics). In previous work, I've considered the
psychological function of hyletic-type perceptions within and given the discontents of
society (*Looking Away: Phenomenality and Dissatisfaction, Kant to Adorno* [Cambridge,
MA: Harvard University Press, 2009]).

ical sensation not yet (and no longer) called time nor divided into past, present, and future.

Spivak appreciates that the novel releases the Creature unextinguished into a site that does not fit an imperial logic. Further, she connects his destination with the novel's address, inhabited by Margaret Saville, Walton's sister to whom all the novel's pages are addressed:

> He is "lost in darkness and distance" (191)—these are the last words of the novel—into an existential temporality that is coherent with neither the territorializing individual imagination (as in the opening of *Jane Eyre*) nor the authoritative scenario of Christian psychobiography (as at the end of Brontë's work) ... Margaret Saville does not respond to close the text as a frame. The frame is thus simultaneously not a frame, and the monster can step "beyond the text" and be "lost in darkness." Within the allegory of our reading, the place of both the English lady and the unnamable monster are left open by this great flawed text. (Spivak, *Critique of Postcolonial Reason*, 139–140)

Agreeing that Shelley is not tempted as Emily Brontë is by "the unique creative imagination of the marginal individualist" (120)—Spivak is careful not to celebrate Shelley as one, either—I wonder whether, even as *Frankenstein* sails away from the Christian family, the reader is sent beyond, to a mythic chaotic origin of all things, so that this origin can be the Creature's end.

Spivak is precise and does not characterize the space toward which the Creature floats. She writes merely that it is neither territorial nor familial. My problem is not with her statement but with the temptation to origin that beckons in Shelley's eschatological structure. The nothingness into which the Creature announces his "very remembrance" will vanish (190) is uncomfortably close to the "midst of ... darkness" (34) out of which he is brought by Victor's secret knowledge. According to Victor, the beyond of the text is the opening from which the events have come. The Creature's animation came through "a passage to life aided only by one glimmering, and seemingly ineffectual, light" (35). Likewise in the chaotic middle, in the storming Jura, "for an instant every thing seemed of a pitchy darkness"; then, lightning had revealed the Creature standing in it (56). In this way, last and first instances happen in the middle. Arguably, the beyond of the text is tethered to the matrix of catastrophic inception, when before the Creature comes to life, Victor feels "dizzy with the immensity" of a fragile prospect (34).

In closing, Shelley does not verify the Creature's end in death, nor his mortality; and to the same extent, she makes it clear enough that she cannot really explain his origin either. Yet, this openness still bids to be a new constitutive chaos myth, similar to other foundational open- · nesses of the radical enlightenment. This mythic quality inflects all the counterfactual, hypothetical, negative, and elliptical spaces of possibility the novel includes. How different is the Creature's Hamlet-like closing soliloquy from his previous argument that in South America, it would be possible for him to be forgotten?

Then, the Creature had demanded "a female for me, with whom I can live in the interchange of those sympathies necessary for my being" (118) and an isolated domestic life in the *sertão*.[35] In his scenario, no one would be threatened; "the sun will shine on us as on man, and will ripen our food" (120). But as he adds too honestly, this *"picture"* of the Creatures' life is "peaceful and human" (120; my italics). In the picture, having minimal, "veiled" relations, he would *appear to become human*— that is, "linked to the chain of existence and events, from which I am now excluded" (121). As in the last instance he hopes to be forgotten, "everyone will be ignorant" of their very existence (121). This stipulation implies that the very thought of their having such an existence would be unbearable; violence would follow any word of it. As Victor Frankenstein perceives, moving to South America would not solve that. The image the speech closes on, of being linked on the great chain of events, is exactly the wrong one to comfort Victor. He concludes that they must be either linked by force or eradicated. It may seem that because the bargain does not come about, Shelley suspends the question of what would have happened if Victor had completed it. But together with the Creature's imagination that "we would be monsters," the reasonable possibility that he might actually be trying for something else, and Victor Frankenstein's reasoning, "How can you, who long for the love and sympathy of man, persevere in this exile?" (120) withdraw the scenario. As we've seen, Shelley rules out possibilities by mooting their points ("No mother had blessed me ... *or if they had*, my past was now a blot" [97; my italics]).

The Creature's idea that moving to South America would be moving away from all human knowledge does not in itself cancel other troubling horizons. The possibility, for instance, that maybe the only thing that could achieve the kind of secrecy the peaceful picture requires would be assimilation to the point of invisibility. Washington points

35. In suggesting the wilds of South America, the Creature again refers to a geography populated by former slaves and their descendants. See, for example, Allan Charles Dawson, *In Light of Africa: Globalizing Blackness in Northeast Brazil* (Toronto: University of Toronto Press, 2014), 118–141.

out that "the creature, in fact, never suggests children nor does he imply that his female 'Eve' be sexed."[36] The assumption that "one of the first results... would be children" (138) is indeed Victor's and is followed by a thinking-through of scenarios that is usually beyond Victor's abilities. Would the children of two creatures look unusual at all? The idea that they would not, does not, if he thinks of it (as someone trained in the life sciences), assuage Victor. He seems to be worried about political ontology too—the possibility that their progeny would be a "race of devils" *because of* what has happened (138).

The fate of these hypothetical possibilities in the novel troubles the idea that Walton's letter and so the novel launch themselves into a free space in which Margaret Saville and the Creature can both exist undefined. It suggests instead that this free space must be read as another fragile thought-balloon among others. The Creature's ending mono-logue is only the last of his speculative fictions: "the very remembrance of us both will speedily vanish ... what I now feel will no longer be felt. Soon these burning miseries will be extinct.... My spirit will sleep in peace; *or if it thinks*, it will not surely think thus" (191; my italics). The wish for forgetfulness, like the capacity to forget the extremity of the Creature's situation when listening to his narratorial voice, and Victor's frequent wish to forget all about the Creature altogether, and the Crea-ture's strong desire to forget himself, is in the "distance" almost elevated into a total longing for what Agamben calls, and longs for as, "the great ignorance" of gnostic withdrawal.[37] Agamben adduces the second-century Egyptian mystic Basilides, who prophesies that after the saved have been saved, "God will bring on the whole world the great igno-rance [megale agnoia], so that every creature may remain in its natu-ral condition [kata physin] and none desire anything contrary to its nature" (89–90).[38]

The Creature's disappearance to a distance beyond Walton's and the reader's capacity to follow his death or life suggests that his discovery or permanent concealment would unlock or lock up the mystery of slav-ery's ground, while the social relations exhibited in its plot say some-thing else. They tell of the allure of such a figure and the suitability of

36. Chris Washington, "Non-Binary Frankenstein?" in *Frankenstein in Theory*, ed. Orrin N. C. Wang, 68.

37. Giorgio Agamben, *The Open: Man and Animal* [2002], trans. Kevin Attali (Stan-ford, CA: Stanford University Press, 2004), 89.

38. As Agamben goes on to muse, Basilides's solution for the unsavable has implica-tions for beings in general, like Nietzsche's hopes for forgetfulness. Instead of the "con-tours of a new creation that would run the risk of being equally as mythological as the other," beings might stay as they are but subside from "the historical task" (92).

the free Black for the role. The law of *Frankenstein* is that the Creature is literally created to be that figure. Thus, when the novel's end disappears into the edge of the world, it seems to describe from the inside what it has previously shown to be wishful. Shelley cannot explore the "last" moment without eschatology's crisis management, as that management, not her invention, is suffused throughout the notion of ending it all. Shelley does not depict fantasmatic reality, though, as Poe and Lovecraft do, as the emanation of a supernatural force operating the puppet state of Geneva. Looking askance at both mysticism and science, *Frankenstein* takes its explanatory power from the everyday.[39] The space in which the Creature has been demanded to exist is not restricted to the Americas, to labor, or to captivity in a narrow sense. It shows the consequence of expanded or "free" borders of slavery's springs, reflected in defenses of the milieu at its most ordinary, in Geneva's progressivism, and Victor's Prometheanism. Can it be anything other than ordinary Geneva, then, that pushes the last/first instance of the Creature beyond itself?

It's possible to take the conflict of interests between the Creature and Victor, instead, as neither mistaken in its terms nor forgettable. Gigante would be right; it could be a matter of survival—that is, "might make the very existence of the species of man a condition precarious and full of terror" (138). Now, Victor Frankenstein finds a reason to conclude that the creature is asking him to risk "sacrific[ing] the whole human race" (156), as he blurts out to his father. On the banal level this hyperbole is just another convenient deflection of his own decision by Victor. Victor Frankenstein's outburst to his father collapses a highly implausible risk of humanity's destruction into certainty: human existence "might" be made "precarious" (138); he bargains with the Creature "at the price perhaps of the existence of the whole human race" (138); and later, he cries, "I could not, my father, indeed I could not sacrifice the whole human race!" (156). On another level, though, if humanism is what Frankenstein has been acting to preserve all along, giving over this counterphantasm would be a sensible request.

Typically, Victor erases his opportunity: it isn't South America that's the possibility and the risk to humanity that's the downside—it's the other way around. He is missing a chance to accept reasonable expo-

39. Part of the task here is holding on to that fact which the Creature may lose sight of, that his singular existence or nonexistence is not the same as the existence or nonexistence of the space that he has been made to fill, so that destroying the one does destroy the other. Nor can Victor break the mold for monstrosity by tearing the female creature to pieces: the womb is not the exemplar of the reproduction Shelley is talking about.

sure to death, which he does not seem ever to have been able to do. Recall that Victor had initially wanted to "render man invulnerable to any but a violent death" (23), a desire that eventuates in Victor's indirect delivery of violent death to his family. Only Victor Frankenstein has access to the thought of risk to the "human race" now, and since he responds uncritically, no one grasps it as a promise. But it is a promise, as Barbara Johnson's question to the novel, "How indeed can one survive humanism?"[40] suggests. In her phrasing, humanism is not what needs protecting but what needs surviving. Taken as a rhetorical question, it may suggest that humanism is interminable because it is too endemic to see one's way around. In that case humanism weathers attempts on its life and keeps killing, as far as can be seen. Taken as a question, however, it suggests that although humanism's survivors, if any, will not be human, there is at least a place from which to pitch Johnson's question. Though in the novel it's fragile, there is a ledge from which Victor's demand to protect humanity comes to seem absurd and questionable, even though the novel never expressly asks what creates such a demand, instead bringing the desire to ask to the surface. The fragile footing for this question is a place that conceives of "risking" humanity.

40. Barbara Johnson, "The Last Man," in *A Life with Mary Shelley*, ed. Judith Butler and Shoshana Felman (Stanford, CA: Stanford University Press, 2014), 3–14, 10.

PART 3

Nonpolitical Distinctions

Consciouslessness comes to designate what separates community from its own realization or from rising to its own concept.

ÉTIENNE BALIBAR, *Citizen Subject: Foundations of Philosophical Anthropology*

Part 3 explores what it's like to occupy spaces and stances that in Hegelian actuality (not simply an invention of Hegel) appear as "nonpolitical"—sublated, disavowing, refusing, failing to cohere, obsolescent, or loosed from a previous political and legal category. These possibilities appear in European political life that is unfree, in civic situations that are themselves hard cases for new realization. Part 3 takes place in Germany, then, with Atlantic slavery and the problem of slavery's borders in the background. These situations help to clarify the relationships between political unfreedom, in which realization may not be possible because it is not socializable, and slavery, in which realization has effected derealization elsewhere. Since part 1 of this book focuses the derealization and destruction of a split-off slave in the background of *The Phenomenology of Spirit*, I am presenting an antidramatic structure—§§ 7 and 8 return Hegel to his living room—that can also, like *Logic* (but I hope not like *Logic!*), be read as a loop or Möbius strip. I conclude with a discussion of early Marx that credits his attention to the delegitimating processes within the state's political legitimation and considers its relation to his reference to North American slavery.

As Hegel's real movement of history transforms entities, from species to institutions and civilizations to new historical ontologies, by externalizing their possibilities, each ideally develops to crack and become the "husk" of a new form. As each realization develops its singular capacity, it experiences its shape and limitation for the first time. For Hegel, radical subjectivity is a self-shattering experience. Hegel calls this space "I=I," meaning that it's a space of "absolute" aloneness. "Beyond itself there is properly speaking *nothing*," Balibar writes, "nothing, at least, that can be lived in common," while that "nothing" itself comprises "the very *experience* of all and each" (Balibar, *Citizen Subject*, 171).

In my terms, the political subject reaches a place where IWWI is not;
but that space is, again, in neither-nor form, not there for anyone and
no one (ANNA), and productive and destructive for each. Hegel turns
the citizen subject, IWWI, so that it confronts, or at least ought to confront, its exposure to history and object status for history. But to IWWI,
derealization can still move a metalevel, to a peak at which it signals
another's insufficient awareness of the universal nonavailability of the
common. To understand what happens here, it's necessary to understand Hegel's genuine interest in self-shattering.

As in part 1, Hegel exhorts self-exposure. He leaves the reader with
outlines of various liminal "forms of life"—never really systematized in
relation to one another, yet thought-provoking for political ontology.
These include "immediate" naturalized forms of life reminiscent of the
threshold of *World History* and suitable for undifferentiated consumption by history. "Immediate life" is a realm to which slaves are assigned
through a process of derealization that is the byproduct of realization.

§ 7 reflects on the production of these "immediate" forms in close
juxtaposition to the "Beautiful Soul" episode in *The Phenomenology of
Spirit*, one of the text's main discussions of complicity and exhorta-
tion of avowed complicity as a favored form of self-realization—the
externalization of one's real unchosen conditions of life as a participant in global violence. It's a particularly popular episode. A kind of
Brave Soul proselytizing negativity encounters a would-be "moralist"
who refuses to affirm his (for it's a feminized male) complicity. Since
Kant is one of the several inspirations for this "shape," a reflection on
Hegel's view of Kant's closeted queerness is fair game. Reading the episode through Kant's queerness raises the question of unchosen, un-
spoken withdrawal from self-presentation. If this form of ambiguous
self-realization displaces pleasure, as Hegel complains, that raises the
question of what a straightforward pleasure is and who or what benefits from the distinction. Yet, this distinction itself draws on the world-
historical account of consumption.

§ 8 reflects on the biographical Hegel's wavering practice of therapeutic negativity in the disappointing Napoleonic and post-Napoleonic
years, when the possibility of political freedom receded from the German states, leaving an unfreedom difficult to describe positively. On the
left, the unfreedom of civil society and the broken self within it come to
form a matrix, not assimilable to classical sovereignty, for realizing political and derealizing subpolitical and nonpolitical ontologies. Against
the background of national projects during this time to institutionalize intra-European forms of racial subordination, self-negation can be
seen maintaining the achievement of political identity as a compensa-

tion for unfreedom. Together §§ 7 and 8 connect a sphere of derealized consumption, in which the subpolitical African Hegel positions in
World History functions as a prop for political identity (including that
of the politically exemplary Black), with derealized depoliticization in
Europe.

Finally, Marx's "On the Jewish Question" (1843) includes a reflection on "non-political distinctions"—social categories created when the
state "annuls" a legal restriction (in this case, restrictions on the rights
of Jewish citizens). In closing I look for the implied functions, for Marx,
of disestablished categories, especially their ability as foils to present a
state's political legitimacy; compare "annulment" in Marx to sublation
in Hegel; interpret Marx's comparative references to voting rights and
slavery in North America; and note the implications of the contrast and
intersection of Hegel's sublation and Marx's annulment for contemporary political ontologies. "On the Jewish Question" indicates that the
political/nonpolitical distinction is mediated by the North American
slave.

§ 7

Beautiful Soul/Brave Soul

It has only a hidden life in God; it is true that God is immediately present in its mind and heart, in its self; but what is manifest, its actual consciousness and the mediating movement of that consciousness, is for it something other than that hidden inner life and the immediacy of God's presence.

HEGEL, *The Phenomenology of Spirit*

In this section I focus on Hegel's discussion of "the moral view of the world" in *The Phenomenology of Spirit* and his lead-up to it in §§ 596–597. In the first part, a sublation of "racialism"—and the ideologeme "tribal"—underwrites Hegel's preference of historico-ontological over moral thinking.[1] Following closely is the Brave Soul's quarrel with the Beautiful Soul. The sequence of events shows Hegel mobilizing historical sublation in the direction of a domestic rival, much as he aims objections to racialism at the German nations. Here, the *Phenomenology*'s framing of "morality" occurs at the expense of romantic writers, especially Kant, who steps into a new "shape" here as an unwilling envoy of queerness. These themes are juxtaposed, it seems, to ask how the Beautiful Soul can possibly act as though he were choosing obsolescence, like the forms that Hegel has just shown passing away. The figure of the closeted queer, performing an enigmatic partial withdrawal, actualizes something and yet poorly exemplifies actualization.

---

1. Hegel distinguishes between performing attachments without realizing them—which he associates with underdevelopment—and the value that they have when performed in response to "many contingencies ... also in play." In the latter case, "differences particularize themselves more and more" and become expressive and educative in comparison to one another (Hegel, *Lectures on the Philosophy of Spirit 1827–28*, ed. and trans. Robert R. Williams [Oxford: Oxford University Press, 2007], 92). Finally, "with cultivated persons these differences are dropped" once again "because these people live according to general determinations" (*Lectures on the Philosophy of Spirit*, 93).

Immediate, Ethical, Legal: The Orders of Diversity

At the opening of his discussion of morality, Hegel places two kinds of being, ethical and legal, at the "cusp of civilization,"[2] where they become historical or not. Even though both have already met their limits, they are "still present" [noch vorhanden] or "still happening" [noch vorkommt]. For instance, Hegel writes that in consciousness the "sense-element is still present [noch vorhanden], but not in the way it was supposed to be in immediate certainty" (PS, § 113). In a fuller treatment of persisting presence,

> What is *thought of,* ceases to be something [merely] thought of, something alien to the self's knowledge, only when the self has produced it, and therefore beholds the determination of the object as its own, consequently beholds itself in the object. Through this activity, the lower determination has at the same time vanished; for the act is the negative that is realized at the expense of something else. *In so far as the lower determination is still present, it has retreated into an unessential aspect; just as, on the other hand, where the lower is still dominant but the higher is also present, the one determination devoid of self has its place alongside the other.* (PS, §§ 417–418; my italics)

To be "still present" encompasses being stored up in memory; vanishing so that something can be realized; standing by, "devoid of self"; and "retreat[ing] into an unessential aspect" or remaining as obsolescent. In the transition to historical life, "Pure Insight," compared here to faith, remains "in relation to the actual world, insofar as it's still positive" (PS, § 535). How positive is that? The only "still positive" form that remains related is "vain consciousness" (§ 535).

Critical discussions of this transition adduce *The Philosophy of Right,* which stands ethics against legality in the tragedy of *Antigone,* since similar issues are involved here as well. As rehearsed by humanities curricula, Sophocles's play contrasts kinship attachment to legal force: Antigone fights to bury her brother, Polynices, since because of Polynices's crimes against the state, the sovereign does not allow him burial rights. The conflict triggers a chain of events that brings down the regime. The parallel discussion in the *Phenomenology,* A. V. Miller notes, "is really characterizing the spiritual life of Germany" as nostalgic for "tribal" intimacy (PS, xii): "spiritual communal life necessarily detaches

2. Tina Chanter, *Whose Antigone? The Tragic Marginalization of Slavery* (Albany, NY: SUNY Press, 2011), 26.

itself from such tribalism, and erects itself into a formally universal 'open society' (term not used by Hegel)" (Miller, note to § 476).
On the strength and precondition of its detachment from "tribalism,"
the state goes on to accommodate "diversity" on its own terms. In this
way, society will have moved from "boring" or "indifferent diversity"
["einen langweiligen Schein der Verschiedenheit," PS, §15; "gleichgültigen Verschiedenheit," § 18]—"compar[ing] a camel to a French dictionary" when "there is no 'difference' between them" (C. L. R. James,
Notes on Dialectics, 84)—to "reflection in otherness within itself" (PS,
§ 18) and difference in relation (§ 125) within a "state," or political collective. Therefore, liberal interpretations turn the ruin of the state in *Antigone* into a cautionary tale that promotes "the diversity that a city must
of necessity encompass"[3]—a good synopsis of postracialist tolerance.

Both the drive to regulate diversity and the larger project of the *Phenomenology* reflect in "the moral view of the world," where, according
to Hegel, "morality" faces off with avowed complicity. Still at the border of the historical world, the "individual self" of ethics, which Hegel explains has "passed away," and the "legal person" with which "the
movement of the world of culture and faith does away," remain present:

> The ethical world showed its fate and its truth to be the Spirit that
> had merely passed away in it, the individual self. This legal person,
> however, has its Substance and fulfillment outside of that world.
> The movement of the world of culture and faith does away with this
> abstraction of the person, and, through the completed alienation,
> through the ultimate abstraction, Substance becomes for Spirit at
> first the universal will, and finally Spirit's own possession. Here, then,
> knowledge appears at last to have become completely identical with
> its truth; for its truth is this very knowledge and any antithesis be
> tween the two sides has vanished, vanished not only for us or in itself,
> but for self-consciousness itself. In other words, self-consciousness
> has gained the mastery over the antithesis within consciousness it
> self. This antithesis rests on the antithesis of the certainty of self
> and of the object. Now, however, the object is for consciousness
> itself the certainty of itself, viz. knowledge—just as the certainty
> of itself as such no longer has ends of its own, is therefore no lon
> ger [contained] within a determinateness, but is pure knowledge.
> (PS, § 596)

3. Vigdis Songe-Møhler, "Antigone and the Deadly Desire for Sameness," in *Birth,
Death, and Femininity: Philosophies of Embodiment*, ed. Robin Schott (Bloomington:
Indiana University Press, 2010), 230.

Societies that are here called "ethical" and glossed by Miller as "tribal" might be just as heterogeneous as modern ones, but without a perspective of state and global relation from which to grasp their internal variety, they are thought unable to appreciate difference. The passage through and beyond legal abstraction realizes difference, as culture produces nature and multiculturalism produces "diversity": "the eidos of the 'postracial' and its corresponding regulatory norms ... arbitrat[e] the threshold in relation to which certain acts are considered political."[4]

Not only do ethical and legal forms pass away in an ongoing sense, Hegel also cultivates *different types* of passing away before "the ultimate abstraction."[5] Different *kinds* of differences subtend the continuum of "difference," as it is known in multiculturalism. Remnants of the individual self and legal person linger at this juncture of the process, still discernible, in contrast with forms of life that Hegel classes as "immediate" and arrays in a spectrum from vegetation to Asians. Sublation entails that they too must be here, but they aren't clearly discernible, implying that consumption of different sorts—from caloric to cultural—fills this realm. Ethical and legal being, in contrast, appear as historical processes always being made from immediate forms of being—which is to say, they are always *making* immediate forms of being. "Germany" is mocked by association with these "immediate" forms of life on which, according to Hegel, ethical forms in general supervene. The immediate forms are not named; correlation with *World History* dares the reader to confirm the stereotypes and guess, with Miller, that again, "tribal" societies are included. As in Shelley, blackness appears not in a proper name but in the absence of any, as in the antiblack *logic* of *World History*, the "forms of life" are singularly significant *en masse*. The mass that history's consumption produces helps us to connect sublation and its indefinite border to Palmer's analysis of blackness' function "as the raw material of the world, as what makes the world possible" in "Europe's domination of the globe."[6]

Immediate, ethical, and legal forms of life not only hold different places in the sequence, they also are not sublated in the same *way*, and

4. M. Ty, "The Resistance to Receptivity: or, Spontaneity from Fanon to Kant," *Cultural Critique* 113 (2021): 1–27, 21.

5. Hegel's ultimate abstraction is interpreted in liberalism as the synthesized collective substance and abstraction of "a state which comes close to the true embodiment of the Idea," as Charles Taylor phrases it in *Hegel* (Cambridge, UK: Cambridge University Press, 1975), 377.

6. Palmer, "Otherwise Than Blackness," 253. On enslaveability, see David Eltis, "Europeans and the Rise and Fall of African Slavery in the Americas: An Interpretation," *American Historical Review* 98 (1993): 1399–1423.

with the sub-Saharans of *World History* in mind, the border is indefinite and *sublated* may not be the right word. It may be that they are not
exactly sublated to the extent to which they are apparently not involved
in collective realization. Hegel's program for Spirit in *Phenomenology*
§ 596 is that "Substance" becomes universal and fully historical. Ethical individuals and legal persons are in the spotlight in and through
their "pass[ing] away," both edifying and being edified. For Hegel, immediate forms of life are also objects of history, but they aren't distinct enough—their history isn't distinct enough—for their possible
edification by historical process to be recounted.[7] More clearly they enable historical process by being (in yet again internally differentiated
fashions) the fuel of it,[8] according to the "clear differentiation of the
grades of objects and the *grades of cognition*" Hegel enables (C. L. R.
James, *Notes on Dialectics,* 166; my italics; the parallelism carries my argument). They are undifferentiated in comparison with the presences
of sublated ethical individuality and legal personhood, nameable even
though their day is being effaced too;[9] their being *alone* can no longer
be differentiated.

Phenomenology is not just a theory of self-realization and educative
undoing but one that frankly celebrates historical subjects' *dependence*
on what might elsewhere have been thought of as alien to history, but in
Hegel is "still present" after it has "passed away." The world continues to
produce vegetables, animals, Africans, and Asians whose potential continues to oscillate. The implication is that history's eventual consumption of the historical self as well, which is quite actual, bids to legitimate
it, but the series reveals the difference between being consumed historically or nonhistorically. Nonhistorical consumption constitutes the
condition for the radical Hegelian to affirm complicity with inevitable
violence and to submit itself to it, either as a price for future relief or,

7. Erin C. Trapp theorizes how work on environmental loss can use psychoanalysis's
supposition of "a primary state of object-relating" that "takes place between an individual *and an environment*," locations that "only later cohere into the positions of subject
and other" ("Human Rights Poetry": 367–394, 373; my italics). She observes that the un-
dialectical dyad of subject and environment "is the operative racialized logic of Europe"
(374). Hegel's natural philosophy thus suggests the need for a more critical psychoanalysis of incorporation. A counter-Hegelian environmental project might reflect on "whatever in the material world can't be made to appear or stand in front of or alongside one
as a singular, person-like entity" (Anne-Lise François, "Passing Impasse," *Comparative
Literature* 72 [2020]: 240–257, 253).

8. Critical notions that might help to explore this unspecific support further include
the anaclitic in psychoanalysis, fungibility in afropessimism, *hylē* in deconstruction.

9. For Spivak, space off the scale of history "*is* a blank, though generative of a text of
cultural identity" inscribed in the West (*Critique of Postcolonial Reason,* 6).

more negatively, in order to assume the present contradiction. In this context, an explicit affirmation of dependency is what Hegel's critique of morality is about to require.

"Morality" as Queer Realization?

How does this proximate organization and sublation of forms of life prepare for the episode narratively close to it, the scuffle between the Brave Soul—a stand-in for the political subject of realization—and a "moralist," a likeness for Kant and other romantic writers?

According to Hegel, the scenes are related because the first is necessary, the stage of all participation in reality, while "moral" thinking exhibits resistances, not to dependency on that violent reality (as all concerned agree) but to affirming its dependency. This dispute can only occur among coparticipants in the legal world, explicitly so. The Brave Soul's rather one-sided dispute with the Beautiful Soul will be a civic dispute, the first of three civic disputes I read in part 3.[10] The term *moral* obscures the fact that other questions are also at issue. In fact, the episode neither surpasses morality nor portrays moralism as only exercised by some–the narrative is moralized on all sides.[11] The Brave Soul exhorts complicity and opposes to that a paraphrase of what Kant writes about morality and individual judgment. The satiric sketch of the Beautiful Soul materializes as a personification of that paraphrase. But it's unclear that the Beautiful Soul says anything having to do with complicity, instead "mutely keeping himself to himself" (§ 667).

According to Hegel the Beautiful Soul, as a personification of "morality," denounces society, like a Social Justice Warrior of "privatized ethics,"[12] and "does not possess the power to renounce the knowledge of itself which it keeps to itself," knowledge of its own complicity. Insofar as it lacks the power of double negativity and consequent self-realization, "the self-certain Spirit, as a 'beautiful soul' ... cannot attain to an identity with the consciousness it has repulsed, nor therefore to a vision of the unity of itself in the other, cannot attain to an objective existence. Consequently, the identity comes about only negatively, as a being devoid of Spirit ... lacking an actual existence, entangled in the

10. In § 8 I'll go on to discuss a version of the same dispute using materials from Hegel's biography and historical details of Napoleonic Prussia.

11. Even within the vocabulary of morality, it would be more accurate to say that two kinds are at stake: the morality of sincerity (Brave Soul) and the morality of authenticity (Beautiful Soul).

12. Drew Milne, "The Beautiful Soul: From Hegel to Beckett," *Diacritics* 32 (2002): 63–82, 65.

contradiction between its pure self and the necessity of that self to externalize itself" (§ 668).

Hegel's sketch of the Beautiful Soul draws biographically on the mystic poet Novalis; the doomed philosopher-poet Hölderlin, who had been acquainted with Hegel; and others. Too brief and anonymized to constitute a dialogue with any one writer, these pages instead indicate how Hegel wants anything like Kant's inner law to be received. According to the Brave Soul, the Beautiful Soul declines to acknowledge its public self; is "forgiven" by the subject of the reader's focalization, the narrator, whom I've called the Brave Soul, who realizes that he is externalizing his own complicity with the Beautiful Soul, in turn; ignores the Brave Soul's apology; and wastes away from his inability to assume a positive existence.

Now, Kant's philosophy arises from his clearly queer alienation from traditionalist conceptions of how social norms work, and his invention of inner law exhibits a permanent conflict between existence and normative ethics.[13] As his exposition of transcendental illusion especially explains, Kant does not believe that self-transformation is always possible, nor that the avowal of the self as is can always be desirable. The self-transformation of a subject whose innermost desire is unrealizable publicly is in doubt: "Experience can only teach him empirically what he is or what he is supposed to be under empirical conditions. Man only knows about himself via pure reason (a priori), he recognizes the ideal of humanity, which, in comparison to him as a human being, makes the character of his species visible and describable through the frailties of his nature that limit the archetypal image."[14] Kant's withholding of an affirmation of social dependency interrupts the celebration of "interdependency" Hegel wishes to orchestrate, not by withholding affirmation of social reality altogether, as Hegel assumes, but through an antagonism between one social reality and another. Similarly, while Hegel avers that Kant's position amounts to a rigid "I=I," it may be rigid, but as "I≠I"—a more Hegelian starting place. The quandary in Kant is that of a self whose existence involves the social foreclosure of its externalization amid the also social demand for it. "Entangled in the contradiction

13. *Looking Away* interprets the Kantian architectonic through queerness (73–113). Clark's "Kant's Aliens" further assesses Kant's queerness in relation to his antiblackness ("Kant's Aliens: The *Anthropology* and Its Others," *CR: The New Centennial Review* 1 [2001]: 201–289).

14. Immanuel Kant, *Anthropology from a Pragmatic Point of View*, trans. Victor Lyle Dowdell (Carbondale: Southern Illinois University Press, 1978), 287n108; my italics.

between its pure self and the necessity of that self to externalize itself" (§ 668), the socially externalized form of inner law does not yet exist.[15]

Within this context, Kant's "dualism" marks the spot of a lose-lose scenario. There is no realization of anything but duality, yet realization as something or other is all society offers: when "others, therefore, do not know whether this conscience is morally good or evil, or rather they not only cannot know... they must take it to be evil" (§ 649). The Beautiful Soul's demise in self-consumption (Novalis died of tuberculosis at the age of twenty-eight; Hölderlin suffered from a debilitating mental illness), and the critical response to it, shows these limited possibilities. Milne points out that Hegel's allusion to Novalis's tuberculosis becomes an occasion for wider moralization, as critics take the opportunity to either call the allusion cruel or imply that the Beautiful Soul deserves it (Milne 2002, 70).[16] Or both. Comay mentions that the "biographical signposts ... cruelly, ludicrously" make fun of Novalis's death. Then, praising the precision of the metaphor, she joins in: "the infinite contraction of a subjectivity withdrawn into itself (as Hegel later characterizes madness [and so Hölderlin too—RT]) presents the mirror image of the infinite dispersal of a body reduced to its elemental atomic particles so as to disappear without a trace" (*Mourning Sickness*, 116). The interest of the metaphor lies in its consistency with Hegel's reality. The consumptive, disintegrating body externalizes its withdrawn condition, an externalization past voluntarism, every degree of recession from participation-in-actuality corresponding to one of physical derealization, as the self's absence becomes the irreal presence of decomposing particles of a mere body. Public morcellation in Hegel's actuality becomes a law of self-retribution for the closeted performer, however much his error is thought to be a condition for a future realization. In the social totality's own terms, closeted desire, as the Brave Soul eventually agrees, does perform[17]—only, the Brave Soul doesn't like what it performs, and especially not being sure what that is.

In a still unrecognized way, the architectonic of global sublation and consumption lies beyond the legally sanctioned privacy of the closeted

15. See Dina al-Kassim's analysis of performances that are not legible before the law in *On Pain of Speech: Fantasies of the First Order and the Literary Rant* (Berkeley, CA: University of California Press, 2010).

16. For a more dynamic account, see Alan Norrie, *Law and the Beautiful Soul* (London and New York: Routledge, 2013).

17. That's why the Brave Soul realizes that they have something in common and apologizes, only to get mad again when his apology goes unreciprocated. All of this has the ring of a real-life experience.

queer. The Kant-Hegel rivalry moves between the world of the noumenon, which grounds reason in a limit at the expense of rendering the
noumenon alien, and a world where inexorable relation in nonrelation
entails historicity's access to locations without reserve.[18] Reapproach-
ing the Kant-Hegel shift, now, through the issue of access to territories puts a spin on post-Kantians' resolve to free philosophy from the
inconvenient "thing in itself ... lying forever beyond the grasp of true
knowledge."[19] Kant doesn't decline to affirm self-negation, and so self-
realization, in solidarity with the colonies. As Judy has diagnosed it,
Kant's epistemological abysses mark the edges of his negrophobia even
before he abandons his epistemology in his anthropology. Ferreira da
Silva notes that "excess figures in Kant's notions of apprehension (in
cognition) and affect (in desire)" and associates the "uncharted territory articulated and negated in Kant's version of knowledge and morality" with feminine sexuality; Moten remarks that the "formulation
of the thing [Ding] to which Kant subscribes" makes it "that to which
nothing can be imputed."[20] When Kant formalizes a sense of himself as
an alien object that would be harmed if it were available to be known,
it serves in the context of Kant's anthropology to place blackness and
Black queerness beyond distance. Allowing that there's more at stake
in "dualism" and "moralism" besides disadvantages for radical activity,
though, is necessary to even start a conversation about these dynamics.

In Kant, the groundless quality of moral law in the Second Critique
entails that moralities have different and incommensurable contents:
that's the Kantian social problem. His solution fatally posits the universality of the form of inner compulsion. Kantian formalism thus leads
to the letdowns of social democracy: the supposed neutrality of legal
formalisms, "separate but equal," and "don't ask, don't tell." Amid the
benefits to centrist liberalism that flow from the formalist "solution,"

18. Frédéric Neyrat's criticism of the "principle of principles of ecology and environmentalism" takes on "the idea, repeated as a mantra, according to which everything
is interconnected" (*The Unconstructable Earth: An Ecology of Separation* [2016], trans.
Drew Burk [Bronx, NY: Fordham University Press, 2019], 12). As Neyrat explains, emphasis on relation may have arisen in response to the "fatal separation between humans
and nonhuman nature established by Descartes" but quickly effects a *"return of dominion"* (137, 138).

19. Gregor McLennan, "Editors' discussion of Part I materials," in Stuart Hall, *Selected Writings on Marxism*, ed. Gregor McLennan (Durham, NC: Duke University
Press, 2021), 158–176, esp. 170. McLennan discusses Hall's concept of "articulation" as a
response to Hegelian problems of determination and relation.

20. Denise Ferreira da Silva, "To Be Announced: Radical Praxis or Knowing (at) the
Limits of Justice," *Social Text* 114 (2013): 57; Fred Moten, "The Case of Blackness," *Criticism* 50 (2008): 177–218, esp. 187.

though, incommensurability of content is never overcome on its own level, as content. It is not extinguished; it is bracketed, and the antagonism that it implies is not relieved by the realization of complicity in time but suppressed in an ominous "peace" more likely to divide space. Because of Kant's formalization, the price for autonomy in the closet is racial segregation on different continents with, as Kant sees it, different resources even for physical existence. Some differences are parted by abysses that nothing can finally and completely integrate and that antagonism cannot exactly confront, since something always remains unseen. There's a tacit insult to the surrounding political possibilities in conciliation as deadpan and lacking in social faith as Kantian formalism.[21] Many readers have been unsatisfied, and indeed Kant does not imagine social reality to be satisfying in and of itself.

Hegel's criticism of Kant underscores the threadbare quality of sociality that incorporates this much alienation. As he points out, there is no clear path from morality to ethics. The Kantian "I" may not be able to care who "you" are (§ 599):

> This otherness, because duty constitutes the sole aim and object of consciousness, is, on the one hand, a reality completely without significance for consciousness. But because this consciousness is so completely locked up within itself, it behaves with perfect freedom and indifference towards this otherness; and therefore the existence of this other-ness, on the other hand, is left completely free by self-consciousness, an existence that is similarly related only to itself. The freer self-consciousness becomes, the freer also is the negative object of its consciousness. The object has thus become... in general, a Nature whose laws like its actions belong to itself as a being which is indifferent to moral self-consciousness, just as the latter is indifferent to it. (§ 599)

Hegel perceives the hazards of a libertarian world of "free" consciousnesses. The indifference this kind of consciousness is capable of producing inspires various political effects depending on who is indifferent to whom and whose perspective one imagines. When Kant is the indifferent consciousness and the other is the Prussian censor, the result is the preservation of queer life; when Kant is the indifferent consciousness and the other is the African of his "Teleological Principles," the result is a fantasy of Black extinction. This variability itself, the fig-

21. See David L. Clark, "Unsocial Kant: The Philosopher and the Un-regarded War Dead," *Wordsworth Circle* 41 (2010): 60–68.

ure eights it traces, the divergent things that "indifference" may mean, connect, and help to bring about, is what Kant's formalism allows and obscures in a fog of sarcastic tact.[22]

As Hegel's subject overcomes alienation by finding itself on both sides of negativity as Kant cannot, Hegel is able to find fear realized and relieved only insofar as he is perceiving and fearing qualities that also exist in himself.[23] Hegel may make the reader feel humble when he writes that it is not possible, much less desirable, to hold oneself apart from others, and when he stresses the radical self's object status in history (the topic of my next section). But on this account the inevitability of object status obscures the power and access to others that that very condition demands the self perpetuate. Across from the Kantian consciousness "locked up within itself" stands the Hegelian consciousness tethered to its others by a chain that it enjoys "acknowledging" very much. The source of the enjoyment is the guaranteed availability, under the sign of common complicity, of others on whom it depends.[24]

So the conflict between transcendental and historical reason includes their common assumption of another scene of mayhem in the world. The transcendental abyss authorizes negative "freedom" and shallow legal symmetry—on which Kant defaults, as Judy observes ("Disappearing Expression," 119–120). Inevitable relation authorizes positive access by history, which defaults to seizure. The Kantian may expose another to death through indifference, perceiving the not-me as "devoid of a self" (PS, §602), and will be afraid of lacking self. The Hegelian self feeds freely on other life, life that it sees as always already common and purchased by its own travails of negativity. It feeds straightforwardly because it truly submits itself to historical process; it pays for membership in history by being abraded by it continually and embracing it. Its awareness of the extent of its own unfreedom legitimates its endorsement of a whole that can be worse than unfree. In contrast to the

22. Kant cultivates "the darkly pleasing way in which the experience of being shamed is balanced by the experience of shaming someone else," as Clark explains ("Kant's Aliens," 259).

23. This is quite the assumption, commonly repeated in the secondary literature— that if it is oneself, one needn't be afraid.

24. With that in mind it becomes possible to see, as otherwise it is not, why for Hegel it is nothing but a problem that "the freer self-consciousness becomes [in the Kantian model], the freer also is the negative object of its consciousness" (§599). Hegel means to criticize a paranoia of "dualistic" separation in which an object split off as not-me comes to be perceived as persecutorial. This criticism, however, takes ground so aggressively that any question about the capacity of complicity comes to look like a disavowal of reality altogether.

provincial Kantian who yearns for the bounded existence of the "self-subsistent" being, ruled by "laws peculiar to itself, as well as an independent operation of those laws," Hegelian self-consciousness, through the generous affirmation of its own lack of autonomy, denies others the possibility of being "indifferent to it" (to paraphrase § 599), no matter how much they beg.

On yet another level, though—and finally—the Beautiful Soul enjoys and co-creates his stance as far as he can, as the Brave Soul complains. His enjoyment suggests that reserved expression is not simply repression but another way—the only one available—of participating in all the things that the Brave Soul participates in. This too agitates the Brave Soul: What if the Beautiful Soul is not a hapless case but an all-too-competent rival architect, however effeminate? In Kant, the autonomy of the inner law with all its secrets is the power with which he builds his own negative version of the Absolute, critical standards for reality, a sublime aesthetic, and the sidereal infinities of Kantian interiority. The battery for this power is the same destruction of colonies, as the Brave Soul objects, who do not hold powers of withdrawal any more than powers of straightforward actualization. The precarity and derealization of the Beautiful Soul—readers really are ready to enjoy his death—produces a cul-de-sac within society that does limit and expose the liabilities of affirmation within it. But the Beautiful Soul's derealization by the Brave Soul's hegemonic realization does not force him, as it forces the African of world history, to actively produce his own negative value, and it does not in and of itself place his depletion at the point of reproduction of the world he and the Brave Soul share.

§ 8

Bearing to Benefit:
Complicity as Therapy

For Hegel the "international" is both a quasi-anarchic realm of radical difference and an institution of *Geist* driving forward universal rapprochement.

ROBBIE SHILLIAM, *German Thought and International Relations: The Rise and Fall of a Liberal Project*

This sliding middle runs through his work.

JACOB TAUBES, *Occidental Eschatology*

Broken Open

If anyone meets the challenge of "dark times" in the German nineteenth century, it would seem to be Hegel. Hegel's account of how Spirit "stays with" the negative in attentive observation and recollection until it "turns it into being [in das Sein umkehrt]" (PS, § 19) amounts to a therapy for damaged political subjects: how to introject objects, overcome narcissism, enter relation, open to nonrelation, and render the present into productivity and what is no longer productive into the past. At once a psychology and a theory of historicity,[1] taken as a whole it is one of the main stories that Western citizens tell of themselves from the early nineteenth century on, in a not merely geographical sense of the so-called West. It is also a story of complicity that bypasses vocabularies of imperialism and sovereignty, telling instead of the death of the illusion of autonomy for a self cracked by "the discipline of the world" and remade only insofar as it accepts itself as an object and a

---

1. This movement depends on acknowledgment that historical process is painfully destructive. The resonance with psychoanalysis is especially visible in theories of object relations, with their objects of fantasy that are inscribed by and ballast reality.

node. The terms of metabolization render the capacity for shattering and being shattered into collective prerequisites, as I suggested in part 1. As self-realizing terms, however paradoxically, these terms derealize; as the shattered self prepares for the political, it splits off foils and props. As the political transposes the racial, racialism, taking over for raciality, becomes the province of split-off features.

Hegel's writing manages dilemmas of nineteenth-century unfreedom that were felt to be disastrous by many European radicals. In doing so, it expresses anxiety about the inadequacy of European societies and states alike to their aspirations. In this tension, slavery and colonization underway before, during, and after the revolutionary activity of the late eighteenth and early nineteenth centuries may at first seem to play the part of no-part. Yet, European progressives' processing of their domestic crises illuminates their rapprochement with global violence. Complicity in that violence comes to be seen as a matter for mature political identities to avow, an evolving ethos for local and international intelligence and activity. The radical subject that emerges in these conditions, at once torn open and hardened by rupture, is able to benefit[2] from what are euphemistically called international relations: it learns

2. Meister substitutes the term *beneficiaries* for *bystanders* in order to emphasize their material gain from others' loss. In transitional justice, "an ongoing beneficiary ... put[s] injustice in the past by embracing the standpoint of a compassionate witness.... Isn't this how European colonists, imbued by classical studies, viewed their unfortunate period of overlap with preexisting cultures, which could be honored and commemorated after they were gone?" (Meister, *After Evil*, 15). Still more clearly, as mentioned above in § 4, "the cost of achieving a moral consensus that the past was evil is to reach a political consensus that the evil is past" (25).

If Meister understands the placement of the past as a necessarily political act, however, he objects not to the limits of its political nature but to the beneficiary-benefiting politics of transitional justice specifically—that is, its evasion of redistribution. He argues that the past/present line be drawn by distribution instead; the reader is "asked to consider *whose* primary loss the melancholic internalizes as his own loss or how this might affect ongoing relations with the real (external) loser" (223). Redistribution, aligned by Meister with revolutionary effects, is the real present, the present that, as in Walter Benjamin, "is *not* a transition" (Benjamin, "On the Concept of History," in *Selected Writings*, vol. 2, part 1, 1927–1940, ed. Howard Eiland, Michael William Jennings, and Gary Smith, trans. Edmund Jephcott and Rodney Livingstone [Cambridge, MA: Harvard University Press, 2003], 396, quoted in Meister, *After Evil*, 352n4, Meister's italics). For Meister, stressing a debt's excess is mostly an excuse that beneficiaries use for never paying anything.

While this excuse does exist, thought *beyond* redistribution is also required. If "after evil" is redistribution, after redistribution there would still be the question of what to do with what could not be compensated. Meister works much more deeply than usual with the psychic structures that form questions of justice. But following on his work,

how to bear to benefit. Middle-class Europeans find ways to weather global violence in the process of convincing themselves to withstand their own injuries.

The assumption of complicity resolves violence into psychic understanding no less than detachment from violence does. Unlike the trite discourses of sovereignty, though, the discourse of the Brave Soul avows *brokenness* as evidence of a shared and mutual subjection to the "discipline of the world." "Self-inflicted violence is everywhere in the *Phenomenology*," as Robyn Marasco points out, "a seemingly unnecessary violence that is also unending" yet "in fact integral to the process."[3] This helps to illuminate certain psychological mechanisms of the uniquely affectable "others of Europe" and Wilderson's "object in a world of subjects" (Wilderson, "Grammar and Ghosts," 123) alike. The designation "affectable" reserves interiority for the hegemonic European psyche: But what kind of interiority? Rather than being whole, the radical subject envisions here that only European interiority is imagined to be *really* violent, really Brave, to really process the discipline of exigent relation, so that it becomes, as Jones suggests, a subjectivity authenticated by its shattering. Without this shattering, "the condition of a meaningful life" disappears (Jones, "Inheritance and Finitude," 298).[4]

Therefore, in nineteenth-century Europe one finds a new self reflecting on affectable others and grammatical objects by arguing for the salutary effects, for consciousness, of being on the *receiving and giving* ends of historical abrasion, so long as one knows how to receive. Enjoyed by the Brave Soul, the twin realizations that (1) the "discipline of the world" does not and should not care about suffering as such, including its own and that (2) in global relation, one is always doing violence,

---

redistributive projects still need a better consideration of what to do with what cannot be compensated than the assumption that what cannot be measured must be bracketed. This act of bracketing itself indicates that the antagonism is still present.

3. Robyn Marasco, *The Highway of Despair: Critical Theory after Hegel* (New York: Columbia University Press, 2015), 45. For Marasco, despair is Hegel's "footing" for thought (56). Noting that "natural consciousness is a sacrificial figure in the dialectic of Spirit, undone at every turn so that the revelatory truth of negativity might be reassimilated into a philosophical retrospective" (50), Marasco does not consider the relationship of sacrifice to sub-Saharan Africa as a domain of faith in nature.

4. "Universal guilt ... is exclusively tied to those who possess the right to exercise it precisely because they are willing to forfeit their particularity. It follows therefore that those who have no special choice of right over mankind cannot feel guilt except through removing what is uniquely singular to them. And for this they are not celebrated, but despised and condemned" (Marriott, *Whither Fanon?*, 79).

combine into a kind of bracing cocktail of which authentic political subjects, and they alone,[5] glowingly partake.

I'll explore these therapeutics below, using Hegel's letters as a case study in acquiring a taste for complicity. It isn't easy. A graduation ritual is necessary: the fractured self has to affirm its assimilation of objectal status as a profound realization of historical dependence. Like other elements of celebratory relation I have mentioned, this narrative retains a Christian valence. It demands that dependency be formalized in conscious avowal and active participation. Affirmation of its objectal status in history vests the historical subject in society; it prescribes complicity to itself and others as a sign of political understanding. In this dynamic, the instructive damage that the "discipline of the world" does to subjects of labor and civil society glosses over noninstructive violence in an other scene. The second-order movement of distinguishing radical identity and relegating its remainder to the place of racial traits runs simultaneously with global violence itself, like a long evening shadow.

From Crisis to Primary Disorder

In the waning days of Napoleon, just after Waterloo and toward the beginning of the "Vormärz"—desolate times for European radicals, when, as Heinrich Heine wrote with gallows humor, "all of Europe became a St. Helena"[6]—Hegel was engaged in demonstrating to himself and others how *The Phenomenology of Spirit* would fare in the years following the battle of Jena. As Hegel's letters show, he is interested in this "middle period" in the survival and extension of his philosophy[7] and

5. Remember A. V. Miller's assimilation of postrevolutionary Germans' domesticity—or what Hegel reduces to domesticity—to "tribalism" (comment on PS, § 476).

6. After his defeat at the Battle of Waterloo, considered by many to be the extinction of already faded postrevolutionary reforms, Napoleon was exiled to the south Atlantic island of St. Helena. Heinrich Heine, *Sämmtliche Werke*, ed. Adolf Strodtmann and Eduard Engel, vols. 13–14 (Hoffmann und Campe, 1876), 423.

7. The major works that correspond to the period are the overlapping *Science of Logic* and *Encyclopaedia* in their various forms. An extension of the principles of the *Phenomenology* to human sciences formed along disciplinary lines, the *Science of Logic* institutionalized Hegel's theory and helped him to acquire his first professorship at Heidelberg in 1816. Thomas Pfau underlines the "palpably bureaucratic" prose and structure of the work: "the interiority of the Hegelian subject must submit to an intricate disciplinary scheme, here set forth in a bureaucratic prose that assigns each psychological state its own category, epistemological rank and relative authority" (*Romantic Moods: Paranoia, Trauma, and Melancholy, 1790–1840* [Baltimore, MD: Johns Hopkins University Press,

he thinks about this issue, in turn, through his ability to live his own theory during crisis.

German radicals did experience the post-Napoleonic years as a disaster. It's difficult to describe, and was difficult for them to describe, exactly what kind of disaster, because although they were of course disappointed that Napoleonic modernizations did not bring democracy to their communities,[8] there was also a positivity to which they objected that resists the conventional vocabulary for ruin. Critics register the difficulty when they call the postwar era in England and Europe a period of "historical chaos" or "historical confusion."[9] As many have pointed out in this connection, the idea that this period was a "restoration" of an old regime doesn't quite work as a descriptor in the absence of a revolution in between. Yet this figure of loss-without-having-had democracy captures left Hegelians' sense of suffocation.[10] Other terms for the

---

2005], 257). Abstract as it is, the grid-like structure of the *Science of Logic* also makes Hegel's philosophy more repeatable and teachable—it tells you how to use it. The system is then condensed and repeated in the *Encyclopaedia*.

8. By "democracy," I mean not only constitutional rights, but also opening of institutions to the public. Reference to "Germany" here indicates that the action is also outside Prussia.

Radicals experienced these years not only as loss of orientation and expectation but also as a positive present of administrative control in police states in which even "liberals" opposed classless suffrage (see David Blackbourn, *History of Germany, 1780–1918: The Long Nineteenth Century*, 2nd ed. [Oxford: Blackwell, 2003], 100). James Sheehan argues that the first three decades of the nineteenth century "deserve to be thought of as the apogee of the *Beamtenstaat* [official state], therefore, not simply because bureaucrats had won decisive victories over their old enemies but also because their new antagonists had not yet begun to take shape" (*German History, 1770–1866* [Oxford: Oxford University Press, 1989], 441). Calling for the termination of the monarchy before the German "Pre-Parliament" in 1848 (and so looking back at the postrevolutionary years I'm concerned with), the radical democrat Gustav von Struve began his address: "A long period of the most profound degradation weighs heavily on Germany" (Gustav von Struve, motion in the German Pre-Parliament, March 31, 1848, in Ernst Rudolf Huber, ed. *Deutsche Verfassungsdokumente 1803–1850*, Vol. 1, *Dokumente zur deutschen Verfassungsgeschichte*, 3rd ed. [Stuttgart: W. Kohlhammer, 1978], 332–334).

9. See James Chandler, *England in 1819: The Politics of Literary Culture and the Case of Romantic Historicism* (Chicago: University of Chicago Press, 1998), 432, and Nicholas Roe, *John Keats and the Culture of Dissent* (Oxford: Oxford University Press, 1999), 60, respectively. Sheehan points out that even Klemens von Metternich, the most powerful diplomat of the period, "lamented that he had been born 'too early or too late.' Earlier he might simply have enjoyed life, later he could have helped build a new society, but 'today I must devote myself to propping up rotten buildings.' A few months later he wrote, 'My most secret thought is that old Europe is at the beginning of the end ... between end and beginning there will be chaos'" (Sheehan, *German History*, 392).

10. Comay argues that the German postwar (and all historicity) is characterized by trauma in the structural sense that it is organized by an ideal revolutionary *now* in com-

postwar period avoid naming it at all. Historians of England tend to call it the "aftermath of Waterloo," and the term *Vormärz* for 1830–1848, the years "before the March" 1848 revolution, complementarily anchors the time in something that hadn't happened yet.[11] But the disaster can't be construed as social "instability" either; the "stability" that replaced this instability was the imperial German state. That was even more disastrous and can't seriously be thought of as less "confused," either, than the "historical confusion" that preceded it.

Historians David Blackbourn and Geoff Eley argued in the 1980s that Cold War histories of Europe composed in the West promoted the hindsight perception that an even longer period of even profounder degradation lay ahead for Germany, one that seemed to culminate at Auschwitz.[12] Clearly, retrospective narratives are part of the problem; the discipline of history is part of the problem and part of a statist notion of setting-to-rights the postrevolutionary "disorder." Since Blackbourn and Eley, historians have approached the German nineteenth century more as a way of life in itself, sometimes discussing how it may have been "liberal" in a different manner after all.[13] Although this kind of approach avoids the problematic notion of historical failure, it still misses the point. Eley's point is not just that scholars should stop being judgmental about the German nineteenth century but that we should ask *who gains* from their judgments.[14] The twentieth-century theory

---

parison with which the time is always too early or too late (Comay, *Mourning Sickness*, 18; for a thoughtful version of the "too early" thesis, see Lewis White Beck, "The Reformation, the Revolution, and the Restoration in Hegel," *Journal of the History of Philosophy* [1976]: 51–61). Although Real traumatic disjuncture explains the phenomena of expectation and disappointment, I would suggest that the Hegelian left—including its Lacanian formations—weaponizes openness and even trauma.

11. There is an element of this inability to actualize a positive term in the term *postwar*.

12. David Blackbourn and Geoff Eley, *The Peculiarities of German History: Bourgeois Society and Politics in Nineteenth-Century Germany* (Oxford: Oxford University Press), 1984.

13. See, for example, Konrad Hugo Jarausch, ed., *In Search of a Liberal Germany: Studies in the History of German Liberalism from 1789 to the Present* (Oxford: Berg, 1990).

Eley's critical tenor is sometimes missing from the writing of Blackbourn alone. When Eley entertains the notion of a German "revolution from above," it matters that it isn't a democratic revolution. Blackbourn, in contrast, can sound more equanimous about a society in which regulation appears as a value just as desirable as that of mutual aid. My aim is not to prescribe to people of the past what would have been good for them but to understand how the therapeutic strategies of radicals transpose antiblack violence.

14. David Scott makes a similar point about criticism of the first anticolonial states in *Conscripts of Modernity: The Tragedy of Colonial Enlightenment* (Durham, NC: Duke University Press, 2004).

of democracy's development from "liberalization" gains the benefit by blaming German exceptionalism for its "failure" to make it work. Similarly, radicals' experience is not disastrous because it fails to match the norms of revolution or even "real" liberalism. As soon as slavery is instead a criterion for disaster, revolutionary and liberal societies must also be disastrous. So—and here I may or may not be departing from the anthropological reflexivity that Blackbourn and Eley bring to their study—this cannot mean that the German police states were really fine. They were positively awful in themselves, awful to the same extent that they can seem functional.

Robbie Shilliam indicates a critical direction to take. Shilliam argues that Hegel's "political philosophy ... sought to guide Germany out of backwardness through an international dimension of social transformation, a dimension he conceptualized through the movement of *Aufhebung*" (89–90). Backtracking from Hegel's lectures on *World History* and *Religion* to earlier work, Shilliam shows that "backwardness" in other countries interlocks circularly with the fear, risen in political "confusion," that Germany is always collapsing in its own. The imperative to learn from international intrusion reflects Germany's need to internalize the lessons of France when otherwise "the pursuit of German-ness (*Deutschtum*) would essentialize and stratify political identity" (Shilliam, *German Thought*, 90). If what is not working in political identity is that it is still too racial, such an open international stance reinforces Europe's distance from Africa aspirationally at the moment when Germany's own political dilemma becomes unbearable. What is interesting here for my purposes is Shilliam's point that the "discipline of the world" is through and through internationalist, as though only the global were really the open. European violence in the colonies is recommended as a worldly discipline after the pattern of Germany's more than merely mental education at the hands of Napoleonic conquest.

Hegel establishes a framework for what it means to succeed politically in which "incorporation of a foreign subject" (Shilliam, *German Thought*, 96) is in high esteem. German citizens learn to see themselves as subjects supposed to learn from the tough love and ironies of history. Achieving this realization requires endurance ("staying with" the negative). As a result, Hegel places a peculiar stress on being able to "bear" things. Words like *ertragen* and *vertragen* (endurance, tolerance) crystallize his descriptions of transformation, and pressure settles on them. His use of *ertragen* connotes constitutional vigor—being able to weather hard knocks—but, especially in his frank letters to friends, also includes a more colloquial sense of being able to stand repulsive events. Transition, and specifically one's own change in it, is the main thing it is necessary to "endure." This self's consciousness of being wrecked by the real movement of history distinguishes it from *World History*'s "natural" sub-Saharan life, as Germany's "stagnation" and Poland's are ominous because they are difficult to distinguish from "natural" societies.[15]

Bearing It: Hegel's Dream

I would like to turn now to Hegel's imagination of these psychic processes of shattering, enduring, and complicity with violence as they appear in his letters to a friend. This will involve descent into the minutiae of everyday life in the German-speaking states, but I would like to inquire into various kinds of relationship between the mundane frustrations of civil society and the real movement of history that traverses it. As a shifting production of distinctions, this movement has been theorized by Chandler through Du Bois's global color line in constant transformation, "the operations of social and historical distinction or forms of relation."[16]

In the first decade of the nineteenth century, Hegel carried on a regular correspondence with Friedrich Immanuel Niethammer, the commissioner of educational administration for Bavaria. In these years liberalization, modernization, and democratization were already coming apart; Hegel and Niethammer are anxious in the midst of liberalization, before Napoleon abdicates in April 1814, and they worry not only about the insecurity of the administration but also of the vacuity of liberalization it offers. In his correspondence Hegel experiments with various ways of managing this worry. Although Hegel eventually converts confrontation with violence into complicity, he has difficulty getting there.

A lot of Hegel's and Niethammer's conversation pertains to the educational system for which they both worked and which was an endless source of aggravation for them both. Briefly, Niethammer was a "neohumanist" who wanted to modernize education while defending it against "utilitarians" who were narrowly interested in professional schools. He had appointed Hegel rector of a gymnasium in Nuremberg because he

15. Julia Lupton narrates the development of the early modern citizen subject as the sacrifice of "particularizing forms of cultural and multicultural identification" (*Citizen-Saints: Shakespeare and Political Theology* [Chicago: University of Chicago Press, 2014], 3). Lupton's paradigmatic citizen-saint is "willing to die for the rule of law" (88). As in her exemplary text *The Merchant of Venice*, the "costs are acknowledged if not lamented" (86).

16. Nahum Chandler, *"Beyond This Narrow Now": Or, Delimitations, of W. E. B. Du Bois* (Durham, NC: Duke University Press, 2022), 73.

knew he would be an ally.[17] Niethammer's enterprises never ran all that smoothly, and as Napoleon's defeat began to seem increasingly likely, he interpreted the newly emboldened attacks on his projects that then occurred as redoubled pressure from conservative and utilitarian forces (i.e., conservative antidemocrats and modernizing antidemocrats). Niethammer was basically right: democratization—parliamentary or otherwise—was not coming in spite of all the "liberalization" and "modernization" that had been accomplished under Napoleon. Seeing that, Niethammer tends to describe his future in apocalyptic terms. Although it is not his letters' only interest, they become a foil for Hegel's therapeutics on the pattern of Hegel's reaction to Kant. Their dynamic too might be stereotyped as structural versus moral.

Hegel was distressed about his own situation and was trying hard not to be. On the night of January 5, 1814, Hegel dreams that he "was in a large group attending a disputation in which two physiologists ... discussed the relative merits of apes and pigs." While the disputants argue about which are more human, apes or pigs,

> a loudmouthed, wide-bodied fellow named Pippel [People?] ... kept wanting to bring up still other matters, even juridical matters such as human rights, constitutions, and so forth. But the moderator, who, so to speak, played the role of fate throughout the whole proceeding, treated all matters of this sort as mere irrelevancies, mere packaging [Emballagen und Allotria]. He disallowed them from being seriously discussed, and held firm in his insistence that the issue was merely preference between the two species. But a super-clever man, murmuring in the corner more to himself, then asked the moderator— this seemed to me unrelated—whether he meant that Pippel, should he someday feel warm in his heart and head, would, as is well known, risk the shirt off his back; that aristocrats would put this to their advantage; and that Pippel would thus play the fool in a game—as in fact occurs quite legally in the name of the Devil, and has always occurred from time immemorial. The historian Zschokke then ran up to jump in, shouting that the people of Bern had already received an answer at least verbally from Zurich, but that there were still many

17. See Terry Pinkard, *Hegel: A Biography* (Cambridge, UK: Cambridge University Press, 2000), 268. Hegel's school was threatened with closure in 1810 as part of a wave of cost-cutting (Pinkard, *Hegel*, 291–292), but it survived and he continued to work there until he received an offer from the university at Heidelberg in 1816 (Pinkard, *Hegel*, 330–331).

other considerations ... and so forth. At that point I woke up and
it seemed difficult to me to have to go to class and lecture on law.[18]

In this oneiric satire on political process, Hegel dreams he is at a debate that isn't really one, and that pretends to seek democracy where
everyone knows it doesn't exist, in one of two unattractive sides. The
dream struggles with impoverished alternatives and vacillates between
them, forming a protective space. There was a Heinrich Zschokke, a
liberal historian, philosopher, and fiction writer, living in Switzerland
at the time of the dream. A local administrator during the Napoleonic
period, he is remembered as having been as enthusiastic as he appears
here (*Letters*, 301). The dream treats his earnestness as though it were as
much a part of the show as the cynicism of the professional moderator
and offstage aristocrats, as though his sincere proceduralism exhibited
the kind of irrelevance the moderator has in mind when he calls juridical issues "mere packaging" [Emballagen, packing matter: styrofoam].
As Pippel is a loudmouth, Zschokke is loquacious; Hegel curtails the
content of his message with the same weary "etc." ["u. s. f."].

In fact, Hegel had been feeling caught between apes and pigs the entire time he taught at Nuremberg. As soon as he gets there, commisera-
tion about assaults on the educational system becomes one of the main
motifs of his correspondence with Niethammer.[19] As early as 1810, Hegel is complaining that "Nobody complains ... the object is simply to
procure treasure, and those who suffered real distress and injustice are
used to the view that everything has gone to the dogs anyway" (*Letters*,
Letter 229, 304). More than any reference to repression, the complaint
that no one is complaining registers the restriction of political space.
Throughout this time Hegel regularly refers to the Allied forces with
dripping irony as "our Liberators": "if *par hasard* there are any liberated individuals to be seen I myself will stand up and watch" (*Letters*,
Letter 225, 299). Although things weren't going very well, Napoleon is
still in Paris on the night of Hegel's dream.[20] It is the Napoleonic administration that has already not left room for complaint. Likewise, the
moderator's "insistence that the issue was merely preference" is absurd

18. Hegel, G. W. F. *The Letters*, trans. Clark Butler and Christiane Seiler (Bloomington: Indiana University Press, 1984), Letter 227, 303. Hereafter *Letters*.

19. The other main topic is Hegel's desire to move on to a university post and his in-
defatigable networking to this end.

20. Napoleon acknowledged the need to take personal charge of the military cam-
paign and left Paris on January 25.

in light of the lack of distinction and merit among the choices. Defending against a void that seems to be opening up here, the possibility of a hidden, deeper rationality in the moderator's behavior furnishes some ballast against the nonevents that crowd the dream.

The highlight of the dream is the part that Hegel selects for attention by calling it "unrelated," the "super-clever" remark that attempts to get beyond the immediate debate to a game played "from time immemorial." The superclever man's observation differs from the others: it's a question, at least rhetorically; it's murmured more in spectation than participation, "more to himself" than to anyone else—which is how Hegel lectured, and how Adorno believes his writing works;[21] and it makes an effort to connect surfaces and depths beyond their immediate costs. It's tempting to see this intervention as the most Hegelian one. The superclever man asks the moderator whether, in his role as "fate," he bars "juridical" topics *because* of the likelihood that the outcome would only play into the hands of aristocrats. At least, he wonders whether this likely outcome is the true meaning of his intransigence.[22] Although in this way the dream aligns itself with supercleverness, Hegel's thoughts on waking imply that his feelings are not identical with that of the superclever man within. It seems difficult—literally, it "hits him hard"— that he must go on with his lectures on law. Now Hegel sees rational law as the only possible means of managing the conflicts of society, and he is soon to take an interest in the particulars of the new constitution, especially regarding the parameters of franchise. So it's interesting that in the dream these matters seem like filler compared to the expropriation that "occurs quite legally," so that as he wakes up it's awful to have to discuss them in public. There is a deficit, a turbulence here that is not contained.

The crushed expectations of historical subjects is the anxious ma-

---

21. Adorno cites the account of H. G. Hotho, who attended Hegel's Berlin lectures: "Exhausted, morose, he sat there as if collapsed into himself, his head bent down, and while speaking kept turning pages and searching in his long folio notebooks, forward and backward, high and low." Hotho recalls Hegel's seeming need to present every thought processively. "Hegel's writings are more like films of thought than texts," Adorno notices (*Hegel: Three Studies*, trans. Shierry Weber Nicholsen [Cambridge, MA: MIT Press, 1993], 121). Nicholsen adds that for Adorno, Hegel's language "murmurs and rustles in mimesis of the nonidentical" (xxxi).

22. Shilliam observes, "Hegel seems to think that the expansionary nature of the system of needs necessarily produces a *Pöbel*—a rabble—that has missed the mediating moment of the corporation ... Hegel warns that, in a sense, civil society can never be rich enough to solve its own problems ... This methodological problem foreshadows a very concrete developmental problem in *Vormärz* Prussia" (*German Thought*, 97–98).

trix for the racist riddle on which readers of Kant and Hegel often focus: philosophy's self-inflicted problem of how to "account for" peoples
who seem unable to gain anything from history. As Bernasconi remarks,
Kant struggles "to answer the question as to why the people of Tahiti
and Lapland bothered to exist,"[23] while for Hegel "colonization is the
solution to the problem of how to include" non-Europeans in history
(Bernasconi, "Philosophy of World History," 190). In a chain of euphe-
mistic substitutions, colonialism appears as international relation, slavery as colonialism, race as culture and "national character" (187). The
intrahistorical problem that troubles Hegel's dreams, in which Europe
is unable to model the useful state, fears the return of "useless suffering"
from overseas, even as Hegel dissolves the latter as a dilemma during his
critique of morality.[24] The difficulty redoubles the demand that Europe
must become more international, less "racial," more committed to "disaccustoming" and transition, less "backward," ad infinitum—a process
of realization in which it continues to need props and foils.

The Invention of Complicity

Something is beginning to happen in Hegel's dream that he opposes
philosophically: the local demands are becoming hard to bear. He overcomes it just as he recommends, by using complicity to place himself on
both sides of his own difficulty. This therapeutic process of integration
complements splitting, healing and returning to splitting.

Hegel's many expositions of what it means to bear something over-
whelmingly associate *ertragen* with that kind of self that comes out of
shattering transformation in the "discipline of the world." His explanations span a tension between transformation and a kind of residual
mass, built up out of former transformations, not simply flexible and
not simply individual, that ballasts transformation. As I mentioned, Hegel phrases the building up of subjectivity through *ertragen* partly as a
matter of constitution or "hardiness" that depends on participation in
absolutely open relation in nonrelation. In part II of the *Encyclopaedia*,
Philosophy of Nature, the basic equipment of an animal, by including
the capacity for sensation, includes the potential to "tolerate itself as
other [als Anderes ertragen]" so that it "can, with the hardiness [Härte]

---

23. Robert Bernasconi, "With What Must the Philosophy of World History Begin?
On the Racial Basis of Hegel's Eurocentrism," *Nineteenth-Century Contexts* 22 (2000):
171–201, 176.

24. G. W. F. Hegel, *Lectures on National Right and Political Science*, trans. J. Michael
Stewart and Peter C. Hodgson (Berkeley: University of California Press, 1995), 307.

of individuality, assimilate it and venture into conflict with other individualities."²⁵ Even this scheme echoes that of the foreign relations, "the
international dimension of social transformation," that, Shilliam clarifies, Hegel leverages against "repulsive" German identity politics (*German Thought*, 101).²⁶

The capacity to bear difference within builds up the "whole mass of
adjustments forming the concrete consciousness,"²⁷ and "a being which
is capable of containing and enduring [ertragen] its own contradiction
is a subject" (*Philosophy of Nature*, § 359). The pairing "containing and
enduring" returns to the understanding that a being may mistakenly
place the contradictions it perceives in objects "outside" itself. To be
able to contain them by attributing them to oneself instead is to be able
to bear them (here enduring is bearing as carrying). While "a psychic
shock produced by grief and pain" or, equally, "sudden excessive joy,"
runs the real risk of "the disruption of the organism, death, or insanity," one who has built up inner resources "is much less exposed [aus-
gesetzt] than others to such effects [Einwirkungen]," and performs better than "the 'natural' man who is poor in imaginative and intellectual
resources and so is unable to endure the negativity of a sudden violent
attack of pain [die Negativität eines plötzlich hereinbrechenden gewal-
tigen Schmerzes zu ertragen]" (*Philosophy of Mind*, § 401). The "natural
man," meanwhile, is always Hegel's own split-off figure. The inability of
the "natural man" to embrace creative destruction stands as a warning
to German society, as societies failing to meet "the standard by which
others were externally pressured to transform internally, else wither and
die" (Shilliam, *German Thought*, 111). "Racialism" in *World History* and
domestic "backwardness" enliven one another; the insufficiently relational activities of sub-Saharan Africa shadow the geographical disadvantages of landlocked Prussia.

"Naturally," Hegel continues, "those who through a life rich in activity and experience have developed a more independent human nature,
are better able to endure [besser zu ertragen] the *loss of a part* [den

25. G. W. F. Hegel, *Philosophy of Nature (Part Two of the Encyclopaedia of the Philosophical Sciences)*, trans. A. V. Miller (Oxford: Clarendon Press, 1970), § 344; henceforward *Philosophy of Nature*.

26. Given the repulsiveness of identity, it may help to restate the point that tends
to be lost in its glare. To the extent that realities other than the political disappear into
identity politics or *racialism*, they are replaced with gratifying fantasy substitutes for the
political identity.

27. G. W. F. Hegel, *Philosophy of Mind (Part Three of the Encyclopaedia of the Philosophical Sciences)*, trans. William Wallace and A. V. Miller (Oxford: Clarendon Press,
1971), § 408; henceforward *Philosophy of Mind*.

Verlust eines Teiles] of what constitutes their world than those who have grown up in simple circumstances" (*Philosophy of Mind*, § 402; my italics). The theory of the building up of subjectivity as the capacity for bearing transformation portrays a "hard," yet complexly layered self up to the task of exposing itself to the agents of change, thus hinting that part of the self up for change (that part *doing* the exposing and weathering) is already able to handle change to the rest. The figure implied—not the usual growth figure for transition but one that's necessarily compatible with its discourse—is that of a substance weathering erosion. Erosion is a form of transformation: response to negativity in the form of erosion would mean experiencing oneself as the partial agent of what would otherwise be "the loss of a part." The self having this experience feels that it is on both sides of a conflict, and so—Hegel interestingly assumes—cannot be simply diminished if it is making cuts to itself.

Identifying oneself in complicity with the sources of one's "grief or pain" can be therapeutically powerful. But alternatives to it are not well presented in the foils that Hegel offers—namely, recourse to an external enemy, a victimized self, or exteriority altogether.[28] Instead, the impression that naive externality is the main alternative arises *when* complicity becomes the norm, just as "individuality" only makes sense with relation. Throughout, the notion that there is no question for the healthy self of a *failure of bearing* negativity depends on Hegel's idea that a "lack" "is a lack only in so far as the lack's overcoming is equally present in the same thing, and contradiction is, as such, immanent and explicitly present in that thing" (*Philosophy of Nature*, § 359). So, things necessarily contain some of their opposites because they exist within the space of relation and nonrelation, and that space refocuses the self because the self is not "outside" it:

> Pain has therefore not reached mind from the outside as is supposed when it is asked in what manner pain entered into the world. Nor does evil, the negative of absolutely self-existent infinite mind, any more than pain, reach mind from the outside; on the contrary, evil is nothing else than mind which puts its separate individuality before all else. Therefore, even in this its extreme disunity, in this violent detachment of itself from the root of its intrinsically ethical nature,

28. Vincent Lloyd groups critics of Hegel into those interested in reconciliation and others interested in "thematizing exteriority," including "a position of exteriority" associated with blackness ("Hegel, Blackness, Sovereignty," in *Nothing Absolute*, ed. Chepurin and Dubilet, 174–187, esp. 178). But he does not cite any such critics.

in this complete self-contradiction, mind yet remains identical with itself and therefore free.... Thus, for example, the idea of "house" is completely contradictory to my "I" and yet the latter endures it. But mind *endures contradiction because* it knows that it contains no determination that it has not posited itself, and consequently that it cannot in turn sublate. (*Philosophy of Mind*, § 382, trans. modified; my italics)

If the mind is able to bear self-contradiction because it knows it participates in negativity, bearable contradiction depends on the debatable assumptions that (a) anything is more bearable that one has participated in oneself and (b) the action of one part of self at the expense of another is freer than action upon oneself. (Kant's hierarchy of causal positions echoes here.) Once these possibilities have been claimed, Hegel can assume that anything that has been posited can be carried to self-negation if one bears with it, painfully changing the self as needed. As above, when the "natural man," without this perspective, served as a warning to German-speaking racialism and as the conflation of sub-Saharan blackness and subpoliticality, complicity appears as an internal assumption of participation in global relation. The self reimagining its abrasion by historicity by finding its own contribution invites everyone to push against a "natural man" as a part of the self.

Isn't this already the disturbing secret of complicity—that it is just as emollient as it is sobering, and as comfortable or uncomfortable as imagining oneself nonviolent? Trapp points out, "the other side of a feeling of complicity that cycles into insight is a feeling of complicity that does not." Within psychoanalysis, she recalls, "[Harold] Searles and [W. D.] Fairbairn make strong cases for the predominance of complicity's defensive function, the way that it protects one from experiencing pain or the 'narcissistic hurts' of others rather than eliciting consciousness or insight."[29] The subject of radical capacity will go on to confess bravely, with a shot of World Spirit spirits, to benefiting from global violence.[30] The statement is both true and psychically profitable.

---

29. Erin C. Trapp, "Children-No-Longer," American Comparative Literature Association, Harvard University, March 18, 2016.

30. Writing in the context of "eco-complicity" (admission of one's contribution to environmental destruction), Chris Malcolm argues that operations of complicity show "that there is a difference between those who can assume their continuance in, and reciprocity, with reality and those who cannot"; the discourse of complicity is "a way of accepting and bearing that difference" ("Eco-Complicity and the Logic of Settler-Colonial Environmentalism," *Resilience: A Journal of the Environmental Humanities* 7 [2020], 106–131).

Returning to Hegel's correspondence with Niethammer, this international therapy is at work in contrast to Niethammer's alternative. While Hegel stresses self-transformation, Niethammer wants to maintain the consistency of his identity in a way that can be at odds with thriving. In the dialectician's language, he is the "natural man" of the story, one who rejects transformation. In November 1815—a few months after the Congress of Vienna, and again with regard to the ongoing controversies in educational administration—Niethammer writes to Hegel to "mobilize" him, he says. For "just as worms, frogs, and other vermin often follow the rain," he writes, "so the Weillers[31] and their ilk follow the dark day now spreading over the entire civilized world" (*Letters*, Letter 254, 319).[32] As in Hegel's dream of apes, pigs, and Pippel the previous year, part of the panic is that Niethammer is not dealing only with energies easily classifiable as human.[33]

It may be perplexing that Niethammer expects Hegel to feel "mobilize[d]" by a presentation of doom. But Niethammer perceives no contradiction, since he sees nothing wrong with fighting losing battles. He continues, "They have become so impudent as to declare teachers of philosophy and even mathematics to be not only dispensable but harmful in the gymnasiums.... But they must not be allowed to settle accounts with us in silence. And they must not mutilate our Protestant educational establishments on the model of the former schools for monks. Against this I want to defend myself to the last man—who I still hope to be" (*Letters*, Letter 254, 319). Niethammer takes a half-Kantian approach to the perceived loss of the human realm for effective action. He turns toward a realm of consciousness that is ultimately in-

31. Kajetan von Weiller, a Catholic theologian, had cowritten a polemic against Hegel and Schelling. See Kajetan von Weiller and Jakob Salat, *Der Geist der allerneuesten Philosophie der HH. Schelling, Hegel, und Kompagnie* [1803–1805] (Brussels: Culture et Civilization, 1974).

32. Ernst Bloch quotes this passage to convey how "everything obsolete drifted back into place" in his own generation: "So those who have apparently been restored reenact what the reaction of a century ago auditioned, as Hegel's friend Niethammer already lamented ... They re-enact that Restoration's recuperation" (*The Spirit of Utopia*, trans. Anthony A. Nassar [Stanford, CA: Stanford University Press, 2000], 235). Bloch's assumption that his generation reenacts a restoration that was already a reaction renders explicit his belief that he belongs to the same era as Niethammer, which is still repeating its favorite plays.

33. Nonhumanity is of course the usual insult to anything that seems unintelligible, and an insult within a polemic. Niethammer's rhetoric, however, serves to indicate that what has happened is on the other side of a line for him. He wishes to register a certain rupture of the frame of perpetual transition. They are living with what "follow[s]" after the dark day (a day that swallowed the world, a time that wouldn't end).

itself if it comes to it, but in the meantime is communicative. According to him, it's important to break "silence" and maintain antagonism. The faint possibility remains that unexpectedly energetic resistance will prevent the worst of the outcomes worth "defend[ing] ... to the last man," but the self is not staked on this chance. In case of the expected failure, it has its Kantianism in reserve, in which case the effort is in and for itself. The thought of being the last man, "who I still hope to be," sustains Niethammer's activity; it seems to be more realistic to "hope" to be the last man—a strange hope, which predicts the cause is lost—than to hope to succeed. In this way Niethammer is able to replace an unreachable goal with an intrinsic satisfaction. A main impetus for resistance is the chance to enact solidarity.

Hegel's reply emerges from the psychic strategy that now sounds stabilized: "The essential point is your belief that it will not get so bad we cannot bear it. Your view coincides pretty much with my own belief that we cannot hope for something good enough to merit any particular praise. This colorless, tasteless middle way [farb- und geschmacklose Mittelwesen], which allows nothing to get too bad and nothing too good, for once rules our world" (*Letters*, Letter 255, 319, trans. modified). Now, Hegel's colorlessness does not really "coincid[e] pretty much" with Niethammer's "dark day." An intermediate state is exactly what Niethammer's apocalyptic language rejects. Niethammer is saying that he *isn't* bearing it. Just as it's unclear why Hegel should find Niethammer's appeal inspiring, it's unclear why Niethammer should find Hegel's reply helpful. For Niethammer, being unable to foresee anything good enough to praise is already "so bad we cannot bear it," and as we've seen, he gets sustenance out of his inability to bear it. They agree, however, that their "world" is the realm at issue and that it is "rul[ed]" by the deactivation of "hope for something good enough." Presenting his disagreement with Niethammer as it might appear in an essential unity they must somehow share, Hegel has already located something good, so that the badness isn't "too bad." He subtly divides goodness that's good enough to praise from *another goodness that merits no praise* but is still there, functioning as a backstop. In the middle of integration splitting is still going on, necessarily. As with this backup goodness, the "middle way" "*allows* nothing to get too bad and nothing too good [welches nichts so arg und nichts so gut werden *läßt*]."

The universal space of mediation is conflated, here, with the recent disappearance of color and taste from the times. It's impossible to tell which one Hegel is talking about when he describes the "middle way" that "rules our world." That "our" world is "for once" ruled by colorlessness and tastelessness seems to make it a historical matter; but Hegel's

is the philosophy in which another middle, the sliding middle of transition, rules a much larger world, and relation is the colorlessness and
tastelessness that allows colors and tastes to be translated into one another. Insofar as what Hegel means by "middle way" has already passed
through the relation that mediates and creates extremes, there can be
no further disagreement, because by disagreeing with Hegel, Niethammer would be disagreeing with the intelligibility of things itself: with
reality, in Hegel's theory of reality. As Hegel presents the debate with
Niethammer as though from its end, his prose presents the grayness of
the times as inseparable from the standpoint of his own assimilation of
it. Hegel returns Niethammer's utterance to him rinsed of its moralized
drama: this thought experiment evokes a world in which everyone realizes that nothing is ontologically too bad or good and can negotiate
differences without hysteria, as Melanie Klein also fleetingly envisions.
Yet, the power of the therapy locates a standard of "*too* bad" suffering
elsewhere.

This limited ability to translate local conflicts corresponds to the
state's redistribution of the energies of individuals from the perspective
of its own subjectivity. It derives its power, further, from international
relations—open relation as a discipline of the world for states and sub-
states. As Marcuse points out, the limit of transformability is that "the
resulting relation between the individuals on the one hand and the state
on the other cannot be the same as that between individuals."[34] Yet citizens are invited to go over the head of the state and sign on, ultimately,
with the real movement traversing them—with its power to ground.
Hegel identifies his own position—*acceptance of* the sidelessness, so to
speak, of complicity—with the *sidelessness of reality itself* and describes
it from the point of view of the colorless "middle way" where positions
would already have appeared as "factors."

Experiencing one's own losses as their agent crests in Hegel's memorable letter of July 5, 1816. This letter upsets Niethammer with its explanation of how to get through postwar reaction:

> I adhere to the view that the world spirit has given the world march-
> ing orders ... no lingering lies or make-believe strokes in the air can
> achieve anything against it. They can perhaps reach the shoelaces
> of this colossus, and smear on a bit of boot wax or mud, but they
> cannot untie the laces. Much less can they remove these shoes of
> Gods—which according to [Johann Heinrich] Voss's *Mythological*

34. Herbert Marcuse, *Reason and Revolution: Hegel and the Rise of Social Theory*, 2nd
ed. (New York: Routledge & Kegan Paul, 2000), 174.

Letters, among other sources, have elastic soles or are even themselves seven-league boots—once the colossus pulls them on. Surely
the safest thing to do (both externally and internally) is to keep one's
eye fixed on the advancing giant. To edify the entire bustling and
eager assemblage [gesamter vielgeschäftigter], one can even stand
there and help smear on the shoe wax that is supposed to bring the
giant to a standstill. For one's own amusement, one can even lend a
hand to the enterprise that is being taken so seriously. (*Letters*, Letter 271; trans. modified)

Hegel repeats some of the material from his 1814 dream: frantic, empty
"bustling" in the foreground, an elastic world spirit "advancing," and a
warily admiring persona standing in Hegel's less elastic shoes. The "discipline of the world," rendered here as though in the imagery of anime,
is anything but romantic. The storyboard is that crude destruction razes
naive posturing. It's a recognizable plot in which awareness of deep
forces can be drawn on to manage what would otherwise cause distress.

Hegel can perceive the continuity of brutality in a way that Niethammer isn't up to. Niethammer takes the contrasting "moral" attitude; he
will be the last man accepting pollution. Hegel can touch the repulsive
commotion, unlike the Beautiful Soul who "flees from contact with the
actual world [flieht es die Berührung der Wirklichkeit]" (PS, § 685).
The Brave Soul's ethos has its benefits: looking the "colossus" in the
"shoelace" if not the eye, allowing aggression within the self (though it
becomes a new prescription), not getting isolated, seeing what people
are doing, knowing you are able to do the same; also feeling "safe . . . externally and internally," feeling superior, and in a certain way remaining incognito.[35] Yet, I suggest this vignette remains a scene of shame,
barely screening the fear of "backwardness," while backwardness re-
names helplessness. Hegel's and Niethammer's interlocking strategies
describe a double bind of activity. These positions together, like those
of Kant and Hegel, organize and reduce the supposed spectrum of pos-

35. In a follow-up, Hegel persists in recommending "Schadenfreude" until Niethammer finally responds with a civil objection:

It is possible that the giant you describe advancing with his seven-league boots
respects good intentions as little as bad, and that he is right to trample down the
work of all equally as something miserable. In any case, it is only by the result that
the individual can know whether he is marching with or against him. But since
the giant merely strides on, leaving to the individual the task of making, pain or
joy over the destiny of individuals is inseparable from hope in the *pleroma*. At
least to me it cannot be a matter of indifference to lose the people with whom I
had hoped to act in common. (*Letters*, Letter 288)

sibilities, which outside Germany are worse as well as better, but not for them. The supposed insularity of the German-speaking territories that can't find their way to democracy defaults to international relations, turning from France to the colonies and back again. As Germany languishes in unfreedom or aspires to learn openness from France, the left Hegelian learns to embrace disjunction itself.

Civil society that is not good enough to praise remains whether they can bear it or not, a fallback world that is supposed to be good enough because of the knowledge that nothing further can be expected, good enough without being at all praiseworthy. As Hegel remarks, the principle of nothing's being too good or bad rules "our world."[36] Like the Beautiful Soul and the Brave Soul, neither Niethammer nor Hegel notices that both the middle way and the rising panic are mediated by the too bad. The letters' debate over stances of complicity and naive resistance rests on the silent question of what violence would be "too" bad—or too good.

36. Marcuse argues that Hegel's underlying concern is perpetuating civil society's quotidian world: "for Hegel, differences in political form between nations did not matter so long as the underlying identity of social and economic relations was uniformly maintained as that of middle-class society" (*Reason and Revolution*, 185–186).

§ 9

Not "Non-political Distinctions": A Phrase in Marx Revisited

> What this people should be in and for themselves, this being-themselves, is what in their own eyes they are not.
>
> HEGEL, *The Phenomenology of Spirit*

Nonpolitical Distinctions

In §§ 7 and 8, I considered how Hegel constructs European civic rivalries between resistance and complicity, in which Hegel argues for the realization capacities of complicity. In this way, contaminated and shattered subjectivity open to historical hurt, rather than one that claims sovereignty, supports its dependence on global violence. At the same time, insufficiently mature domestic political stances are pressured with comparison to the "racialist" subpolitical colonies. In § 9, I turn to a counter-Hegelian exploration of the mechanisms that render domestic foils nonpolitical in early Marx and Marx's deployment of slavery and franchise in North America. Together, the three sections of part three form the European circuit of a loop back to the beginning of this book in Hegel's direct charges of African "racialism" and his antiracist incorporation of a political protagonist slave of dialectic at the expense of other slaves.

In the first part of "On the Jewish Question" (1843),[1] Marx responds to his left Hegelian friend Bruno Bauer, who, himself involved in another exchange, had argued that Prussian Jews should consider themselves as universal subjects and, consistently with that, should aban-

---

1. "On the Jewish Question," in *Collected Works*, vol. 3, by Karl Marx and Friedrich Engels, trans. Clemens Dutt (London: Lawrence Wishart, 1974), 146–174. Henceforward OJQ.

don their demands for emancipation as Jews.[2] In this context Bauer calls on the German-speaking nations likewise to abandon Christianity. Marx replies by questioning the bounds of merely political emancipation: "What kind of emancipation is in question? What conditions follow[?]" (OJQ 149). Marx points out that political emancipation is as limited "for us" as religious emancipation seems limited to Bauer. Political emancipation no less than Christianity retains the function of "the intermediary to which man transfers all his non-divinity and all his *human freedom*" (OJQ 152).

Jared Rodriguez's "The Blackness of Marx's Jewish Question, a Theo-Political Remix" explores the extent to which a transposition of Marx's essay to North America can help to express why political goals are inadequate for Black Americans.[3] I am also interested in what "On the Jewish Question" has to say about the relationships between what Marx calls "non-political distinctions" (which can also be translated "non-political differences") in a narrow juridical sense that appears in Marx's essay and a wider sense, drawn from contrast and comparison with Hegel, in which any political identity is the product of a larger order of realization and derealization. In the narrow sense, Marx's analysis of Prussia's creation of Jewishness as "non-political" clarifies that political excess is racial. In the wider sense, Marx is interested in what happens when a polity "lifts" [hebt] a legal restriction, for which he uses the language of "annulment" [Annullation]. He brings out how the lifting of the law creates "non-political"—in this instance, no longer political—"distinction" as a space in which people live—a fragile space at risk from both polity and civil society. When a polity "annul[s]" a law, the power that formalized the distinction continues to exist, first as a threat to make law (demonstrated in its ability to unmake law); second, as reconfigured legal pressure; and third, as extralegal violence. The lifting of discriminatory law is the condition of possibility for the vigilante if the law is so idealized that the social sources of its power are erased. In practice, the liberalization of antisemitic restrictions after the Edict of 1812 exposed Prussian Jews to vacillations in their legal rights (which Marx's family experienced) and to conditions attached to rights that reshaped Jewishness to the advantage of the state and Christian society. Patchen Markell explains how, even as the Edict "liberated Jews from

2. Bruno Bauer, *The Jewish Problem* [1843], trans. Helen Lederer (Cincinnati, OH: Hebrew Union College-Jewish Institute of Religion, 1958).

3. Jared Rodriguez, "The Blackness of Marx's Jewish Question, a Theo-Political Remix," *An und für sich*, October 8, 2018, unpaginated, https://itself.blog/2018/10/08/the-blackness-of-marxs-jewish-question-a-theo-political-remix/.

some restrictions, it also subjected them to novel forms of subordination precisely in order to secure the sovereign self-image of Germans."[4]

In this context, Marx reflects that canceling political distinctions
produces "non-political distinctions":

> the political annulment of private property [for voting] not only fails
> to abolish private property but even presupposes it. The state abol-
> ishes, in its own way, distinctions of *birth, social rank, education*, and
> *occupation* when it declares that birth, social rank, education, and
> occupation are *non-political distinctions*, when it proclaims, without
> regard to these distinctions, that every member of the nation is an
> *equal* participant in national sovereignty, when it treats all elements
> of the real life of the nation from the standpoint of the state. Nev-
> ertheless the state allows private property, education, and occupa-
> tion to act in their way, i.e., as private property, as education, as oc-
> cupation, and to exert the influence of their special nature. Far from
> abolishing these *factual* distinctions [diese faktischen Unterschiede
> aufzuheben], the state only exists on the presupposition of their ex-
> istence; it feels itself to be a *political* state and asserts its universal-
> ity only in opposition to these elements. (OJQ 153, trans. modified)

This passage implies more than that a state needs to be the state of a
society. Introducing that point and hanging over it indefinitely is the
state's act of annulment, its simultaneously negative and positive "de-
clar[ation]" of the *existence* of "non-political distinctions," differences
that no longer need to be contested legally. Marx contends that this
kind of declaration of nonpolitical distinction has a special function in
binding civil society to the state.

The implications of nonpolitical distinction as a special private and
state-sponsored zone are expanded by the proximity of "annulment" to
sublation.[5] *The Phenomenology of Spirit*, as we've seen, describes sublated entities in terms of their continuation. While Marx's better-known
idea about sublation is that it "displaces ... entities from 'their actual ex-

4. Patchen Markell, *Bound by Recognition* (Princeton, NJ: Princeton University
Press, 2003), 127–142, 127.

5. Marx distances the comparison. He uses the word, but only in its meaning of "abolition" rather than in its meaning of sublation, when grammatically it can have both
meanings. "Annulment [Annullation] ... not only fails to abolish [aufgehoben] ... but
presupposes," Marx writes. Yet, Marx's annulment is for exactly that reason closer to the
other sense of Aufhebung, sublation.

istence' and transform[s] each of them into a philosophical concept,"[6] sublation, like annulment, entails continued existence. Sublation and its interpretations variously emphasize preservation and supersession. If we take sublation to be the loosing of Spirit from its husk, its dislodgment from a confining structure, the entity contributes to a new form of life. Pippin therefore develops sublation into an image of emancipation (e.g., Pippin, *Hegel's Realm of Shadows*, 140). When sublation is taken as having a bearing on emancipation, then there is strain between this liberatory register and the implication that sublation cannot be *only* abolition from the previous structure, even if it would like to be. Sublation is also afterlife and remainder. In the case of transition from ethical to legal forms of life I considered in § 7, the reader may imagine the scatter of ethical practices being replaced by legal formalizations while instances of those same practices continue unaware that theirs is no longer the single force, and other practices that were once legal continuing after they are no longer legal. In the transition to legality, should the persistence of parallel ethical practices be considered husks of a formerly central ethical life? And what is the husk of a lapsed law? In Pippin's consideration of Hegel's treatment of Roman slavery, it's clear that slavery "contravenes [the Romans'] own conception of law" (*Hegel's Realm of Shadows*, 151) but less clear how the reader should imagine the afterlife of the institution nonetheless. Not only does Hegel allow for the persistence of regressive entities such as people who aren't ready to live a new dispensation; to Hegel's bitterness the German nations are one enormous regressive persistence. Marx pauses over the question of what to call the heaviness of a lifted restriction.

In "annulment" Marx deals with the uncanny effects for those enveloped in a disestablished legal distinction. An "annulment" in law declares the invalidity of a previous law. It may declare that it never was legitimate; yet it is *unable to make it nothing at all*.[7] Speech act philos-

---

6. Ranajit Guha, *History at the Limit of World-History* (New York: Columbia University Press, 2002) 3.

7. "On the Jewish Question" builds on Marx's "On a Proposed Divorce Law" two years earlier. Marx argues that divorce at will is individualistic, and that a "dead" marriage is dead not because it has been legally ended but because people have killed it. "The legislator," then, "can only determine when it *may* be dissolved, though essentially it already is dissolved" ("On a Proposed Divorce Law," in *Writings of the Young Marx on Philosophy and Society*, ed. and trans. by Lloyd D. Easton and Kurt H. Guddat [New York: Anchor/Doubleday, 1967], 141). The marriage here resembles Rousseau's state of popular sovereignty, which ceases to exist—whatever persists after it—in the moment it loses social legitimacy.

opher Laura Caponetto points out that what is annulled is commanded by authorities to lose all present and future force, as if it were nothing. But at a minimum, it retains its powers in the past tense and in the effects of its specific past. "Since the past is not open, nobody can 'make undone things that have once been done,'" she writes, quoting Aristotle: "Agathon is right in saying, 'For this alone is lacking even to God, to make undone things that have once been done.'"[8]

The newly nonpolitical distinction of Prussian Jews is neither a kind of content nor a degree of intensity. According to Marx, he is concerned with distinction that persists "factual[ly]" beyond its annulment. (I will come back to the problematic word *factually*.) For Caponetto, strictly speaking, no annulled distinctions lie entirely outside this category. Marx's exploration enriches the understanding of polities invested in the achievement of a postracial society: *legally disestablished discriminatory categories contribute through their disestablished quality*[9] to the "self-awareness" of the "political state." Further, Marx's point bears repercussions for Hegel that show in his other criticisms of Hegel. Pausing on the concrete instance of annulment, finding annulled spaces still occupied, Marx gives us fuel to question the effects *of sublation*, which is not just a legal process but also a historical and material one. What prevents the categories created by sublation from operating at the level of history, in the way that nonpolitical distinctions function for the state—as foils for the self-awareness *of history*?

From here, there are two simultaneous tasks: to pause on what it means to talk about the state or history as having *self-awareness*, and to locate the difference Marx is making in comparison to Hegel. It will be easier to talk about the latter first, as it lays a ground to talk about self-awareness after. So what kind of intervention is Marx making? First, Hegel, and similarly Bauer, often treats the "non-political" as a position *not yet* political, not *fully* political. This is not simply a chronological matter but a retroactive one—that is, one of realization. Regardless, Hegel's illustrations of the nonpolitical are often what he believes to

8. Caponetto quotes Aristotle, *Nicomachean Ethics*, VI; see the translation by David Ross and W. D. Ross (Oxford: Oxford University Press, 1980), 139–141. She goes on to discuss how some "illocutionary acts appear to invalidate, at least to some extent, the logic of the 'closed past'" ("Undoing Things with Words," *Synthese* 97 [2020]: 2399–2414). Rather, pasts are made different by futures, but not simply by a decree.

9. Viren Murthy remarks that "with these words, Marx develops a politics of depoliticization" ("Beyond Particularity and Universality: Moishe Postone and the Possibilities of Jewish Marxism," *Jewish Social Studies: History, Culture, Society* 25 [2020]: 127–167, 139). As the phrase implies, however, *politicization* works through the politics of depoliticization.

be the isolationist and "racialist" practices of religions and kinship societies from Africa to Prussia that have not yet constellated awareness
of global relation and complicity. Marx points out now, in keeping with
the retroaction above, that Hegel does acknowledge the state's creation
of nonstate society in general. In *Critique of Hegel's Philosophy of Right*,
Marx notes, "it is the state which divides itself into ... family and civil
society" to return to itself through them:

> It is the state which *divides* itself into them and *presupposes* them, and
> does this "in order to leave behind its ideality and to become *explic-
> itly infinite* actual spirit." "It divides itself in order to ..." [um aus ihrer
> Idealitat fur sich endlicher werklicher Geist zu senn]. It *thus lends* to
> these spheres the materiality of its actuality, *in such a way that* this
> lending, etc., *appears* mediated [*vermittelt* erscheint] ... the logical,
> pantheistic mysticism is strikingly apparent. (CHPR, 155)

For Hegel, the solidity of these categories is "lent" by the state: "it lends
to these spheres the material of its actuality, *in such a way that* this lending, etc. *appears mediated*" (CHPR, 155). And Marx thinks that Hegel
is wrong about this: Marx distinguishes between the superficial mediation of the state and the real mediation of society. He reads these
sentences as a "pantheistic" reversal of the truth that the state borrows
its actuality from social practices. Hegelians might want to condescend
to Marx when he refers to the nonpolitical distinctions as "factual distinctions," as if mediation had halted and their given existence were revealed. If we do, though, it becomes harder to see that Marx is beginning to work on value by working on nonpolitical differences.

The most general level of nonpolitical distinction involves all social
categories, on a plane that Derrida calls "racination" (*Of Grammatology*, 101)—any projection of the given reality of an entity as its structure or genesis. Marx uses "race" in this way, to satirize the reification
of relations into identities in general. In the German states, property
qualifications and regulation of occupations controlled access to citizenship,[10] and so antisemitic professional restrictions were layered on

---

10. This situation is closely connected to debates on slavery and capitalism through
the idea of "varieties of capitalism," "the 'stickiness' of existing political economy institutions and their inability to change" (Marcel Hoogenboom, Christopher Kissane, et al.,
"Guilds in the Transition to Modernity: The Cases of Germany, United Kingdom, and
the Netherlands," *Theory and Society* 47 (2018): 255–291, 257. According to Hoogenboom
et al., after the "formal abolition of guilds," social practices often kept up "the old regulatory mechanisms ... far into the nineteenth century." This logic again takes up the mechanisms of social marking and naturalization.

an already reified order: "What a sight! Society is forever splitting into the most varied races opposing one another with petty antipathies, bad consciences, and brutal mediocrity, and precisely because of their mutually ambiguous and distrustful situation they are all treated by their rulers as merely licensed existences, without exception, though with varying formalities."[11] Occupations here lend the absurd form of licensed toleration to more general forms of life and, for Marx, demean what it means to exist in Prussia. I cannot tell whether Marx's irony supposes that race usually has a deeper basis than Prussian law's petty production of types, or whether the pettiness, for him, characterizes what race is anyway. At any rate, these "licensed existences" had shaky connections to social necessity and yet operated, and the obverse condition was also obvious, that distinctions "lifted" from legality continue to work. Even if the processes are unthematized, in the essay's reflection on legal withdrawal the overlap between sublation and nonpolitical distinction is making room for a political ontology of human difference. It can sometimes feel like there is only one conscious radical enlightenment theory of race, one that proposes that race is the tool of juridical and economic bounds. Yet the reader can see in the essay that in 1843, Jewishness cannot be fully explained by law or, as Marx goes on to remark, by religious activity. Nor is Jewishness ever exhausted by law and religion in Hegel, as Marx helps to illumine.[12]

To go any further into the dimension of lifted distinctions, I need to return now to Marx's comment that the state "feels itself to be a *political state* and asserts its universality only in opposition to" social phenomena. With "feels itself," Marx seems to be doing the same "pantheistic" thing he criticizes Hegel for doing when, in the section of *Philosophy of Right* I quoted, Hegel makes it sound as though the state is *staging* the private spheres. Marx stresses the state's dramaturgy in Hegel: "the polity *thus lends* to these spheres the materiality of its actuality, in such a way that this lending, etc., *appears* mediated" (CHPR, 155). Both He-

11. "Toward the Critique of Hegel's Philosophy of Law: Introduction," in *Writings of the Young Marx*, 252–253, trans. modified.

12. David Lloyd's *Under Representation*, studying the persistence of "a racial 'regime of representation'" in contemporary institutions, argues that subaltern subjects who cannot be captured by representation in the larger sense of aesthetic perception become targets of state pedagogy and the foregone conclusion that "their ineradicable difference" in representational terms will leave them always subjected. The two halves of Marx's phrase, "Unable to represent themselves, they must be represented" (describing the masses in *The Eighteenth Brumaire of Louis Bonaparte*) correspond to the double bind of the colonial intellectual (*Under Representation*, 115).

gel and Marx, then, work on the problem of state "self-awareness." One nonpantheistic way of explaining this effect is to suppose that the polity's metalevel legitimations (including its legal stratigraphy) need foils to bring its political legitimacy into perceptibility; that is, that *perceptibility is constitutive in the notion of political legitimacy, and that raciality is the foil of the political.* Marx shows that the polity broadcasts its legitimacy *in the form of a shift from "exclusion" to "inclusion,"* in the parlance of minority rights. It cannot generate awareness of itself *as political* in opposition to "elements" that it is openly dominating.[13] Domination is like the master in the dialectic: it cannot "know"—that is, describe itself—as political but only as tyrannical, and if it "knew" itself as tyrannical, it would "know" itself as nonpolitical and, in that sense, delegitimate itself. These are the effects that Hegel, at least, would predict given his assumption that negativity is dynamic.

Marx's "annulment" suggests something more unexpected, namely, that if the inclusiveness of the state were perfect, it not only would not be able to "feel" its own generosity—it would also not be a state at all. It would have "passed away" as Hegel likes to say, lost its identity in its success. It would also pass out—lose consciousness. Between domination and vaporization, the political state maintains perceptibility of its universality through nonpolitical distinctions. Race may model these distinctions, or perhaps they model race; either way their nonpolitical aspect is their active ingredient. Then, when "awareness," public demonstration, is necessary to realize a capacity, it opens the desire to *keep* an object, the object that proves the capacity. Giving the state a criterial "self-awareness"—which I have interpreted to mean a metalevel of thematized perceptibility that is not simply secondary, in that it's necessary for its "primary" existence—reveals its special and one-way dependence on nonpolitical distinctions. Suppose that there had been a "complete" legal emancipation: Jews would still have been encouraged to disappear *as* their former distinction and yet remain identifiable so that the state's political legitimacy could remain identifiable. Markell notes that for Jews in the period, dealing with a patchwork of riders and effects, the result was "a vigilant surveillance. . . . The imper-

---

13. Hegel's position for Jewish emancipation, like his criticism of Roman slavery, evaluates the ill effects of subjugation *for the state*: if the Jewish population "remained in that isolation with which they have been reproached . . . this would rightly have brought blame and reproach upon the state which excluded them" (*Lectures on National Right and Political Science*, trans. J. Michael Stewart and Peter C. Hodgson [Berkeley: University of California Press, 1995], 298).

ative of emancipation becomes, paradoxically, that *the state must see at all times that each Jew has ceased to be Jewish*" (Markell, *Bound by Recognition*, 146).

Marx cites Hegel's *Philosophy of Law* at this point to clarify that he is commenting on Hegel's approval of secular polities' dependence on "non-political distinctions" of religion:

> In order ... that the state should come into existence as the *self-knowing, moral reality* of the mind, its *distinction* from the form of authority and faith is essential. But this distinction emerges only insofar as the ecclesiastical aspect arrives at a *separation* within itself. It is only in this way that the state, above the *particular* churches, has achieved and brought into existence *universality* of thought, which is the principle of its form. (Hegel, *Philosophy of Law*, 346 [§ 270])

> Exactly! Only in this way, above the *particular* elements, does the state constitute itself as universality. (OJQ, 153, trans. modified)

"Exactly [Allerdings]!" Marx exclaims. Of course: what political life brings is "only" anything insofar as it is suspended "above" the "material life" of man (OJQ, 153).

Although material life may self-sufficiently loan reality to abstractions in Marx's ontology of the moment and not later when the difference between them does not hold, his criticism of Hegel holds even when his ontology changes. The location of the political "above" the material is not important, and that is already true in "On the Jewish Question." If political life is not suspended like a religion "*above*" other practices, in a more immanent reality of social life within the political state one still "leads a double life, a heavenly and an earthly life, not only in thought or consciousness but also in *actuality* [nicht nur im Gedankenn, im BewuStsein, sondern in der Wirklichkeit, im Leben ein doppeltes, ein himmlisches und ein irdisches Leben]" (OJQ, 154, trans. modified). "Not only in thought or consciousness"—Marx refers to Hegel's complaint that Kant located the parameters of reality in his head. Hegel's improvement over Kant here is that while Kant divides social life from what he thinks it ought to be, in Hegel the diremption is "actual" on both sides, in the contrast between political relations and social relations. People can no more reach their political freedom in their social relations than Kant can live in his thoughts. It might even be less than living in one's thoughts, if investment in political life makes one think that in political forms society possesses the methods to advance well-being. As Pippin writes of Hegel's view of Kant's moral conception of freedom, the political conception of freedom is for Marx "a concept of freedom whose actualization makes the agent less free" (Pippin, *Hegel's Realm of Shadows*, 150n15). It is by viewing the nonpolitical distinction as an inhabited territory that we can find in it the foil for the violence, not of the state's domination, but of its inclusiveness—whether that inclusiveness is for anyone or for no one.

Not Nonpolitical Distinctions

The domestic nonpolitical foil is an object in reserve—an object of past and future political formation, antagonistic or collaborative, and Marx indicates that this object is raced. Marx knows that he needs to ask about this object's social as well as juridical, political, or nonpolitical formation. And there is also a further issue. Noting that the Jewish Question means different things in different national circumstances, Marx hazards that "only in the North American states—at least in some of them—does the Jewish question lose its *theological* significance and become a really *secular* question" (OJQ, 150).[14] The free states, at least some of them, enter "On the Jewish Question" as the only contemporary example of "complete political emancipation" (OJQ, 151)—meaning in the parameters of the essay that they theoretically allow all men to vote. In fact, as you know, while property requirements for franchise lifted in the 1820s in the United States, antebellum suffrage in the North was a patchwork of state laws that usually excluded Black men, while social violence was brought to bear on their every movement. Joy James presses the Marxian point that "*the state does not create legal categories in abstraction....* In the very act of (re)naming involuntary servitude [in the Thirteenth Amendment], the United States recreated rather than abolished slavery."[15] In the northern states that did not formally restrict suffrage, would the situation of Black men holding rights to vote be for Marx that of the nonpolitical distinction "tossed among the multitude of private interests" (OJQ, 155, trans. modified), caught between "*political emancipation*" and "*human* emancipation" (OJQ, 155)?

14. It's not completely clear how the North is more secular than the South in 1843. While the Confederate constitution did declare its Christian identity, this did not happen until 1861. Is Marx referring to not yet formalized affirmations of Christian identity in the slave states that he might have known about in 1843?

15. Joy James, "Introduction: Democracy and Captivity," in *The New Abolitionists: (Neo)Slave Narratives and Contemporary Prison Writings*, ed. Joy James (Albany, NY: SUNY Press, 2005), xxiv.

Rodriguez's strict parallels between Marx's criticisms of Bauer and US antiblackness imply that the essay opens in this direction. Casting a left American, so to speak, in the role of Bauer's left Hegelian, Rodriguez finds a version of Bauer's error still being made: "if America asks the Blacks: Have you, from your standpoint, the right to want *political emancipation*? We ask the converse question: Does the standpoint of *political* emancipation give the right to demand from the Black the abolition of Blackness and from man the abolition of religion?" (Rodriguez, "The Blackness of Marx's Jewish Question").

Part II of "On the Jewish Question," hailing North America and bracketing the slave states, underlines that the entire essay confines itself as a matter of course to the possibilities of those who *can* be political subjects—however misguided that commitment might be—in contradistinction to slaves. One could ask Marx "the question of the *relation of human emancipation to the emancipation of slaves*." The bracketing of the southern states on account of their not being political enough in their voting laws to be primed for human emancipation, as opposed to their not being political as slave states, expresses this restrictive relation. Like Jews in Bauer, who, Bauer writes, are not even as protopolitical as Christians, and therefore two steps away from political emancipation, slaves here have no reason to be considered—I mean diegetically, narratively in the essay's terms of "human emancipation"[16]—since they are not even yet included in the political emancipation that northern states have achieved. Obviously, slaves do not inhabit the field where, as for Kant, Rousseau, Hegel, and Bauer, subjects of emancipation assume their political responsibilities or not. Marx's desire to locate the social basis of Jewishness in "practical need" is likewise irrelevant in the case of slaves who are not in charge of their practical needs (247), as opposed to the practical need, and ability to use its proceeds, that leads Prussian Jews, in Marx's account, to the few forms of labor legally available to them. Slave labor may contain a need or desire for the fruits and energies of work, and yet not one that originates in slaves. Imagining the desires that the slave's work expresses as future fulfillments of the slave for the slave, as Hegel does, runs through a hypothetical extrapolation, a detour from situation. The understanding of mediation that leads the political subject to a place of leveraged complicity leads the slave around in a circle. Thus slavery in "On the Jewish Question" marks the limit of nonpolitical as well as political distinctions: because slaves are not political in the same way as rights-bearing subjects, slaves are

16. That is, I am not characterizing Marx's views on slavery but pointing out the discursive terms of the essay.

also not nonpolitical. Ferreira da Silva's matheme for blackness, "an account of opposition that figures *nullification* instead of *contradiction*,"[17] is helpful here. Marx places the accounts side by side.

Chandler, in a two-part essay starting from Du Bois's "Die Negerfrage in den Vereinigten Staaten [The Negro Question in the United States]"[18] and working on a later period of German statehood, argues that German polities continue then to construct state legitimacy by drawing a shifting "color line" out of "the relations between different human groups within one political and economic horizon."[19] For Max Weber, Chandler writes, the problem of the color line "took the form of the so-called 'Polish question' in late nineteenth-century Germany," which is in turn connected to the "so-called Eastern question," where "the so-called 'Jewish question' was also interwoven" (Chandler, "Form of an Interlocution," Part 2, 233). Weber views these various "questions" as the state's struggles with its very possibility of existence ("Form of an Interlocution," Part 2, 241, 248–249). According to Chandler, Weber parts ways with Du Bois when he becomes unable to imagine any alternative "horizon of becoming" potentially as comprehensive and legitimate as that of the state: "that is to say, Polish could not announce for him, for example, the futural form of an ultimate accomplishment of possibility within the German Reich. The pivotal issue here is a matter of capacity or the sense of ability as possibility" (Chandler, "Form of an Interlocution," Part 2, 249). The state wields power here only because it incorporates other capacities in its therefore "ultimate" capacity, "in the sense of *being the singular historical form of the passage beyond limit*" ("Form of an Interlocution," Part 2, 250). Beyond the state, Weber posits relationality itself as his final authority. Note the effect if "state" is taken as standing in for any legitimate "collective" as it is in generous readings of Hegel. Here we have the figure of contradiction.

In this way, according to Chandler, the Prussian-dominated German nations find themselves with contradictory desires for race not neces-

---

17. Denise Ferreira da Silva, "1 (life) ÷ 0 (blackness) = ∞—∞ or ∞/∞: On Matter Beyond the Equation of Value," *e-flux* 79 (February 2017): unpaginated, https://www.e-flux.com/journal/79/94686/1-life-0-blackness-or-on-matter-beyond-the-equation-of-value/.

18. "The Negro Question in the United States" [1906], trans. Joseph Fracchia, *CR: The New Centennial Review* 6 (2006): 241–290. See Chandler, "The Possible Form of an Interlocution: W. E. B. Du Bois and Max Weber in Correspondence, 1904–1905," Part 1, *CR: The New Centennial Review* 6.3 (2006): 193–239.

19. Nahum Chandler, "The Possible Form of an Interlocution: W. E. B. Du Bois and Max Weber in Correspondence, 1904–1905," Part 2, *CR: The New Centennial Review* 7.1 [2007]: 213–272, 228.

sarily voiced by the same actors. In one, political realization must come about by *incorporating* capacities for human difference: If the state cannot do this, how is it different from a local community? In that view, "if the Polish could be understood to be or become a full citizen of the *Reich*, in equal measure to anyone, then they would be welcomed" (Chandler, "Possible Form of an Interlocution," Part 2, 250). Another voice responds: unfortunately, the Polish happen not to show this capacity. And the state also needs them to remain unincorporated (this pattern restates the logic of nonpolitical difference again).

The next problem, Chandler continues, is reflected in the second-order solution to the first: understanding "the fundamental heterogeneity of the 'German' nation ... as remarking an expansion of historical possibility" ("Form of an Interlocution," Part 2, 250). What other than the necessity that there be *no* limit to Germany's historical becoming, that "the futural form of ultimate becoming" in total openness be the only real horizon (249), an imperative that requires constant self-transformation and expansion or else proves the state inadequate, makes Germany's relation to Polishness so tortuous? Germany's rejection of its own "backwardness" makes it horrid to let Poland be and horrid to interact with it. The anxiety can be dispelled by blaming Polish racialism (*its* lack of capacity to be more than itself). As part of the longer history of genocidal policies against "indigenous" Poles, David Blackbourn mentions the Prussian perception that Poland was "stagnating," "superstitious," and uninterested in land development.[20] In this way, "the premise of the capacity to *stand at the limit* of historicity" makes it impossible for Polishness to be *either* "welcomed" or rejected (Chandler, "Form of an Interlocution," Part 2, 250). If this premise is often racial, it is metaracial, I've argued, when relational openness becomes the medium in which Poland's "stagnation" appears as its persistence in an insufficiently political stance.

For Marx in 1843, there isn't obviously a problem with dialectic and negativity itself, only with political form as their imagined terminus. Revolutionary subjectivity can elude the dead end of political form. It can live in the "contradiction between the political state and civil society" (OJQ, 159–160), and between civil society in the form of institutions and social relations informally. Marx's revolutionary subjectivity can be to Hegel's historical subjectivity what Hegel was to Kant's by taking back for social relations the desire and energy that Hegel outsources to the state. In the second half of "On the Jewish Question" Marx tries

20. David Blackbourn, "Conquests from Barbarism: Interpreting Land Reclamation in 18th Century Prussia," International Congress of Historical Sciences, 2000.

to carry out the plan by going back to pick up an "actual" Jew (OJQ 169) that Bauer had seemingly forgotten. But, famously, the second half of the essay falls apart into antisemitic stereotypes and rather fragmentary statements.

For Bauer, Jewishness *is* religious identity and therefore sheerly fantasmatic. Marx disagrees. He points out that Bauer seems unaware of the secular Jew: he "saw in it 'merely' a religious significance" (OJQ 169). Marx knows that religiosity is only part of being Jewish, that there is also the "*social* element," "the *everyday Jew*" (OJQ 243). In seeking the "everyday Jew," Marx tries to demonstrate how emancipation could focus on a core human ability that he glosses as "social," "everyday," "secular," and "practical." For Marx, these qualities along with others compose the "actual." Yet, in the rest of the essay Marx cannot find a nontheoretical Jew. He decides to represent "practical, real Judaism" in work, and from there in "money and bargaining" (OJQ 170, trans. modified), which he recommends are not simply to be rejected as unwholesome stereotypes but taken in and taken to their end as part of communism's reclamation of all labor and life fashioned by modernity. Marx reasons that since the financial stereotype is grounded in need, it contains a reality and desire that can be deployed. But Marx maintains a structure parallel to Bauer's to argue that it is the Jew who idealizes his circumstances into Jewish identity, a "chimerical nationality" (OJQ 172), to deflect confrontation with actual Jewishness based in "*practical need, self-interest*" (OJQ 172, trans. modified). While the chimera is no longer religion as in Bauer but *nationality*, the target of the charge of irreality remains Jewishness.

So in the failed second half of the essay, the "factual" criterion for the continued existence of nonpolitical distinctions takes over the narrative to its demise, causing Marx to hunt for the "actual" Jew. He inherits Bauer's target, Jewishness, in spite of himself. Instead of positioning the political at the expense of the religious, as Bauer does, he attempts to find a social actuality that could derealize political form *and* ethno*nationality*—stances that would then count as null and irreal in comparison with social life. From Hegel's vantage, Marx has traveled in the wrong, precritical direction away from Bauer, and it might seem as though a better understanding of Hegelian actuality, as "absolutely" mediated, would have helped Marx avoid this cul-de-sac. But if Marx had arrived at a richer construction of the "actual" as absolute mediation, the outcome could still have been parallel: as in Hegel, Jewishness could figure as a deceived *belief in* and *practice of* tribal identity that is null and irreal in comparison with negative historicity. Marx is already aiming the same accusation at Jewishness by calling it a "chimerical nationality." Bauer's essay too already mobilizes this Hegelian arrangement, in which the problem with Jewishness is its racialism (degree of separatism). And Rodriguez highlights the transposed racism of Bauer's argument in his text's ventriloquy of a similar voice indulging the antiblack fantasy of criticizing Black separatism. While from Bauer's Hegelian perspective Marx's error is not referring to Jewishness as "chimerical" but opposing a given-sounding "factual' reality to it, from another perspective, one that watches realization's wake of derealization, what matters is not the initial claim but its recreation of the same racialized target. The effect, rendering Jewishness chimerical, would have occurred just the same. In fact, Hegel and Bauer have already done it, both in a politically radical way.

Despite its rejection of political *form*, then, "On the Jewish Question" remains within Hegelian political identity and Wynter's *homo politicus*. Like the political state Marx criticizes, it materializes the legitimacy of its project against a foil—namely, Jewishness—whose distinction, or difference, it both overrides and summons to appear as such. More negativity would only continue the pattern on a metalevel. But if the range of the term *nonpolitical* is expanded—from "not legally relevant" to "that which allows the properly political to appear legitimate"—then an understanding of how political identities are coconstitutive with "nonpolitical" foils is furnished in the first part of "On the Jewish Question," when the state is seen to materialize its political legitimacy by creating nonpolitical racialist life.

What the second half of Marx's essay tells is that it isn't only the state, not only legality, that does this. Marx's political will goes beyond political *form* entirely, and yet in the service of "human emancipation" he still materializes the radical orientation of the actor working toward emancipation by making Jewishness into a "chimerical nationality" in comparison to the community of man. As Rodriguez demonstrates, a version of this move insinuates that interest in antiblackness is interest in something insufficiently grounded or—in the negatively Hegelian mode—insufficiently aware of common groundlessness.

This argument, including the Hegelian rendition, is the one I've been probing in radical enlightenment theories that slavery itself is "null" while the slave of the dialectic models the possibility in the radical's antiracist reality. Todd McGowan argues that the Nazi regime "require[d] the Jew to function as the universal that gives an identity to its particularity" (McGowan, *Emancipation*, 194) and at the same time, because it was a "particularist" empire, saw itself as duty bound to eradicate Jews. It makes sense that Nazis, as overt murderous racists, would demean as "universalist" a people on whom they wished to demonstrate their power. Correspondingly, however, it also makes sense that left Hegelians portray as "racialist" what they use for purposes of their own political legitimation, since Hegelian leftists like McGowan, diametrically, stake their political identities on their freedom from racism. What McGowan's analysis of Nazi antisemitism occludes is that if Nazis could not stand universality, what they *really* couldn't stand was universality *through Jewishness*. When the slave's political potential serves as proof of openness itself, Hegel's slave in the dialectic will be the most popular figures of political identity.

This dynamic, including its Hegelian rendition, also gives rise to common radical enlightenment theories that a social form is "null" because it is out of touch with actuality. (For McGowan, Nazism is "not just morally or politically abominable but logically doomed to failure" [McGowan, *Emancipation*, 194]). I've lingered over Rousseau's assumption that because of its poor connections to reason and need, slavery must perish. Hegel's observation of "the nullity of a rigid distinction between races that have rights and those that have none" (EPR, § 393A) succumbs to similar problems. Citing this passage, Karen Ng observes that it "is complicated by the fact that it is followed by an extended, highly speculative, and extremely racist discussion of the characteristics of different races based on a distinction Hegel draws between the old and new worlds."[21] She does not make a connection between the conception of racial distinction as nullity and the passage that follows it, instead urging the reader to remodel Hegel's antiracist mode with more consistency. Rather, we can see by now that these statements of nullity are consistent with the transposition of racial attributes to stances toward antiblackness.

When nonpolitical distinctions derealize—and in a reality given standing by polity in the largest sense, they do—the apparently groundless position they are required to hold turns them into derealized props and foils for real social transformation taking place around them. Part I of "On the Jewish Question"glimpses a version of this problem, before Marx attempts to reorient himself. Marx's 1840s criticism of Hegel, in general, follows rounds of antisemitic political distinction-making whose mediated production Marx perceives, and whose premise of anterior and ongoing violence he rejects. In his apprehension of the diremption of the political from the social within the actual, he expresses the precarity of actuality via its use of race, where, in Hegel, raciality

---

21. Karen Ng, "Hegel and Adorno on Negative Universal History: The Dialectics of Species-Life," in *Creolizing Hegel*, ed. Michael Monahan (New York: Rowman & Littlefield, 2017), 113–133, esp. 130.

remains a symptom of insufficient understanding of actuality. In Hegelianism, this kind of insufficient understanding cannot be separated
from insufficient actuality itself.

At the same time, the chain of criticism Marx constructs suggests
further questions for Marx of the type of Marx's questions for Bauer.
Antisemitism in "On the Jewish Question" shows its metafunction in
a specifically political field, that is, a debate over the political and nonpolitical, where restrictions are "lifted" or not in demonstrations of
the state's legitimacy. The reference to North American slavery shows
that slavery as such does nothing to legitimate the United States politically, domestically or internationally. The state is not demonstrating
its power to move its political borders back and forth. Emancipation
when it comes is not a demonstration of state power over what counts
as Black. And if we decide, as various paradigms of the radical enlightenment propose, that race is a matter of marks for economic channel-
ing and/or demonstration of state power, then blackness, in its entan-
glement in slavery, unstable in origin and cause, begins to push further
than what those theories call race. The radical enlightenment record
of transformations suggests that the point now is not to write a new
formulation but to ask where formulations are located with regard to
the antiblackness of political longing in conditions of desperate unfreedom. Marx's essay suggests that a decision about what role slavery plays
in capital (cause or effect? primary or secondary? technology or value
form?) is less needed than a critical reflection on antiblackness's living
pressure on the radical imaginary.

AFTERWORD

I began with Wynter's schematic overview of enlightenment, then descended into the texts to try to inhabit their unconscious elaboration of antiblack political logics. This procedure involves interpretive as well as explanatory work, and inhabitation as something different from explanation. There is more here than I "explain," because it is not possible to see around one's own position, so I hope that readers can find the material fruitful to work on further.

Dwellling in the literature of the radical enlightenment, even to this limited extent, indicates that racial slavery raises the anxiety of the unfree political subject in need of human emancipation. I've suggested that Hegel's proposal of a political reality of conditions in totality, not finally navigable by anyone, even as that realization ought therefore to be available to anyone, is a systematic and therapeutic acknowledgment of that anxiety. I feel the attraction of indeterminate negations—the double negative utopian category of "neither nor," for instance, which rejects a limitation and imposes no new one. Yet I want to say in the end that the "neither nor" realm is not abstractable from its context in the destructive history that produces the need for it. Similarly, the texts I read seem to find the unstable origins and causality of racial slavery disorienting, but I find I can't say that that necessarily shows how blackness has leverage on categories that get opposed to it. I have not been trying to remap the "discipline of the world" but to make visible the limits of the antiracism with which radicals approach it. I've suggested that this antiracism contains a transformation of antiblackness that is deflected by underexamined principles of the genuinely radical enlightenment.

It might be helpful to offer a neo-Wynterian frame for the questions I've raised, situating them within a sequence of transformations in intellectual history and differentiating the problems that enlightenment radicals face from hegemonic conflicts. This may be the more helpful given that my discussions have not been chronological. The relationships I propose here do not correlate with the narrative order of my discussions but indicate how moves in the intellectual history of these centuries are inspired by problems unsolved in their antecedents, displace rather than solve them in turn, and create work that needs to be done. To understand relations between white supremacist imperialism, postracialist statist liberalism, and antiracist antistate radicalism, we can follow a sequence of three problems:

1. In formulations of white supremacy that precede Hegel *argumentatively*, there's no contradiction between rac(ial)ism and political activity. Out of its own transatlantic conflicts, though, the natural law tradition generates a debate that begs to be stabilized, the first of the three thresholds. In the environment dominated by the white supremacist natural law of Locke, there necessarily arises a debate about the humanity of Black chattel slaves insofar as human being is seen as political being, as Black Studies scholarship on the concept of humanity has shown. Racial science resolves this question biologically, thereby distributing rights according to biological hierarchies, such that the Black chattel slave could possess none. But radicals in the eighteenth and nineteenth centuries, for their part, resolve this question in favor of one humanity of *homo politicus*, as Wynter avers, each member of which is theoretically an abstract political subject of their own political organization.

2. Therefore, there arises simultaneously with the postracialism of radical communities[1] *a new debate about the quality of the reality that should be attributed to race*—the race it leaves ambiguous given its monist view of humanity. Clearly this debate, and the one "before," is ongoing and has many possible permutations, including romantic multiculturalism. Nonetheless, with a deeper critique of the given, radical discourse more or less resolves this debate for itself in the direction of a historical ontology of social relations and the significance of all realities, including that of race, as lived structural conditions. "Identity" now needs to be understood under erasure, as a historically contingent position open to continual transformation by real movement and novel encounter. It is understood as a nonsubstantive position of political identity only. This radical identity discursively *demands* Black political identities as the structural effects of racism are incorporated into historical ontology, on the understanding that race is not an illusion but a social reality.

   But in the eighteenth century, nascent antiracism splits off a portion

---

1. Discursive communities, not necessarily formal polities.

of slavery when it creates exemplary Black political identities. To return to Sorentino's formulation, there immediately come to be "good slaves and bad slaves": those who "demonstrat[e] their anthropological political potential" and those who do not (Sorentino, *Idea of Slavery*, 177). This is a way to manage ambivalence and limit anxieties about the difficult, and therefore still politically unstable, origins of the marriage of slavery and blackness. As debates about humanity were resolved on the left by being incorporated into political identity, the nexus of slavery and blackness could only be partially apprehended through these—and perhaps any—revisions. Rousseau and Hegel do not believe they are leaving anything aside when they argue as though slavery will wither away: as a result of its poor apprehension of reality, it is an issue taken care of in advance. They engage it without the aspects that seem to them not worth considering useless imposition and unconsciousness. Liberal abolitionism focuses on legal emancipation and suffrage; radical abolitionism takes up property and wage relations as well. But aspects of slavery that could not be turned toward liberation in the radical frame were foreclosed in the radical enlightenment as irreal. Thus to the extent that afropessimist writing, for example, foregrounds this imposition and unconsciousness, afropessimism too continues to be suppressed and moralized as subpolitical. Radical antiracism has staked a great deal on a relatively narrow understanding of slavery in a way that was not visible in a phase of overconfidence.

3. For, to the extent that it envisions a real movement of history that abolishes the present state of things the Hegelian left posits a nonracial—because ungraspable—causal force that destroys and creates social forms. The nonraciality of historical process is taken to be entailed in its indetermination: real movement is open to anything in a way that capitalism is not. Amid the transformation of chattel slavery into Black imprisonment and everyday death, a politics that has staked itself on the necessity to avow and assume subjection to real movement for collective purposes will necessarily struggle over the bounds of slavery, because theories of reality are at stake. There arises a debate about what slavery is. The previous rounds of argument suggest that the current controversy does not concern the magnitude of slavery in and of itself. Theories of reality will be at stake not to the extent that the *function* of slavery is in play (is it a motive or a mechanism of capitalism?) but to the extent that the borders of slavery call the grounds of *homo politicus* into play.

I have not focused on what, if anything, pressures Hegel's "discipline of the world," much as I would like there to be something pressuring it,

but rather on the radical Hegelian imaginary of unfreedom and its splitting of slavery to select, with an antiracist energy, a "slave, that is, the
subject" (Balibar, *Citizen Subject*, 214). To Hegelians this concern might
look like a concern for what Hegel leaves out or where he contradicts
himself, whereas in fact he's all about self-contradiction. But looking
for the functions of Hegelian avowals of contradiction, emptiness, and
self-shattering rather than for their difference from the violent episte-
mologies they superceded suggests that they manage quandaries of origin and causality that racial slavery illumines and for which blackness
continues to pay. To displace those problems, and possibilities for the
worse and the better with them, antiblackness in radical circles needed
transposition to a metaracial logic. It's helpful to study this logic because it supports violence in and of itself, foreclosing possibilities for
better and worse that reside in the tension of antiblack antiracism.

ACKNOWLEDGMENTS

The last time I wrote a set of acknowledgments, I said that I hoped the public universities would act in solidarity with their communities, meaning that I knew they wouldn't. This work eventually grew out of the following years of activism across the University of California system, which consisted almost entirely of student protest. This activity took up the better part of seven years, which I continue to cherish, especially its UC Irvine manifestation. I was writing then about the unfreedom of postrevolutionary Europeans, especially radical writers' tendency to phrase their unfreedom metaphysically. Meanwhile, in the system-wide activity of university protest, "racism for radicals" showed itself to be very persistent. I was familiar with the phenomenon through decades of institutional work, and in fact it has permeated all the institutions I have been associated with. My introduction to the limits of antiracism came through years of conversations I had with Sandra Gunning at the University of Michigan, for which I continue to be grateful, even as I had never written directly about these consuming institutional struggles. The same years of student protest after the financial crisis saw an efflorescence of Black critical thought, available in African American Studies at Irvine especially through the work of Nahum Chandler, Jared Sexton, and Frank Wilderson. Their conceptual vocabularies helped to explain the political contexts and not at all the other way around. So I began to see that these concerns were related and that my project should account differently for radical anxiety, despite or because of the fact that I am involved in my topics of investigation. If nothing else, exploration of that limit is given here. I would most like to thank (alphabetically) Linette Park, Morgan Slade, Sara-Maria Sorentino, and Parisa Vaziri, who always dared to talk through the intellectual questions within the environment we shared and whose work encourages everyone to participate in locating and creating necessary vocabularies.

It's difficult to acknowledge all the contributions to ten years of work, and I will err on the spare side. I'm very grateful to the anonymous readers for the University of Chicago Press. They engaged in detail while remaining honest and levelheaded, none of which could have been easy. I'm unusually fortunate to have had these graceful and responsible readings. The following people kindly commented on parts of the manuscript or associated writings: Eyal Amiran, Joe Diaz, John Gillespie, Grace Lavery, David S. Marriott, Linette Park, Sara-Maria Sorentino, Morgan Slade, Erin Trapp, M. Ty, and Parisa Vaziri. David C. Lloyd read the entire manuscript and has been exceptionally generous for many years on many levels. I appreciate the long-term friendship of Dina al-Kassim, Anne-Lise François, and Eliza Richards, and I benefited from affection and ideas during various phases of the project from— among many others—Ana Baginski, James Bliss, Daniel Carnie, Williston Chase, Charles Fisher, Mehra Gharibian, Carlos Colmenares Gil, Kim Icreverzi, Eric Johnston, Claire Jean Kim, Chris Malcolm, Louis-Georges Schwartz, Saniya Taher, and Ameeth Vijay. My visit to JNU and Delhi, arranged by Brinda Bose and Sneha Chowdry, has turned out to be a permanent resource in life. Aloe, Dactyl, Imogen, Meno, and Poa made innumerable creative contributions.

Eyal Amiran is a person of remarkable perception, stamina, unpredictability, and capacity to care. The most really.

Portions of § 1 were published in "Hegel's Racism for Radicals," *Radical Philosophy* 2, no. 5 (2019): 11–22 and "Impasse as a Figure of Political Space," *Comparative Literature* 72, no. 2 (2020): 144–158 (copyright 2020, University of Oregon, all rights reserved, republished with permission of the publisher, www.dukeupress.edu); portions of § 4 in "The Racial Grammar of Kantian Time," *European Romantic Review* 28, no. 3 (2017): 267–278 (reprinted with permission of the publisher, Taylor & Francis Ltd, www.tandfonline.com); portions of § 5 in "Blackness and Anthropogenesis in *Frankenstein*," in *Frankenstein in Theory: A Critical Anatomy* (Bloomsbury, 2020), edited by Orrin N. C. Wang; portions of § 6 in "Hegel and the Prehistory of the Postracial," *European Romantic Review* 26, no. 3(2015): 289–299 (reprinted with permission of the publisher, Taylor & Francis Ltd, www.tandfonline.com); and portions of § 7 on the University of Colorado's *Romantic Circles* website (2012). Thanks to Peter Hallward and Orrin N. C. Wang for their very helpful editorial suggestions. The preparation of the manuscript was supported by research assistance from the Humanities Center at UC Irvine, and my university work was always enabled and steadied by Bindya Baliga and Suzanne Bolding.

The best thing about this disaster of a decade has been listening to very brilliant, much younger people. I always write with you primarily in mind.

This book is dedicated to Joe Krall—"Here's to insufficiency."

WORKS CITED

Aching, Gerard. *Freedom from Liberation: Slavery, Sentiment, and Literature in Cuba*. Bloomington: Indiana University Press, 2015.

———. "No Need for an Apology: Fanon's Untimely Critique of Political Consciousness." *South Atlantic Quarterly* 112 (2013): 23–38.

Adorno, T. W. *Hegel: Three Studies*. Translated by Shierry Weber Nicholsen. Cambridge, MA: MIT Press, 1993.

———. *History and Freedom: Lectures 1964–1965*. Edited by Rolf Tiedemann, translated by Rodney Livingstone. Cambridge, UK: Polity, 2006.

———. *Negative Dialectics*. Translated by E. B. Ashton. London and New York: Routledge & Kegan Paul, 1973.

Agamben, Giorgio. *The Open: Man and Animal*. Translated by Kevin Attali. Stanford, CA: Stanford University Press, 2004.

Alexander, Claire. "Breaking Black: The Death of Ethnic and Racial Studies in Britain." *Ethnic and Racial Studies* 41 (2018): 1034–1054.

al-Kassim, Dina. *On Pain of Speech: Fantasies of the First Order and the Literary Rant*. Berkeley: University of California Press, 2010.

Allison, Henry. *Kant's Transcendental Idealism: An Interpretation and Defense*. 2nd ed. New Haven, CT: Yale University Press, 1983.

Althusser, Louis. *Lessons on Rousseau*. Translated by G. M. Goshgarian. New York: Verso Books, 2019.

———. *Philosophy of the Encounter: Later Writings, 1978–1987*. Edited by François Matheron, translated by G. M. Goshgarian. London: Verso Books, 2006.

Aristotle. *Nicomachean Ethics*. Translated by David Ross and W. D. Ross. Oxford: Oxford University Press, 1980.

Arthur, Chris. "Hegel, Feuerbach, Marx and Negativity." *Radical Philosophy* 35 (1983): 10–19.

————. "Hegel's Master-Slave Dialectic and a Myth of Marxology." *New Left Review* 142 (1983): 67–75.

Asad, Talal. "Are There Histories of Peoples Without Europe? A Review Article." *Comparative Studies in Society and History* 29 (1987): 504–607.

————. *Genealogies of Religion: Discipline and Reasons of Power in Christianity and Islam*. Baltimore, MD: Johns Hopkins University Press, 1993.

Austin, J. L. *How to Do Things with Words*. 2nd ed. Edited by J. O. Urmson and Marina Sbisà. Cambridge, MA: Harvard University Press, 1975.

Bakan, Abigail B. "Marxism and Anti-Racism: Rethinking the Politics of Difference." In *Theorizing Anti-Racism: Linkages in Marxism and Critical Race Theories*, edited by Abigail B. Bakan and Enakshi Dua, 97–122. Toronto: University of Toronto Press, 2015.

Balibar, Étienne. *Citizen Subject: Foundations of Philosophical Anthropology*. Translated by Steven Miller. Bronx, NY: Fordham University Press, 2017.

Barber, Daniel. "World-Making and Grammatical Impasse." *Qui Parle* 25 (2016): 179–206.

Barbeyrac, Jean. Notes on Samuel Pudendorf, *Of the Law of Nature and Nations: Eight Books*. Edited and translated by Basil Kennett and George Carew. London: Walthoe & Wilkin, 1729.

Barrett, Lindon W. *Blackness and Value: Seeing Double*. Cambridge, UK: Cambridge University Press, 1999.

————. *Racial Blackness and the Discontinuity of Western Modernity*. Edited by Justin A. Joyce, Dwight A. McBride, and John Carlos Rowe. Urbana: University of Illinois Press, 2014.

Bauer, Bruno. *The Jewish Problem*. Translated by Helen Lederer. Cincinnati, OH: Hebrew Union College-Jewish Institute of Religion, 1958.

Beck, Lewis White. "The Reformation, the Revolution, and the Restoration in Hegel." *Journal of the History of Philosophy* 14 (1976): 51–61.

Benjamin, Walter. "On the Concept of History." In *Selected Writings, vol. 2, part 1, 1927–1930*, edited by Howard Eiland, Michael William Jennings, and Gary Smith, translated by Edmund Jephcott and Rodney Livingstone. Cambridge, MA: Harvard University Press, 2003.

Bernasconi, Robert. "With What Must the Philosophy of World History Begin? On the Racial Basis of Hegel's Eurocentrism." *Nineteenth-Century Contexts* 22 (2000): 171–201.

Biddick, Kathleen. *Make and Let Die: Untimely Sovereignties*. New York: Punctum Books, 2016.

Binder, Guyora. "Mastery, Slavery, and Emancipation." *Cardozo Law Review* 10 (1989): 1435–1480.

Blackbourn, David. "Conquests from Barbarism: Interpreting Land Reclamation in 18th Century Prussia." In *Proceedings: Reports, Abstracts and*

Round Table Introductions. 19th International Congress of Historical Sciences. Oslo: ICHS, 2000. Full text at www.oslo2000.uio.no.

———. *History of Germany, 1780–1918: The Long Nineteenth Century*. 2nd ed. Oxford: Blackwell, 2003.

Blackbourn, David, and Geoffrey Eley. *The Peculiarities of German History: Bourgeois Society and Politics in Nineteenth-Century Germany*. Oxford: Oxford University Press, 1984.

Bloch, Ernst. *The Spirit of Utopia*. Translated by Anthony A. Nassar. Stanford, CA: Stanford University Press, 2000.

Blunden, Andy. *Hegel for Social Movements*. Leiden: Brill, 2019.

Brahm, Felix, and Eve Rosenhaft. *Slavery Hinterland: Transatlantic Slavery and Continental Europe, 1680–1850*. Woodbridge, UK: Boydell and Brewer, 2016.

Brassier, Ray. "Strange Sameness: Hegel, Marx, and the Logic of Estrangement." *Angelaki* 24 (2019): 98–105.

Brennan, Timothy. *Borrowed Light: Hegel, Vico, and the Colonies*. Stanford, CA: Stanford University Press, 2014.

———. "Hegel, Empire, and Anti-Colonial Thought." In *The Oxford Handbook of Postcolonial Studies*, 142–161. Oxford: Oxford University Press, 2013.

Buck-Morss, Susan. *Hegel, Haiti, and Universal History*. Pittsburgh, PA: University of Pittsburgh Press, 2009.

Bugg, John. "'Master of Their Language': Education and Exile in Mary Shelley's *Frankenstein*." *Huntington Library Quarterly* 68 (2005): 655–666.

Capener, Sean. "Time in the Middle Passage: Race, Religion, and the Making of Modernity's 'Second Moment' in Kant and Hegel." University of Toronto, February 10, 2022.

Caponetto, Laura. "Undoing Things with Words." *Synthese* 97 (2020): 2399–2414.

Carter, J. Kameron. *Race: A Theological Account*. Oxford: Oxford University Press, 2008.

Casas Klausen, Jimmy. *Fugitive Rousseau: Slavery, Primitivism, and Political Freedom*. Bronx, NY: Fordham University Press, 2014.

Chandler, James. *England in 1819: The Politics of Literary Culture and the Case of Romantic Historicism*. Chicago: University of Chicago Press, 1998.

Chandler, Nahum. *"Beyond This Narrow Now": Or, Delimitations, of W. E. B. Du Bois*. Durham, NC: Duke University Press, 2022.

———. "The Economy of Desedimentation: W. E. B. Du Bois and the Discourses of the Negro." *Callaloo* 19 (1996): 78–93.

———. "Paraontology: Or, Notes on the Practical Theoretical Politics of Thought." Lecture at Cornell University, October 15, 2018.

————. "The Possible Form of an Interlocution: W. E. B. Du Bois and Max Weber in Correspondence, 1904–1905." Part 1. *CR: The New Centennial Review* 6.3 (2006): 193–239.

————. "The Possible Form of an Interlocution: W. E. B. Du Bois and Max Weber in Correspondence, 1904–1905." Part 2. *CR: The New Centennial Review* 7.1 (2007): 213–272.

————. *Toward an African Future: Of the Limit of World*. London: Living Commons Collective, 2013.

————. *X—The Problem of the Negro as a Problem for Thought*. Bronx, NY: Fordham University Press, 2013.

Chanter, Tina. *Whose Antigone? The Tragic Marginalization of Slavery*. Albany, NY: SUNY Press, 2011.

Chun, Wendy Hui Kyong. "Introduction: Race and/as Technology; or How to Do Things to Race." *Camera Obscura* 70 (2009): 7–35.

Cicciarello-Maher, George. *Decolonizing Dialectics*. Durham, NC: Duke University Press, 2017.

Clark, David L. "Kant's Aliens: The Anthropology and Its Others." *CR: The New Centennial Review* 1 (2001): 201–289.

————. "Last Words: Voice, Gesture, and the Remains of *Frankenstein*." In *Frankenstein in Theory: A Critical Anatomy*, edited by Orrin N. C. Wang, 13–32. New York: Bloomsbury, 2020.

————. "Unsocial Kant: The Philosopher and the Un-regarded War Dead." *Wordsworth Circle* 41 (2010): 60–68.

Cole, Andrew. *The Birth of Theory*. Chicago: University of Chicago Press, 2015.

Comay, Rebecca. *Mourning Sickness: Hegel and the French Revolution*. Stanford, CA: Stanford University Press, 2011.

Crawford, Margo. *Black Post-Blackness: The Black Arts Movement and the Twenty-First Century*. Champaign: University of Illinois Press, 2017.

Crockett, Clayton, and Creston Davis. Introduction to *Hegel and the Infinite: Religion, Politics, and Dialectic*, edited by Slavoj Žižek, Clayon Crockett, and Creston Davis. New York: Columbia University Press, 2011.

Cutrofello, Andrew. *Discipline and Technique: Kant, Poststructuralism, and the Problem of Resistance*. Albany, NY: SUNY Press, 1994.

Dawson, Allan Charles. *In Light of Africa: Globalizing Blackness in Northeast Brazil*. Toronto: University of Toronto Press, 2014.

Dawson, Michael. *Blacks in and out of the Left*. Cambridge, MA: Harvard University Press, 2013.

Dean, Jodi. *Comrade: An Essay on Political Belonging*. New York: Verso Books, 2019.

Denson, Shane. *Postnaturalism: Frankenstein, Film, and the Anthropotechnical Interface*. Bielefeld: Transcript Verlag, 2014.

Dent, Jerome. "Athazagoraphilia: On the End(s) of Dreaming." *InVisible Culture* 31 (2020): unpaginated. www.invisibleculturejournal.com /pub/athazagoraphilia/release/1?readingCollection=56e19667.

Derrida, Jacques. *The Animal That Therefore I Am.* Edited by Marie-Louise Mallet, translated by David Wills. Bronx, NY: Fordham University Press, 2008.

———. *Edmund Husserl's "Origin of Geometry": An Introduction.* Translated by John P. Leavey Jr. Lincoln: University of Nebraska Press, 1978.

———. *Glas.* Translated by John P. Leavey Jr. Lincoln: University of Nebraska Press, 1986.

———. *Of Grammatology.* Translated by Gayatri Chakravorty Spivak. Baltimore, MD: Johns Hopkins University Press, 1976.

———. *Positions.* Translated by Alan Bass. Chicago: University of Chicago Press, 1982.

———. *The Problem of Genesis in Husserl's Philosophy.* Translated by Marian Hobson. Chicago: University of Chicago Press, 2003.

Douglass, Patrice D. "The Claim of Right to Property: Social Violence and Political Right." *Zeitschrift für Anglistik und Amerikanistik* 65.2 (2017): 145–159.

———. "On (Being) Fear: Utah v. Strieff and the Ontology of Affect." *Journal of Visual Culture* (December 17, 2018).

Du Bois, W. E. B. *Black Reconstruction in America: An Essay Toward a History of the Part Which Black Folk Played in the Attempt to Reconstruct Democracy in America, 1860–1888.* Oxford: Oxford University Press, 2014.

———. "The Negro Question in the United States." Translated by Joseph Fracchia. *CR: The New Centennial Review* 6.3 (2006): 241–290.

———. *The Souls of Black Folk.* New York: Pocket Books, 2005.

Dussel, Enrique. "Beyond Eurocentrism: The World-System and the Limits of Modernity." In *The Cultures of Globalization,* edited by Fredric Jameson and Masao Miyoshi, 3–31. Durham, NC: Duke University Press, 1998.

———. *Politics of Liberation: A Critical World History.* Translated by Thia Cooper. London: SCM Press, 2011.

———. "Transmodernity and Interculturality: An Interpretation from the Perspective of Philosophy of Liberataion." *Transmodernity: Journal of Peripheral Cultural Production of the Luso-Hispanic World* 1 (2012): 28–59.

Edelman, Lee, and Calvin Warren. "Conversation." Department of Women's, Gender, and Sexuality Studies, Emory University, October 30, 2020.

Eltis, David. "Europeans and the Rise and Fall of African Slavery in the Americas: An Interpretation." *American Historical Review* 98 (1993): 1399–1423.

Fairbairn, W. D. "The Repression and the Return of Bad Objects (with Special Reference to the 'War Neuroses')." In *Psychoanalytic Studies of the Personality*, 59–81. London and New York: Routledge, 1994.

Falaky, Fayçal. "Reading Rousseau in the Colonies: Theory, Practice, and the Question of Slavery." *Small Axe* 46 (2015): 5–19.

Fanon, Frantz. *Black Skin, White Masks*. Translated by Richard Philcox. New York: Grove Press, 2008.

Farley, Anthony Paul. "The Colorline as Capitalist Accumulation." *Buffalo Law Review* 56 (2008): 953–963.

Fenves, Peter. *The Messianic Reduction: Walter Benjamin and the Shape of Time*. Stanford, CA: Stanford University Press, 2011.

Ferrarin, Alfredo. "Hegel on Recognition: Self-Consciousness, Individuality, and Intersubjectivity." In *"I That Is We, We That Is I": Perspectives on Contemporary Hegel*, edited by Italo Testa and Luigi Ruggui, 253–270. Leiden, Netherlands: Brill, 2016.

Ferreira da Silva, Denise. "1 (life) ÷ 0 (blackness) = ∞—∞ or ∞/∞: On Matter Beyond the Equation of Value." *e-flux* 79 (February 2017): unpaginated. https://www.e-flux.com/journal/79/94686/1-life-0-blackness-or-on-matter-beyond-the-equation-of-value/.

———. "To Be Announced: Radical Praxis or Knowing (at) the Limits of Justice." *Social Text* 31 (2013): 43–62.

———. *Toward a Global Idea of Race*. Minneapolis: University of Minnesota Press, 2007.

———. *Unpayable Debt*. New York: Sternberg Press, 2022.

Ferreira da Silva, Denise, and Paula Chakravartty. "Accumulation, Dispossession, and Debt: The Racial Logic of Global Capitalism—an Introduction." *American Quarterly* 64 (2012): 361–385.

Fishkin, Shelley Fisher. *Was Huck Black? Mark Twain and African-American Voices*. Oxford: Oxford University Press, 1994.

François, Anne-Lise. "Passing Impasse." *Comparative Literature* 72 (2020): 240–257.

Garba, Tapji, and Sara-Maria Sorentino. "Slavery Is a Metaphor: A Critical Commentary on Eve Tuck and K. Wayne Yang's 'Decolonization is Not a Metaphor.'" *Antipode* 52 (2020): 764–782.

Gigante, Denise. "Facing the Ugly: The Case of *Frankenstein*." *ELH* 67 (2000): 565–587.

Gilroy, Paul. *Against Race: Imagining Political Culture Beyond the Color Line*. Cambridge, MA: Harvard University Press, 2002.

———. *The Black Atlantic: Modernity and Double Consciousness*. Cambridge, MA: Harvard University Press, 1995.

Glissant, Edouard. *Poetics of Relation*. Translated by Betsy Wing. Ann Arbor: University of Michigan Press, 1997.

Gordon, Jane Anna. "Unmasking the *Big Bluff* of Legitimate Governance and So-Called Independence: Creolizing Rousseau through the Reflections of Anna Julia Cooper." *Critical Philosophy of Race* 6 (2018): 1–25.

Gordon, Jane Anna, and Neil Roberts, eds. *Creolizing Rousseau.* New York: Rowman & Littlefield, 2014.

Gordon, Lewis R. *Fanon and the Crisis of European Man: An Essay on Philosophy and the Human Sciences.* London and New York: Routledge, 1995.

Gramsci, Antonio. "Equilibrium with Catastrophic Prospects." In *Selections from the Prison Notebooks.* 2nd ed. Edited and translated by Quentin Hoare and Geoffrey Nowell-Smith. New York: International Publishers, 1997.

Grumley, John. *History and Totality: Radical Historicism from Hegel to Foucault.* London and New York: Routledge, 2016.

Guha, Ranajit. *History at the Limit of World-History.* New York: Columbia University Press, 2002.

Habib, M. A. R. *Hegel and Empire: From Postcolonialism to Globalism.* New York: Palgrave Macmillan, 2017.

Haider, Asad. *Mistaken Identity: Race and Class in the Age of Trump.* New York: Verso Books, 2018.

Hall, Bruce. "The Question of 'Race' in the Pre-Colonial Southern Sahara." *Journal of North African Studies* 10 (2005): 339–367.

Hall, Stuart. *Essential Essays, vol. 1: Foundation of Cultural Studies.* Durham, NC: Duke University Press, 2018.

———. *Selected Writings on Marxism.* Edited by Gregor McLennan. Durham, NC: Duke University Press, 2021.

Hamacher, Werner. *Premises: Essays on Philosophy and Literature from Kant to Celan.* Translated by Peter Fenves. Cambridge, MA: Harvard University Press, 1999.

Han, Sora. "Slavery as Contract: *Betty's Case* and the Question of Freedom." *Law and Literature* 27 (2015): 395–416.

Harper, Philip Brian. "Nationalism and Social Division in Black Arts Poetry of the 1960s." *Critial Inquiry* 19 (1993): 234–255.

Hartman, Saidiya V. *Scenes of Subjection: Terror, Slavery, and Self-Making in Nineteenth-Century America.* Oxford: Oxford University Press, 1997.

Hartman, Saidiya V., and Frank B. Wilderson III. "The Position of the Unthought." *Qui Parle* 13.2 (2003): 183–201.

Hegel, G. W. F. *Aesthetics.* Vol. 1. Oxford: Oxford University Press, 1975.

———. *Elements of the Philosophy of Right.* Translated by H. B. Nisbet, edited by Allen Wood. Cambridge, UK: Cambridge University Press, 1991.

———. *Lectures on National Right and Political Science.* Translated by J. Michael Stewart and Peter C. Hodgson. Berkeley: University of California Press, 1995.

————. *Lectures on the Philosophy of Religion*. Vol. 2, *Determinate Religion*. Edited by Peter C. Hodgson, translated by R. F. Brown, P. C. Hodgson, and J. M. Stewart. Berkeley: University of California Press, 1987.

————. *Lectures on the Philosophy of Spirit 1827–28*. Edited and translated by Robert R. Williams. Oxford: Oxford University Press, 2007.

————. *Lectures on the Philosophy of World History*. Vol. 1. Edited and translated by Robert F. Brown and Peter C. Hodgson. Oxford: Oxford University Press, 2011.

————. *Lectures on the Philosophy of World History. Introduction: Reason in History*. Translated by H. B. Nisbet. Cambridge, UK: Cambridge University Press, 1975.

————. *The Letters*. Translated by Clark Butler and Christiane Seiler. Bloomington: Indiana University Press, 1984.

————. *The Phenomenology of Spirit*. Translated by A. V. Miller. Oxford: Oxford University Press, 1977.

————. *Philosophy of History*. Translated by J. Sibree. Kitchener, Ontario: Batoche Books, 2001.

————. *Philosophy of Mind. Part Three of the Encyclopaedia of the Philosophical Sciences*. Translated by William Wallace and A. V. Miller. Oxford: Clarendon Press, 1971.

————. *Philosophy of Nature. Part Two of the Encyclopaedia of the Philosophical Sciences*. Translated by A. V. Miller. Oxford: Clarendon Press, 1970.

————. *Science of Logic. Part One of the Encyclopaedia of the Philosophical Sciences*. Translated by William Wallace. Oxford: Clarendon Press, 1975.

————. *Werke in zwanzig Bänden*. Edited by Eva Moldenhauer und Karl Markus Michel. Frankfurt: Suhrkamp, 1970.

Heine, Heinrich. "From the Introduction to 'Kahldorf on the Nobility in Letters to Count M. von Moltke.'" In *On the History of Religion and Philosophy in Germany and Other Writings*, edited by Terry Pinkard. Cambridge, UK: Cambridge University Press, 2007.

————. *Sämmtliche Werke*. Edited by Adolf Strodtmann and Eduard Engel, vols. 13–14. Hamburg: Hoffmann und Campe, 1876.

Heng, Geraldine. *The Invention of Race in the European Middle Ages*. Cambridge, UK: Cambridge University Press, 2018.

Hesse, Barnor. "Preface: Counter-Racial Formation Theory." In *Conceptual Aphasia in Black: Displacing Racial Formation*, edited by P. Khalil Saucier and Tryon P. Woods. Lanham, MD: Lexington Books, 2016.

Holsclaw, Geoffrey. *Transcending Subjects: Augustine, Hegel, and Theology*. Chichester, UK: John Wiley & Sons, 2016.

Holt, Thomas C. "Marking: Race, Race-making, and the Writing of History." *American Historical Review* 100 (1995): 1–20.

Hoogenboom, Marcel, Christopher Kissane, Maarten Prak, Patrick Wallis, Chris Minns. "Guilds in the Transition to Modernity: The Cases of Germany, United Kingdom, and the Netherlands." *Theory and Society* 47 (2018): 255–291.

Hyppolite, Jean. *Genesis and Structure of Hegel's* Phenomenology of Spirit. Translated by Samuel Cherniak and John Heckman. Evanston, IL: Northwestern University Press, 1979.

Jackson, Zakiyyah Iman. "Losing Manhood: Animality and Plasticity in the (Neo)Slave Narrative." *Qui Parle* 25 (2016): 95–136.

James, C. L. R. *Notes on Dialectics: Hegel, Marx, Lenin.* Westport, CT: Lawrence, Hill & Co., 1980.

———. "Rousseau and the Idea of the General Will." In *You Don't Play with Revolution: Montreal Lectures,* edited by David Austin. Chico, CA: AK Press, 2009.

James, Joy. "Introduction: Democracy and Captivity." In *The New Abolitionists: (Neo)Slave Narratives and Contemporary Prison Writings,* edited by Joy James, xxi–xlii. Albany, NY: SUNY Press, 2005.

———. "The Womb of Western Theory: Trauma, Time Theft, and the Captive Maternal." *Carceral Notebooks* 12 (2016): 253–296.

Jarausch, Konrad Hugo, ed. *In Search of a Liberal Germany: Studies in the History of German Liberalism from 1789 to the Present.* Oxford: Berg, 1990.

Johnson, Barbara. "The Last Man." In *A Life with Mary Shelley,* edited by Judith Butler and Shoshana Felman, 3–14. Stanford, CA: Stanford University Press, 2014.

Johnson, Robert. "Was the British Empire Racist or Racialist?" In *British Imperialism,* 107–121. Houndmills, UK: Palgrave Macmillan, 2003.

Johnson, Walter. "The Pedestal and the Veil: Rethinking the Capitalism/Slavery Question." *Journal of the Early Republic* 24 (2004): 299–308.

Jones, Donna. "Inheritance and Finitude: Toward a Literary Phenomenology of Time." *ELH* 85 (2018): 289–303.

———. *The Racial Discourses of Life Philosophy: Negritude, Vitalism, and Modernity.* New York: Columbia University Press, 2010.

Jubb, Robert. "Rawls and Rousseau: Amour-Propre and the Strains of Commitment." *Res Publica* 17, (2011): 245–260.

Judy, R. A. *(Dis)forming the American Canon: African-Arabic Slave Narratives and the Vernacular.* Minneapolis: University of Minnesota Press, 1993.

———. "Kant and Knowledge of Disappearing Expression." In *A Companion to African-American Philosophy,* edited by Tommy L. Lott and John P. Pittman, 110–224. Oxford: Blackwell, 2003.

———. "Kant and the Negro." *Surfaces* 1.8 (1991): 4–70.

Kant, Immanuel. *Anthropology from a Pragmatic Point of View.* Translated by Victor Lyle Dowdell. Carbondale: Southern Illinois University Press, 1978.

———. *Critique of Pure Reason.* Translated by Norman Kemp Smith. New York: St. Martin's Press, 1965.

———. *Kritik der reinen Vernunft.* In *Gesammelte Schriften* [Akademie-Ausgabe], I–XXIII, Electronic Edition.

———. *Lectures on Metaphysics.* Edited and translated and by Karl Ameriks and Steve Naragon. Cambridge, UK: Cambridge University Press, 1997.

———. *The Metaphysics of Morals.* Edited by Lara Denis, translated by Mary Gregor. Cambridge, UK: Cambridge University Press, 2017.

———. "On the Use of Teleological Principles in Philosophy." In *Anthropology, History, and Education*, edited and translated by R. B. Louden and G. Zoller. Cambridge, UK: Cambridge University Press, 2007.

———. "Religion within the Boundaries of Mere Reason." In *Religion and Rational Theology*, edited and translated by Allen W. Wood and George di Giovanni. Cambridge, UK: Cambridge University Press, 1996.

Karera, Axelle. "Blackness and the Pitfalls of Anthropocene Ethics." *Critical Philosophy of Race* 7 (2019): 32–56.

———. "Paraontology: Disruption, Inheritance, or a Debt That One Often Regrets." Cooper Union, November 17, 2020.

Kistner, Ulrike, Philippe van Haute, and Robert Bernasconi, eds. *Violence, Slavery and Freedom between Hegel and Fanon.* Johannesburg: Wits University Press, 2020.

Kitson, Peter. "'Bales of Living Anguish': Representations of Race and the Slave in Romantic Writing." *ELH* 2 (2000): 515–537.

Klein, Melanie. *Envy and Gratitude and Other Works, 1946–1963.* New York: Free Press, 1975.

———. *Love, Guilt, and Reparation and Other Works, 1921–1945.* New York: Free Press, 1975.

Kojève, Alexandre. *Introduction à la lecture de Hegel: Lecons sur la Phénomenologie de l'Esprit Professées de 1933 à 1939 à l'École des Hautes Études.* Assembled by Raymond Queneau. Paris: Éditions Gallimard, 1947.

———. *Introduction to the Reading of Hegel: Lectures on the Phenomenology of Spirit.* Assembled by Raymond Queneau, edited by Allan Bloom, translated by James H. Nichols Jr. Ithaca, NY: Cornell University Press, 1980.

Kolodny, Niko. "The Explanation of Amour-propre." *Philosophical Review* 119.2 (2010): 165–200.

Levinas, Emmanuel. *Existence and Existents.* Translated by Alphonso Lingis. Pittsburgh, PA: Duquesne University Press, 2001.

Lloyd, David C. "Civil War: Race under Representation." UCHRI Podcast, December 18, 2019. https://www.listennotes.com/podcasts/uchri-podcast/civil-war-race-under-c8xh2QuDMUH/.

————. "The Social Life of Black Things: Fred Moten's *Consent Not to Be a Single Being*." *Radical Philosophy* 2.07 (Spring 2020): unpaginated. https://www.radicalphilosophy.com/article/the-social-life-of-black -things.

————. *Under Representation: The Racial Regime of Aesthetics*. Bronx, NY: Fordham University Press, 2019.

Lloyd, Vincent. "Hegel, Blackness, Sovereignty." In *Nothing Absolute: German Idealism and the Question of Political Theology*, edited by Kirill Chepurin and Alex Dubilet, 174–187. Bronx, NY: Fordham University Press, 2021.

Locke, John. *Treatise of Civil Government [Treatise Concerning the True Original and Extent of Civil Government*, edited by Andrew Bailey. Peterborough, ON: Broadview Press, 2015.

Losurdo, Domenico. *A Brief History of Liberalism*. Translated by Gregory Elliott. New York: Verso Books, 2011.

Lupton, Julia. *Citizen-Saints: Shakespeare and Political Theology*. Chicago: University of Chicago Press, 2014.

Malchow, H. L. "*Frankenstein's* Monster and Images of 'Race' in Nineteenth-Century Britain." *Past and Present* 139 (1993): 90–130.

Malcolm, Chris. "Eco-Complicity and the Logic of Settler-Colonial Environmentalism." *Resilience: A Journal of the Environmental Humanities* 7 (2020): 106–131.

Marasco, Robyn. *The Highway of Despair: Critical Theory after Hegel*. New York: Columbia University Press, 2015.

Marcuse, Herbert. *Reason and Revolution: Hegel and the Rise of Social Theory*. 2nd ed. London and New York: Routledge & Kegan Paul, 2000.

Markell, Patchen. *Bounds of Recognition*. Princeton, NJ: Princeton University Press, 2002.

Marriott, David S. "En Moi: Frantz Fanon and Rene Maran." In *Frantz Fanon's* Black Skin, White Masks: *New Interdisciplinary Essays*, edited by Max Silverman, 146–179. Manchester, UK: University of Manchester Press, 2005.

————. *Haunted Life: Visual Culture and Black Modernity*. New Brunswick, NJ: Rutgers University Press, 2007.

————. *Lacan Noir: Lacan and Afro-Pessimism*. Cham, Switzerland: Palgrave Macmillan, 2021.

————. "On Decadence: *Bling Bling*." *e-flux* 79 (February 2017): unpaginated. https://www.e-flux.com/journal/79/94430/on-decadence -bling-bling/.

————. *Whither Fanon? Studies in the Blackness of Being*. Stanford, CA: Stanford University Press, 2017.

Marx, Karl. *Critique of Hegel's Philosophy of Right*. In *Writings of the Young*

Marx on Philosophy and Society, edited and translated by Lloyd D. Easton and Kurt H. Guddat, 151–202. New York: Anchor/Doubleday, 1967.

———. *First Writings of Karl Marx*. Edited and translated by Paul M. Schafer. Brooklyn, NY: Ig Publishing, 2006.

———. *Grundrisse: Introduction to the Critique of Political Economy*. Translated by Martin Nicolaus. New York: Vintage Books, 1973.

———. "On a Proposed Divorce Law." In *Writings of the Young Marx on Philosophy and Society*, edited and translated by Lloyd D. Easton and Kurt H. Guddat, 136–142. New York: Anchor/Doubleday, 1967.

———. "On the Jewish Question." In *Collected Works*, vol. 3, by Karl Marx and Friedrich Engels, translated by Clemens Dutt, 146–174. London: Lawrence Wishart, 1974.

———. "Toward the Critique of Hegel's Philosophy of Law: Introduction." In *Writings of the Young Marx on Philosophy and Society*, edited and translated by Lloyd D. Easton and Kurt H. Guddat, 249–265. New York: Anchor/Doubleday, 1967.

Marx, Karl, and Friedrich Engels. *The German Ideology*. Translated by W. Lough, C. Dutt, and C. P. Magill, edited by Chris [C. J.] Arthur. New York: International Publishers, 1970.

Masayesva, Victor Jr., dir. *Itam Hakim, Hopiit*. Documentary Educational Resources, 1984.

McCarney, Joseph. "Hegel's Racism? A Response to Bernasconi." *Radical Philosophy* 119 (2003): 32–37.

McGowan, Todd. *Emancipation after Hegel: Achieving a Contradictory Revolution*. New York: Columbia University Press, 2019.

McLane, Maureen. *Romanticism and the Human Sciences*. Cambridge, UK: Cambridge University Press, 2000.

McLaughlin, Kevin. *Poetic Force: Poetry after Kant*. Stanford, CA: Stanford University Press, 2014.

McLennan, Gregor. "Editor's Discussion of Part I Writings." In *Selected Writings on Marxism*, by Stuart Hall, edited by Gregor McLennan, 158–176. Durham, NC: Duke University Press, 2021.

McLendon, Michael Locke. "Rousseau and the Minimal Self: A Solution to the Problem of Amour-Propre." *European Journal of Political Theory* 13.3 (2014): 341–361.

Meister, Robert. *After Evil: A Politics of Human Rights*. New York: Columbia University Press, 2011.

———. *Political Identity: Thinking Through Marx*. Oxford: Blackwell, 1990.

Mikkelsen, Jon M. *Kant and the Concept of Race: Late Eighteenth-Century Writings*. Albany, NY: SUNY Press, 2013.

Mills, Charles. *The Racial Contract*. Ithaca, NY: Cornell University Press, 2014.

———. "Rousseau, the Master's Tools, and Anti-Contractarian Contractarianism." In *Creolizing Rousseau*, edited by Jane Anna Gordon and Neil Roberts. New York: Rowman & Littlefield, 2014.

Milne, Drew. "The Beautiful Soul: From Hegel to Beckett." *Diacritics* 32 (2002): 63–82.

Morton, Timothy, and Hans Ulrich Olbrist. "[C]onversation held on the occasion of the Serpentine Galleries' Extinction Marathon: Visions of the Future." *Dis Magazine* (October 2014): unpaginated. http://dismagazine.com/disillusioned/discussion-disillusioned/68280/hans-ulrich-obrist-timothy-morton/.

Moten, Fred. "Blackness and Nothingness (Mysticism in the Flesh)." *SAQ* 112 (2013): 737–780.

———. "Knowledge of Freedom." *CR: The New Centennial Review* 4 (2004): 269–310.

———. "Notes on Passage (The New International of Sovereign Feelings)." *Palimpsest: Journal on Women, Gender, and the Black International* 3 (2014): 51–74.

———. *Stolen Life*. Durham, NC: Duke University Press, 2018.

———. *The Universal Machine*. Durham, NC: Duke University Press, 2018.

Mouffe, Chantal. "Citizenship and Political Identity." *October* 61 (1992): 28–32.

Murthy, Viren. "Beyond Particularity and Universality: Moishe Postone and the Possibilities of Jewish Marxism." *Jewish Social Studies: History, Culture, Society* 25 (Winter 2020): 127–167.

Nesbitt, Nick. *Universal Emancipation: The Haitian Revolution and the Radical Enlightenment*. Charlottesville: University of Virginia Press, 2008.

Neyrat, Frédéric. *The Unconstructable Earth: An Ecology of Separation*. Translated by Drew Burk. Bronx, NY: Fordham University Press, 2019.

Ng, Karen. "Hegel and Adorno on Negative Universal History: The Dialectics of Species-Life." In *Creolizing Hegel*, edited by Michael Monahan, 113–133. New York: Rowman & Littlefield, 2017.

Norrie, Alan. *Law and the Beautiful Soul*. London and New York: Routledge, 2013.

Oaklander, L. Nathan. *The Ontology of Time*. New York: Prometheus Books, 2004.

Ogle, Vanessa. *The Global Transformation of Time, 1870–1950*. Cambridge, MA: Harvard University Press, 2015.

Okiji, Fumi. *Jazz as Critique: Adorno and Black Expression Revisited*. Stanford, CA: Stanford University Press, 2018.

Olaloku-Teriba, Annie. "Afro-Pessimism and the (Un)logic of Anti-Blackness." *Historical Materialism* 26 (2018): 96–122.

Palmer, Tyrone. "Otherwise Than Blackness: Feeling, World, Sublimation." *Qui Parle* 29 (2020): 247–283.

Park, Linette. "The Eternal Captive in Contemporary 'Lynching' Arrests: On the Uncanny and the Complex of Law's Perversion." *Theory & Event* 22 (2019): 674–698.

Park, Peter. *Africa, Asia, and the History of Philosophy: Racism in the Formation of the Philosophical Canon, 1780–1830*. Albany, NY: SUNY Press, 2013.

Pateman, Carole. *The Sexual Contract*. Cambridge, UK: Polity, 2018.

Patterson, Orlando. *Slavery and Social Death: A Comparative Study*. Cambridge, MA: Harvard University Press, 1982.

Persram, Nalini. "Pacha Mama, Rousseau, and the Femini: How Nature Can Revive Politics." In *Creolizing Rousseau*, edited by Jane Anna Gordon and Neil Roberts, 225–251. New York: Rowman & Littlefield, 2014.

Pfau, Thomas. *Romantic Moods: Paranoia, Trauma, and Melancholy, 1790–1840*. Baltimore, MD: Johns Hopkins University Press, 2005.

Pinkard, Terry. *Hegel: A Biography*. Cambridge, UK: Cambridge University Press, 2000.

Pippin, Robert. *Hegel's Realm of Shadows: Logic as Metaphysics in the* Science of Logic. Chicago: University of Chicago Press, 2019.

———. *Idealism as Modernism: Hegelian Variations*. Cambridge, UK: Cambridge University Press, 1997.

Pudendorf, Samuel. *Of the Law of Nature and Nations: Eight Books* [1672]. Edited and translated by Basil Kennett and George Carew. London: Walthoe & Wilkin, 1729.

Raphael-Hernandez, Heike, and Pia Wiegmink. "German Entanglements in Transatlantic Slavery: An Introduction." *Atlantic Studies* 14 (2017): 419–495.

Rawls, John. *Lectures on the History of Political Philosophy*. Cambridge, MA: Harvard University Press, 2007.

Reed, Adolph. "The Post-1965 Trajectory of Race, Class, and Urban Politics in the United States Reconsidered." *Labor Studies Journal* 41 (2016): 260–291.

Regnault, François. "Hegel's Master and Slave Dialectic in the Work of Lacan." *Quarto* 64 (1998). London Society of the New Lacanian School. http://www.londonsociety-nls.org.uk.

Roberts, Neil. *Freedom as Marronage*. Chicago: University of Chicago Press, 2015.

———. "Rousseau, Flight, and the Fall into Slavery." In *Creolizing Rousseau*, edited by Jane Anna Gordon and Neil Roberts. New York: Rowman & Littlefield, 2014.

Robinson, Cedric. *Black Marxism: The Making of the Black Radical Tradition*. Chapel Hill: University of North Carolina Press, 2021.

———. *Terms of Order: Political Science and the Myth of Leadership*. Chapel Hill: University of North Carolina Press, 2016.

Rodriguez, Dylan. "Black Studies in Impasse." *Black Scholar* 44 (2014): 37–40.

Rodriguez, Jared. "The Blackness of Marx's Jewish Question, a Theo-Political Remix." An und für sich, October 8, 2018. https://itself.blog/2018/10/08/the-blackness-of-marxs-jewish-question-a-theo-political-remix/.

Roe, Nicholas. *John Keats and the Culture of Dissent*. Oxford: Oxford University Press, 1999.

Rose, Gillian. *The Broken Middle: Out of Our Ancient Society*. Oxford: Blackwell, 1992.

———. *Hegel Contra Sociology*. New York: Verso Books, 2009.

Rose, Paul Lawrence. *German Question/Jewish Question: Revolutionary Antisemitism in Germany from Kant to Wagner*. Princeton, NJ: Princeton University Press, 1990.

Rosenberg, Justin. *The Empire of Civil Society: A Critique of the Realist Theory of International Relations*. New York: Verso Books, 1994.

Rousseau, Jean-Jacques. *Discourse on the Origin of Inequality*. In *The Discourses and Other Early Political Writings*, edited and translated by Victor Gourevitch. Cambridge, UK: Cambridge University Press, 1997.

———. *Oeuvres Completes*. 3 vols. Edited by Robert Derathé, François Bouchardt, Jean Starobinski, Sven Stelling-Michaud, Jean-Daniel Candaux, and Jean Fabre. Paris: Éditions Gallimard, 1964.

———. *On the Social Contract, or Principles of Political Right*. In *The Basic Political Writings*. 2nd ed. Edited and translated by Donald A. Cress. Indianapolis, IN: Hackett Publishing, 2012.

Sala-Molins, Louis. *Dark Side of the Light: Slavery and the French Enlightenment*. Translated by John Conteh-Morgan. Minneapolis: University of Minnesota Press, 2006.

Saucier, P. Khalil, and Tryon B. Woods, eds. *Conceptual Aphasia in Black: Displacing Racial Formation*. London: Lexington Books, 2016.

Scott, David. "Antinomies of Slavery, Enlightenment, and Universal History." *Small Axe* 33 (2010): 152.

———. *Conscripts of Modernity: The Tragedy of Colonial Enlightenment*. Durham, NC: Duke University Press, 2004.

———. *Omens of Adversity: Tragedy, Time, Memory, Justice*. Durham, NC: Duke University Press, 2014.

———. "The Theory of Haiti: The Black Jacobins and the Poetics of Universal History." *Small Axe* 18 (2014): 35–51.

Sexton, Jared. "Affirmation in the Dark." *Comparatist* 43 (2019): 90–111.

——. *Amalgamation Schemes: Antiblackness and the Critique of Multiracialism*. Minneapolis: University of Minnesota Press, 2008.

——. "The *Vel* of Slavery: Tracking the Figure of the Unsovereign." *Critical Sociology* 42 (2014): 583–597.

Sheehan, James. *German History, 1770–1866*. Oxford: Oxford University Press, 1989.

Shelley, Mary. *Frankenstein; or, The Modern Prometheus*. Edited by Marilyn Butler. Oxford: Oxford University Press, 1993.

Shilliam, Robbie. *German Thought and International Relations: The Rise and Fall of a Liberal Project*. Houndmills, UK: Palgrave Macmillan, 2009.

Siemerling, Winfried. "Du Bois, Hegel, and the Staging of Alterity." *Callaloo* 24 (2001): 325–333.

Singh, Nikhal Pal. "On Race, Violence, and So-Called Primitive Accumulation." *Social Text* 34 (2016): 27–50.

Smallwood, Stephanie E. *Saltwater Slavery: A Middle Passage from Africa to American Diaspora*. Cambridge, MA: Harvard University Press, 2008.

Songe-Møhler, Vigdis. "Antigone and the Deadly Desire for Sameness." In *Birth, Death, and Femininity: Philosophies of Embodiment*, edited by Robin Schott, 211–232. Bloomington: Indiana University Press, 2010.

Sorentino, Sara-Maria. "The Abstract Slave: Anti-Blackness and Marx's Method." *International Labor and Working-Class History* 96 (2019): 17–37.

——. "The Idea of Slavery: Abstraction, Analogy, and Anti-Blackness." PhD diss., University of California, Irvine, 2018.

——. "Natural Slavery, Real Abstraction, and the Virtuality of Anti-Blackness." *Theory & Event* 22 (2019): 630–673.

Spillers, Hortense. *Black, White, and in Color: Essays on American Literature and Culture*. Chicago: University of Chicago Press, 2003.

Spivak, Gayatri Chakravorty. *A Critique of Postcolonial Reason: Toward a History of the Vanishing Present*. New York: Columbia University Press, 1999.

Stovall, Tyler. *White Freedom: The Racial History of an Idea*. Princeton, NJ: Princeton University Press, 2021.

Taubes, Jacob. *Occidental Eschatology*. Translated by David Ratmoko. Stanford, CA: Stanford University Press, 2009.

Taylor, Charles. *Hegel*. Cambridge, UK: Cambridge University Press, 1975.

Terada, Rei. *Feeling in Theory: Emotion after the "Death of the Subject."* Cambridge, MA: Harvard University Press, 2001.

——. *Looking Away: Phenomenality and Dissatisfaction, Kant to Adorno*. Cambridge, MA: Harvard University Press, 2009.

Testa, Italo. "Spirit and Alienation in Brandom's *A Spirit of Trust: Entfremdung, Entäußerung*, and the Causal Entropy of Normativity." In *Reading*

Brandom: On A Spirit of Trust, edited by Gilles Bouché, 140–165. London and New York: Routledge, 2020.

Tomba, Massimiliano. *Marx's Temporalities*. Leiden, Netherlands: Brill, 2013.

Trapp, Erin C. "Children-No-Longer." American Comparative Literature Association, Harvard University, March 18, 2016.

———. "Human Rights Poetry: Ferida Durakovic's *Heart of Darkness*." *Journal of Narrative Theory* 44 (2014): 367–394.

———. "Human Rights Poetry and the Poetics of Nonhuman Being: Dunya Mikhail's Writing of Disaster." *Social Text* 36.4 (2018): 81–110.

Ty, M. "The Resistance to Receptivity: or, Spontaneity from Fanon to Kant." *Cultural Critique* 113 (2021): 1–27.

UC Humanities Research Institute. "Session 2014: Archives of the Nonracial: A Mobile Workshop in South Africa." UCHRI Seminar in Experimental Critical Theory IX / Johannesburg Workshop in Theory and Criticism. http://sect.uchri.org/apply.

Vaziri, Parisa. "Arba'īn and Bakhshū's Lament: African Slavery in the Persian Gulf and the Violence of Cultural Form." *Antropologia* 7 (2020): 191–214.

———. "No One's Memory: Blackness at the Limits of Comparative Slavery." *Racial Formations in Africa and the Middle East: A Transregional Approach* 44 (2021): 14–19.

———. "On 'Saidiya': Indian Ocean World Slavery and Blackness beyond Horizon." *Qui Parle* 28.2 (2019): 241–280.

von Struve, Gustav. "Motion in the German Pre-Parliament, March 31, 1848." In *Deutsche Verfassungsdokumente 1803–1850*, vol. 1, edited by Ernst Rudolf Huber, 332–334. *Dokumente zur deutschen Verfassungsgeschichte*. 3rd ed. Stuttgart: W. Kohlhammer, 1978.

von Weiller, Kajetan, and Jakob Salat. *Der Geist der allerneuesten Philosophie der HH. Schelling, Hegel, und Kompagnie*. Brussels: Culture et Civilization, 1974.

Walcott, Rinaldo. "Middle Passage: In the Absence of Detail, Presenting and Representing a Historical Void." *Kronos* 44 (2018): 59–68.

Walker, Nicholas. "Review of Brown and Hodgson's translation of Hegel." *Lectures on World History, Notre Dame Philosophical Reviews* (December 14, 2011): unpaginated. https://ndpr.nd.edu/news/lectures-on-the -philosophy-of-world-history-vol-i-manuscripts-of-the-introduction -and-the-lectures-of-1822-3/.

Warren, Calvin. "Barred Objects (o): Police Brutality, Black Fetishes, and Perverse Demonstrations." *Comparatist* 45 (2021): 29–40, 31.

———. *Ontological Terror: Blackness, Nihilism, and Emancipation*. Durham, NC: Duke University Press, 2018.

Washington, Chris. "Non-Binary Frankenstein?" In *Frankenstein in Theory*, edited by Orrin N. C. Wang. New York: Bloomsbury, 2020.

Wilderson, Frank B. III. "Grammar and Ghosts: The Performative Limits of African Freedom." *Theatre Survey* 50 (2009): 119–125.

———. *Red, White & Black: Cinema and the Structure of U.S. Antagonisms*. Durham, NC: Duke University Press, 2010.

Williams, Eric. *Capitalism and Slavery*. Chapel Hill: University of North Carolina Press, 2021.

Williams, Patricia J. *The Rooster's Egg: On the Persistence of Prejudice*. Cambridge, MA: Harvard University Press, 1995.

Winant, Howard. "The Dark Matter: Race and Racism in the 21st Century." *Critical Sociology* 41 (2015): 313–324.

Winnicott, D. W. "Aggression, Guilt, and Reparation." In *Deprivation and Delinquency*, 116–123. London and New York: Routledge, 1990.

———. *Playing and Reality*. London and New York: Routledge, 1991.

Wollstonecraft, Mary. "Review of *Narrative of the Interesting Life of Olaudah Equiano*." In Wollstonecraft, *The Vindications: The Rights of Men* and *The Rights of Woman*, edited by D. L. MacDonald and Kathleen Scherf, appendix A. Peterborough, ON: Broadview, 1997.

Wood, Allen W. "Hegel on Education." In *Philosophers on Education*, edited by Amélie O. Rorty, 312–329. London and New York: Routledge, 2005.

Wright, Michelle. *Physics of Blackness: Beyond the Middle Passage Epistemology*. Minneapolis: University of Minnesota Press, 2015.

Wynter, Sylvia. "Beyond the Word of Man: Glissant and the New Discourse of the Antilles." *World Literature Today* 63 (1989): 637–648.

———. "'A Different Kind of Creature': Caribbean Literature, the Cyclops Factor and the Second Poetics of the Propter Nos." *Annals of Scholarship* 12 (2002): 153–172.

———. "On How We Mistook the Map for the Territory, and Re-Imprisoned Ourselves in Our Unbearable Wrongness of Being, of Désêtre: Black Studies Toward the Human Project." In *Not Only the Master's Tools: African-American Studies in Theory and Practice*, edited by Lewis Gordon and Jane Anna Gordon, 107–172. Boulder, CO: Paradigm, 2006.

———. "Unsettling the Coloniality of Being/Power/Truth/ Freedom: Towards the Human, After Man, Its Overrepresentation—An Argument." *CR: The New Centennial Review* 3 (2003): 257–337.

Yagoda, Ben. "Racists and Racialists—What's the Difference?" *Chronicle of Higher Education* (June 9, 2016).

Young, Elizabeth. *Black Frankenstein: The Making of an American Metaphor*. New York: NYU Press, 2008.

Yousef, Nancy. *Isolated Cases: Anxieties of Autonomy in Enlightenment Phi-

losophy and Romantic Literature. Ithaca, NY: Cornell University Press, 2018.

———. "The Monster in a Dark Room: *Frankenstein*, Feminism, and Philosophy." *MLQ* 63 (2002): 197–226.

Zambrana, Rocío. "Boundary, Ambivalence, Jaibería, or, How to Appropriate Hegel." In *Creolizing Hegel*, edited by Michael Monahan, 24–42. New York: Rowman & Littlefield, 2017.

———. "Hegel, History, and Race." In *The Oxford Handbook of Philosophy and Race*. Oxford: Oxford University Press, 2017.

Žižek, Slavoj. "Hegel versus Heidegger." *e-flux* 32 (February 2012): unpaginated. https://www.e-flux.com/journal/32/68252/hegel-versus-heidegger/.

———. *Less Than Nothing: Hegel and the Shadow of Dialectical Materialism.* New York: Verso Books, 2012.

INDEX

Absolute, 22, 26–29, 147

access: to divinity, 35; globalism and, 26, 29–30, 46, 102–3, 105n28, 144, 146; prescribed value of, 20, 23–25, 31, 66, 92. *See also* globalism: openness and accumulation, 63, 67, 77–78, 84, 87

Aching, Gerard, 51

actuality, 49, 63, 85, 110; degrees of reality and, 30n23; derealization and, 43, 133, 143, 181, 183; morality vs., 145, 156, 165, 176–77, 183; negativity and, 27, 30; raciality and, 20, 183–84; state and, 173–74, 176. *See also* actualization; derealization; realization

actualization, 43, 47, 66, 134, 136, 147, 177. *See also* actuality; derealization; realization

Adorno, T. W., 4–5, 57, 158n21, 158

aesthetics, 110, 147; humanity and, 121n31

affirmation, 20, 66, 141–42, 147, 151

Africa, North, 22–24; Europe and, 23–24

Africa, sub-Saharan: antiblackness and, 20–29; geographical imagination of, 22–24, 160; German-speaking nations and, 21, 24n8, 38–40, 154–55, 159–60; globalism and, 24–25, 30, 160; imagined connection to nature of, 150n3; "racialism" and, 25, 29–30, 173; slave trade and, 30; "tribalism" and, 20–21, 25–26

afropessimism, 48n10, 140n8, 187

Agamben, Giorgio, 127

Alexander, Claire, 17

al-Kassim, Dina, 143n15

allegory, 123, 125

Allison, Henry, 97

Althusser, Louis: *Lessons on Rousseau*, 67, 70–73, 75, 90

amalgamation, 6, 14, 48, 67. *See also* Sexton, Jared: *Amalgamation Schemes*

America, North, 133, 135, 177, 184

America, South, 126

amour-propre, 68–69, 74, 79. *See also* dependency

annulment, 169–75; sublation and, 135, 170–72

antiblackness: antiracism and, 9, 11, 16, 20, 25, 83, 99, 185–88; Hegel and, 21–22, 25, 29, 48–49, 52, 91, 139; Kant and, 91, 142; of political desire, 7, 17, 184; of political ontology, 109nn8–9; vs. racism, 9, 16–17, 22, 32; reception of Shelley and, 103, 106–7, 112; repetition and, 49, 65–66, 119; Rousseau and, 82; Shelley and, 112, 118–19, 139; sub-Saharan Africa and, 20–29; transposition and, 32, 66, 153n13, 182; US, 178

Antigone (Sophocles), 137

Antilles, 57

antiracism: antiblackness and, 9, 11, 16, 20, 25, 83, 99, 185–88; blackness and, 183; enlightenment, 5, 10, 99, 104,

relation; shattered self; slave; slavery; sublation; world spirit

Heine, Heinrich, 151

Heng, Geraldine, 78

Hesse, Barnor, 15

hierarchy, racial, 21–22; transposition of, 10, 18, 25, 30n23, 32, 36–37, 63, 78 (*see also* metaracial logic); in Wynter, 1–2

historical ontology. *See* ontology: historical

historicity (phenomenological category), 148; body and, 121; destructive power of, 5, 35; globalism and, 31, 144; limit of, 180; negativity of, 5, 21, 24, 28, 44–45, 162, 181; trauma and, 152n10

history, 20, 26, 65, 66, 70, 76, 90, 98, 185–86; German, 149–54, 180; human, 120–23; imaginary, 34–36; indeterminate, 64, 73, 75; nonteleological, 5, 21; ontology and, 109n9; "real movement" of, 49, 133, 155, 187; of religion, 32; slave as subject of, 48; slavery and, 118; sublation and, 43, 53, 58, 134, 139–40, 146, 172; unknown of, 140n9. *See also* Hegel, G. W. F.: *Lectures on the Philosophy of World History*; prehistory

Hobbes, Thomas, 76

Hölderlin, Friedrich, 142

Holsclaw, Geoffrey, 45

Holt, Thomas C., 78n19

homo politicus, 1–5, 46, 56, 182. *See also* political identity; Wynter, Sylvia

Hoogenboom, Marcel, 173n10

Hotho, H. G., 158n21

humanism, 8–9, 100, 108n5, 128–29; blackness and, 41; posthumanism and, 26–27, 29

humanity, 12, 74, 111, 114–17, 128, 183; aesthetic criteria for, 121n31; animality and, 69, 95, 156; blackness and, 41; common, 19, 20, 78n19; cultural criteria of, 112; difference and, 174, 179–80; emancipation of, 177–78, 181–82, 185; end in property of, 79; freedom of, 97–98, 169; historically ontological criteria for, 118, 120–24, 126, 160; lack and, 58;

natural signs as criteria for, 98; negative universality and, 47; negativity and, 48–49; noninstrumental, 102–3; objects and, 53, 55–56; origin of, 69; physical and geographical criteria for, 24n8; political criteria for, 1–2, 7, 93, 186; potential and, 27, 106; relational character of, 32, 49, 52, 67–71, 120–21, 126; slavery and, 42, 83, 90, 108–9; social agreement as, 73; spatiotemporal criteria for, 93, 97–98; as variations on European conditions, 4; "wildness" and, 74–75, 79–81

Husserl, Edmund, 93–94n7; *hylē* in, 124, 124n34

Hyppolite, Jean, 49, 56

identity, 33, 35, 38, 45, 122, 123, 163; Christian, 177; cultural, 140n9; of difference, 58; lost, 175; middle class, 167n36; negative, 141; of the object, 58; open, 186; racialism and, 17–18, 160n26. *See also* political identity

identity politics, 6, 10, 160

India, 25, 28, 34–35, 40n4

interdependence, 46, 66, 71, 99. *See also* dependency

interiority, 5, 74, 147, 150, 151n7

international relations, 33, 38–39, 99, 149, 154, 159–60, 165, 167. *See also* relation: global

"I that is We, We that is I" [IWWI], 46–48, 65, 75, 134

Jackson, Zakiyyah Iman, 109n8

James, C. L. R., 45, 52, 76n15, 138, 140

James, Joy, 72n10, 119n29

Jefferson, Thomas, 8–9n18

Jewishness, 174, 178, 181, 183; antisemitic figures of, 31n28, 31n30, 78n19; Christianity and, 31, 169; as foil, 182; as "nonpolitical identity," 135, 169, 176, 181–82. *See also* Bauer, Bruno: "The Jewish Problem"; Marx, Karl: "On the Jewish Question"

Johnson, Barbara, 129

Johnson, Robert, 4n6

Jones, Donna, 30, 92n3, 150